YE·LIBRARIE OF

Don and Irene Dow

HUMAN DESTINY

Lecomte du Noüy

HUMAN
DESTINY

LONGMANS, GREEN AND CO.

New York · London · Toronto

1947

LONGMANS, GREEN AND CO., INC.
55 FIFTH AVENUE, NEW YORK 3

LONGMANS, GREEN AND CO. Ltd.
OF PATERNOSTER ROW
43 ALBERT DRIVE, LONDON, S.W. 19
NICOL ROAD, BOMBAY 1
17 CHITTARANJAN AVENUE, CALCUTTA 13
36A MOUNT ROAD, MADRAS 2

LONGMANS, GREEN AND CO.
215 VICTORIA STREET, TORONTO 1

HUMAN DESTINY

PUBLISHED SIMULTANEOUSLY IN THE DOMINION OF CANADA
BY LONGMANS, GREEN AND CO., TORONTO

PRINTED IN THE UNITED STATES OF AMERICA BY
KINGSPORT PRESS, INC., KINGSPORT, TENNESSEE

TO MY WIFE

faithful collaborator and friend,
with all my gratitude, my admiration,
and my love

P. L. N.

PREFACE

THIS book is simply written, and technical terms have been avoided whenever it was possible to do so without affecting the accuracy of the ideas, so that it is accessible to any educated man or woman.

Nevertheless, as it brings to light new ideas, new interpretations, and as it calls for thought, it may require an unwonted effort of concentration on the part of the reader. He may have to read slowly, and to go over certain passages twice. There is nothing in them that an intelligent person cannot understand if he or she is willing to try.

Just as food cannot be digested without being masticated, so ideas cannot be assimilated without having been thought over and understood. The author has done his best to be lucid. But no matter how clear are the directions given for the use of an instrument, one cannot master it by simply reading them through. One must handle it. We beg the reader to make the effort of "handling" the ideas which are not familiar to him by criticizing them, by taking them to pieces, and by trying to replace them by others.

The problems of today have become so complex that a superficial smattering of knowledge is inadequate to enable the cultivated layman to grasp them all, much less to discuss them. This fact has been occasionally exploited in order to twist truth and to mislead the public. The time has come for all men of good will and of good faith to become conscious of the part they can and must play in life, if our present Christian civilization is to endure.

Everyone shares a responsibility in the future. But this responsibility can materialize into a constructive effort only if people realize the full meaning of their lives, the significance of their endeavors and of their struggles, and if they keep their faith in the high destiny of Man.

As the purpose of this book is to substantiate this faith by giving it a scientific basis, the writer hopes that the effort imposed on the reader will be rewarded by a clearer outlook on the most important problems of all times.

P. L. N.

Tee-La-Wuket Ranch
   Colorado, 1945
La Quinta, Altadena
   California, 1946

CONTENTS

BOOK II

The Evolution of Life

BOOK III

The Evolution of Man

INTRODUCTION

THE human race has just passed through one of the darkest periods of its history. It may even prove to be the most tragic of all, due to the fact that the conflict penetrated into the remotest corners of the world and that its unprecedented violence destroyed whatever illusions we might have had as to the solidity and permanence of the civilization man was so proud of.

A general uneasiness had spread over all the occidental countries ever since the first world war. This was not a new phenomenon but simply an awakening of the human conscience which had been anesthetized by the mechanical progress of the preceding fifty years.

The rapid development of the material side of civilization had aroused the interest of men and kept them in a kind of breathless expectation of the next day's miracle. Little time was left for the solving of the true problems: the *human* problems. Men were hypnotized by the incredibly brilliant display of new inventions following one another almost without interruption from 1880 on, and were like children who are so fascinated by their first view of a three-ring circus that they even forget to eat or drink.

This prodigious spectacle became the symbol of reality, and true values, dimmed by the glitter of the new star, were relegated to second place. The shift was easy and painless because philosophers and scientists of the nineteenth century had already prepared the minds of the thinking public by setting up question marks without answers.

Many people had a presentiment of the danger and gave the alarm, but it remained unheeded. It remained unheeded because a strange new idol had been born and a true fetishism, the cult of novelty, had taken hold of the masses. On the other hand, the discerning minds—the Cassandras—only had anachronic arguments at their disposal. The world was changing every day, replacing yesterday's garb by a more brilliant and unexpected one. While the dazzled children of men opened wide their eyes in an admiring ecstasy which insensibly turned into a true faith in the unlimited power of science and invention, the wise men fought only with venerable but outworn arguments, words stripped of the prestige of youth, and appeals for the awakening of a conscience which nobody wanted and many thought strangely old-fashioned and useless.

The Churches made a great effort but without rejuvenating their teachings. The results were not successful enough to halt the universal demoralization or even the disaffection and uneasiness of the crowd. It could not be otherwise. Compulsory education had opened up new paths, highways, and lanes in the intelligence of men. Without becoming much more intelligent, men had learned to employ the tricks of rational thought. An infinitely seductive tool, a new toy had been put in their hands and they all had the illusion that they knew how to use it. This tool had obtained sensational results which gradually transformed their material life and raised unlimited hopes. It was natural that the respect, heretofore bestowed on the priests, should be transferred progressively to those who had succeeded in harnessing the forces of nature and in penetrating some of her secrets.

Thus materialism spread not only amongst technicians but, alas, in the masses. Rational thinking should have been employed to fight this disease of reason. A mathematical argument can only be fought by other mathematical arguments, a scientific reasoning can only be destroyed by a reasoning of the same kind. If a lawyer tries to demonstrate that you are in the wrong it is no use pleading your case sentimentally or even logically. He will only be convinced if you confront him with other laws which contradict those he has invoked. It makes no difference if you are right and if, equitably, you should win. It is just as impossible to overcome his objections by subjective and psychological statements as it is to open a door with the wrong key.

We must use the right key if we want to fight paralyzing skepticism and destructive materialism which are by no means the inevitable consequences of the scientific interpretation of nature, as we have been led to believe. Therefore, we must attack the enemy with his own weapons and on his own ground. If we are unable to convince the skeptic, because of his bad faith or simply because of his negative faith, there is hope that the honest and impartial spectator who has followed the vicissitudes of the struggle will recognize the victor.

In other words, nowadays we can hardly expect to destroy atheism by using the sentimental and traditional arguments which could arouse the ignorant masses of the past. We cannot fight tanks with cavalry, nor planes with bows and arrows. Science was used to sap the base of religion. Science must be used to consolidate it. The world has evolved in the last five hundred years. It is important to recognize this and to adapt ourselves to the new conditions. We no longer travel from New York to San Francisco in a "prairie schooner," nor do we burn witches as they did in some places during the seventeenth century. We no longer treat infectious diseases by purging and bleeding, but we still use the same weapons as two thousand years ago to fight the greatest peril which has ever menaced human society, and we do not realize that large quantities of powerful arms are within our reach, capable of ensuring a certain if not immediate victory.

The purpose of this book is to examine critically the scientific capital accumulated by man, and to derive therefrom logical and rational consequences. We shall see that these consequences lead inevitably to the idea of God.

The present work, therefore, will not help convinced believers, except for the fact that it will give them new scientific arguments which they may use to advantage. It is not primarily meant for them. It is meant for those who, as a result of certain conversations, or experiences, have, at some moment of their existence, felt a doubt arising in their minds. It is meant for those who suffer from the conflict between what they *think* is their rational self, and their spiritual, religious, or sentimental self. It is meant for all men of good will who have understood that the aim of human life is the realization of a superior conscience and the perfection of self by a harmonious fusion of all the specifically human qualities; for all those who strive to understand the meaning of their efforts and of their trials. It is meant for those who would wish these efforts to be integrated in the cosmic order, and who are eager to contribute to it in a certain measure, thus conferring to their existence and aspirations a real value transcending the narrow frame of their individual interests. It is meant for all those who believe in the reality of human dignity and of man's mission in the universe, and for those who do not believe in it yet, but who are anxious to be convinced.

To achieve this result we will first study some mechanisms of human thought, so as to know what real value can be attributed to our concepts, to our reasoning, and to those of the materialists. Some of the latter are sincere and have an absolute and naive faith in their cerebral processes; others, however, are not so sincere and deem that the public should not be admitted back of the scientific stage lest they realize that the scenery is sometimes of pasteboard and canvas. They often avoid showing up obscurities and contradictions. They may not see them themselves. Indeed, it is the philosophers of science rather than the laboratory workers who should point out the difficulties of interpretation, the gaps and the relativity of the theories. Such men unfortunately are rare, and their language is often incomprehensible even to the cultivated public.

In our opinion it is imperative for the layman to know something of modern scientific and philosophic thought, and to learn how to use it so as to avoid being misled and impressed by the reasoning of materialistic scientists who, even if they are of good faith, are not always free from error.

We hope the reader will understand that, if he is interested in the destiny of man, he cannot attack this immense question without knowing the handicaps attached to human thought which enable us to study it. When physicists make measurements with the aim of verifying a hypothesis, when astronomers check the position of a star, they know exactly the degree of precision of their instruments, and the mean error introduced into their observations. They take that into account, and the calculus of errors constitutes an important chapter in all the sciences. Our problem is Man. The instrument used is the brain. It is, therefore, necessary to know the limitation of the instrument before trying to solve the problem. We will see that this investigation will reveal grave weaknesses in the scientific and mathematical reasoning of materialists. These weaknesses are so serious that, in the actual state of our knowledge, they take away all scientific value from their arguments.

We shall next examine man in the universe, and this will lead to an attentive study of evolution. This in turn will lead us to expound a hypothesis which incorporates human evolution into evolution in general, and to develop its logical consequences.

The aim of the author is specifically human. He is convinced that the modern uneasiness arises mainly from the fact that intelligence has deprived man of all reason for existence by destroying, in the name of a science still in the cradle, the doctrines which up till now gave a meaning to individual life, a reason for effort, a transcendent end to attain: namely, the religions.

The negation of free will, the negation of moral responsibility; the individual considered merely as a physico-chemical unit, as a particle of living matter, hardly different from the other animals, inevitably brings about the death of moral man, the suppression of all spirituality, of all hope, the frightful and discouraging feeling of total uselessness.

Now, what characterizes man, *as Man,* is precisely the presence in him of abstract ideas, of moral ideas, of spiritual ideas, and it is only of these that he can be proud. They are as real as his body and confer to this body a value and an importance which it would be far from possessing without them.

If, therefore, we want to give a meaning to life, a reason for effort, we must try to revalorize these ideas scientifically and rationally, and it seems to us that this can only be achieved by trying to incorporate them into evolution, by considering them as manifestations of evolution, in the same way as the eyes, the hands, and articulate speech.

It must be demonstrated that every man has a part to play and that he is free to play it or not; that he is a link in a chain and not a wisp of straw swept along by a torrent; that, in brief, human dignity is not a vain word, and that when man is not convinced of this and does not try to attain this dignity, he lowers himself to the level of the beast.

These are the ideas propounded by the author in the following pages with the help of our present scientific knowledge.

ARCHEOZOIC		PROTEROZOIC	PALEOZOIC	
(Archean)	(Algonkian)	(Primary) Age of Invertebrates	Age of Fishes	Age of Amphibians
	Pre-Cambrian	Silurian / Cambrian	Devonian	Permian / Carboniferous
Traces of life in the form of local deposits of coal.	Bacteria (Microscopic organisms: Leptothrix)	Traces of worms (Annelida) Crustaceans—Trilobites (Arthropodes) First ganoid Fish—Marine plants. Mollusks—Cephalopodes Crustaceans—Trilobites—Polyps	Fish—Ostracodermi—First Ferns. First batrachians (?) Insects—	First Ammonitidae (Mollusks); Sphenodon Batrachians (Stegocephalia) Selachii—Ferns, Cordaites—First Reptiles
		Estimated duration (after W. A. Parks, F.R.S.C.): About 800 million years or 2/3 of the age of Life on the Earth and 1/2 of the age of the Earth itself. (very approximately) All figures in this column are approximate but based on the most authoritative modern works. 130 million years 70 million years	50 million years	25 million years 85 million years
1200 million years			360 million years	

THE AGES OF LIFE ON EARTH

Eras	Ages	Periods		Approximate duration
CENOZOIC	(Tertiary) (Quaternary) Age of Mammals	RECENT	First men—Glacial period	1 million years
		PLEISTOCENE		
		PLIOCENE	Elephant—Rhino—Deer	6 million years
		MIOCENE	Mastodon	12 million years
		OLIGOCENE	Paleotherium—(Seasons appear)	16 million years
		EOCENE	Placental mammals—Primates	20 million years
MESOZOIC	(Secondary) Age of Reptiles	CRETACEOUS	Flowering plants—Apogee of Dinosaurs—Ostriches—First snakes—many insects	40 million years
		JURASSIC	Swimming and Flying Dinosaurs—First Reptilelike birds: Archaeopterix—(No seasons)	60 million years
		TRIASSIC	Reptiles, Dinosaurs, Tortoises, Crocodiles—First mammals (Marsupials)	35 million years

CENOZOIC: 54 million years

MESOZOIC: 135 million years

BOOK I

The Methods

1

OUR SUBJECTIVE IDEA OF THE UNIVERSE • RELATIVITY OF
THIS IMAGE • THE NOTION OF CAUSE • THE SCALE OF
OBSERVATION

Two different paths may eventually lead to the comprehension of man. The first, revelation, is a direct road, but
is closed to a great many people and independent of
rational thought. Those who can make use of it are fortunate. The second, on the contrary, is strictly rational and
scientific. It leads us to consider man as one of the elements
of the whole, the universe, and to study this element as a
function of the external world. This method requires a
description of the universe as it is perceived and conceived
by the human brain. If this description is broad enough,
man must perforce take his place in it, and the picture thus
obtained should enable us to place him in his proper environment. Unfortunately, we must take into account the
fact that this picture is constructed *by the mind,* and that
as a consequence it is dependent on the structure of the
brain, on the sense system which puts us in contact with
the outside world, and on the logical mechanisms which
are at the base of the interpretations of direct sensorial
observations.

The foregoing requires an explanation, as the reader is, perhaps, unfamiliar with these ideas.

The external world, nature, is revealed to us through our sense organs. We see the stars, the sun, the mountains, the animals, and other men by means of the eye which is constructed like a photographic apparatus. The inverted image of things is projected onto the retina at the back of the eye. The retina is composed of an immense number of sensitive elements, the so-called cones and rods. The reactions of these elements are transmitted through the optic nerve to certain brain centers. These reactions are the cause of what we call visual impressions. It is, therefore, not the eye which sees, but the brain.

Now, it is not always true that the visual impression corresponds exactly to the external reality. For instance, some people see colors differently from others; they are color-blind. When we speak of a red flower or a green field, we do so with the mental reservation: for the majority of observers. It is this majority which constitutes what we call *normality*.

There are also many optical illusions: a stick plunged in water looks broken; parallel lines separated by others disposed in herringbone formation seem to diverge; white figures appear larger than black figures, etc. The sense of touch is not always reliable either. When we cross the index and the middle finger and roll a ball between them we "feel" two balls. The organ of hearing does not determine identically the same reactions in everybody. Musicians perceive a false note instantaneously and understand melodies which non-musicians do not find in the least melodious. There is no way of comparing the reactions of taste in different individuals. Finally, we all have the impression, whether we are at the North Pole, the South Pole, or the Equator, that we walk, with our heads *up,* and there are still some people who refuse to admit that the earth is round.

A direct and superficial examination of things does not, therefore, always enable us to conclude that reality is identical with perception. Reasoning and experience must intervene to correct the direct impression of the senses and to construct in our brains a picture which corresponds to what we call the external world, the objective world, in opposition to the subjective idea which is the result of the information given by the senses. That is why we wrote above that our image of the world depends on the structure of our sensorial system and of our brain. In short, this picture is *relative* and not *absolute.* We must take this fact into account when we try to describe the external universe.

We have also mentioned the logical mechanisms of thought. Many people wrongly think that these mechanisms are "standard" and that logical reasoning, and all the more so mathematical reasoning, are inevitably "true." This is not always the case. We must beware of the process of human thought because, in the first place, the starting point is often a sensorial observation (therefore of doubtful value) or an observation based on common sense. Now, common sense cannot be trusted. It is common sense that leads us to think that the earth is flat; that two plumb lines are parallel (they are both directed toward the center of the earth and consequently form an angle); that motion in a straight line exists, which is absolutely false as we have to take into consideration not only the motion of the earth around its axis and around the sun, and that of the entire orbit of the earth, but also the motion of the whole solar system toward the constellation Hercules, etc. As a result, a bullet, or an airplane, which seem to move in a straight line, with respect to the earth, for a certain length of time, in reality follow a trajectory more closely resembling a kind of corkscrew with respect to a vaster system of reference, the nearest stars for instance. Common sense tells us that the edge of a razor blade is a continuous straight line, but if we examine it under a microscope it resembles the wavy line drawn by a child. Common sense tells us that a piece of steel is solid: X-rays show us that it is porous, and the modern theories of matter teach us that it is in reality made up of trillions of animated, miniature universes having extraordinarily rapid movements and no contact with each other.

If, therefore, the starting point, the premise, of a reasoning is false, the conclusion will, necessarily, logically, be false. The Greek philosophers called these reasonings sophisms. It is not always easy to distinguish a sophism from the logical and sound reasoning which is constantly used in science and philosophy: the syllogism.

As we have no other means of knowing and describing nature but those given us by our senses and our reasoning faculties—i.e., by our brain cells—we must be extremely cautious and never forget the *relativity* of the picture which we construct—a relativity with respect to the recording instrument, man.

Human science is based on the physical study of phenomena. We try to link these facts together by means of laws, that is to say, by qualitative and sometimes quantitative relations. But these phenomena only exist, as such, in our brains. Each has an external, objective cause, and we cannot affirm that there is an identity between this cause and the phenomenon which results from it within ourselves.

We have made use of the word "cause." It is one of those words which everybody thinks he understands. Yet it gives rise to any number of questions. When we examine this notion from the simple point of view of common sense (of which, as we have seen, we must beware), it is extremely complex. Strange to say, it is difficult to define exactly. At first glance each event has a cause, or more often several causes. However, let us take a cannon shot, for instance. Shall we say that the firing of the shell is "caused" by the small percussion cap, or by the movement of the soldier's hand which has pulled the string? Shall we say that the cause is the charge of powder? But without the movement of the hand this charge could have remained inert for centuries. Anyway, the movement of the hand can be replaced by a different mechanism and the explosion of the percussion cap could have been brought about by a very slight action, such as, for instance, the momentary interception of a feeble ray of light by the wing of a fly. This ray of light might have been chosen amongst the stars, by means of a telescope, and would suffice, after amplification, to project the ton of steel, which the shell weighs, about thirty miles. The Chicago Exposition in 1933 was thus entirely lighted by the closing of an enormous switch commanded by a weak ray of light emitted forty years earlier by the star Arcturus. As far as the cannon shot is concerned, it would seem absurd to make the star responsible for the damage done by the shell, and yet this slight ray of light, emitted long before, will have played as important a part in the shooting as the charge of powder.

Neither can we say that the workers who manufactured the powder, or the chemical engineers who invented it, or the builders of the factory, or the capitalists who gave the funds to build it, or their parents, or their grand-parents, etc., are responsible. And yet each one of them, each of these men who contributed to the construc-tion of the cannon, shoulders a part of the responsibility, which gradually crumbles away, without ever disappear-ing totally, and reaches back to the origin of the world.

We thus automatically arrive at the First Cause, and the problem passes imperceptibly from the material realm into the philosophical and religious realms. It is impossible to avoid this passage from the material to the immaterial when seeking the causes, for it is evident that we should have mentioned the psychological causes, the *motives* which led to the manufacture of the gun and the powder and to the firing of the shot. Without them there would have been no shell, no cannon, no charge, no percussion cap, no shooter, and no continuity of coordinated effort with the *aim* of making the shot go off.

From the material point of view we are, therefore, obliged to bring causality back to mere precedence. Every phenomenon, act, or thought which invariably precedes another phenomenon could be considered as its cause. Ex-perimentally, it is no more than an order of succession in time. However, this is not very satisfactory and restrains in a singular manner the value which we generally attribute to the word: cause.

Thus, without even taking into consideration the crea-tion of universes, whenever man intervenes, it is generally necessary to consider his intention, his will, as the efficient cause. But this cause is itself the result, the end of one or several series of such extraordinarily complex anterior "causes" that the word loses all significance. This becomes even more apparent when we envisage longer intervals of time. If we consider extremely slow phenomena (with respect to ourselves) such as those which took place in the course of the geological periods, we no longer can look for an efficient primitive cause in a will, unless we leave the realm of science to penetrate into that of religion. That is why the materialist denies an efficient cause and falls back entirely on chance. We shall see that this hypothesis is not satisfactory and leads to grave contradictions which have generally been passed over in silence up till now.

In the preceding pages we touched on some of the questions dealing with the relations between the objective, external world and the human brain, or, if one prefers, between the "cause" of our sensations and of our ideas and the ideas themselves. In this case the definition of precedence applies. We have seen that when we seek the cause of any event which brings human activity into play, we are generally led back to a psychological fact, that is, as far as we can *actually judge,* an immaterial fact. For the pure materialist a psychological phenomenon is evidently of material origin, as it manifests itself through the activity of the brain cells. However, not only are we incapable, in the present state of our science, of appreciating in units of energy the work represented by a single thought or sentiment which results in an act of the will, but, what is more, the notion of quality will probably always escape us. It will be impossible for us to discern the "cause" of the choice between two decisions; one constructive, the other destructive; one good, the other bad; and from a human point of view that is the only thing which counts. There are some men who have always, to the detriment of their interests, their health, and at the risk of their lives, chosen and executed the action which was good. Others, having only their immediate welfare in view, or obeying their passions, have chosen the nefarious act. Assuming that the energy spent in their thought could one day be expressed quantitatively, this would not greatly increase our knowledge, for it is doubtful whether a materially appreciable energy difference can be found between the words: yes and no.

Even if it were found, the question would still arise as to what the cause was which had motivated the yes or the no. Before leaving the subject we particularly want to draw attention to an observation which is brought out by some of the examples cited above (pp. 4, 5). Certain of our mental illusions are due to the fact that we consider a phenomenon, as we observe it, in the frame of our current life. Motion in a straight line, for instance, is real with respect to the earth, and false with respect to the universe. This does not only apply to sensory illusions. It applies to all our human observations which are always relative to the *system of reference* chosen. By system of reference we simply mean the *scale of observation*. This demands an explanation.

Let us suppose that we have at our disposal two powders. One white (flour) and the other black (finely crushed charcoal or soot). If we mix them we will obtain a gray powder which will be lighter in color if it contains more flour and darker if it contains more soot. If the mixture is perfect, *on our scale of observation* (that is, without the help of a microscope) the phenomenon studied will always be a gray powder. But let us suppose that an insect of the size of the grains of flour or of soot moves around in this powder. For him there will be no gray powder, but only black or white boulders. On *his* scale of observation the phenomenon, "gray powder," *does not exist*.

The same is true of any print or engraving. When examined with a magnifying glass, the nose of George Washington will look to us like a succession of black and white points. Under the microscope, we will see nothing but the grain of the paper, gray, black, or white according to whether it has been covered by ink or not. The principal phenomenon, the design, the portrait of Washington, has disappeared. It only existed *on our normal scale of observation.*

In other words, one can say that from the standpoint of man *it is the scale of observation which creates the phenomenon.* Every time we change the scale of observation we encounter new phenomena.

On our scale of human observation, as pointed out before, the edge of a razor blade is a continuous line. On the microscopic scale, it is a broken but solid line. On the chemical scale we have atoms of iron and carbon. On the sub-atomic scale we have electrons in perpetual motion which travel at the rate of several thousand miles per second. All these phenomena are in reality the manifestations of the same basic phenomenon, the motions of the electrons. The only difference which exists between them is the scale of observation.

This fundamental fact was first pointed out by a brilliant Swiss physicist who died in 1942, Professor Charles-Eugène Guye. It enables one to understand many things and to avoid grave philosophical errors. We shall come back to it several times in the course of this book, for we will frequently bring in the scale of observation in order to explain certain apparent contradictions.

2

Now that the reader has been warned against certain errors, which have their source in the human brain, we can examine the methods used by the mind to describe the universe and to foresee future events. This study is indispensable, as we expect to base our arguments on scientific methods and on mathematical reasoning to demonstrate that they both lead to the necessity of admitting the intervention of a transcendent, extra-earthly force in order to explain Life.

Man, in whose fate we are interested, is part of an immense cosmos and is capable, alone amongst the animals, of observing nature, of experimenting and of establishing relationships and laws between facts. He is at the same time the subject of the experiment and the observer. If we admit that knowledge of the laws which govern the living world can throw some light on the significance of man by explaining his appearance on earth, the ties which unite him to the other living forms and the differences which characterize him, we must study the evolution of the whole world from the beginning, without forgetting that our observations can be warped by our instrument of observation.

Similarly, when we arrive in an unknown country and wish to study its economic, social and intellectual life, we have to examine in detail its resources, industries, traditions, ambitions; its commercial, scientific and artistic production; its education and religion. To accomplish this we must take into consideration the broad lines as well as the small details; the material facts and the moral causes. If we fail to do this the picture will be incomplete and inadequate.

The reader must not overlook the fact that the materialists and the so-called freethinkers—who strangely enough do not admit free will—have always claimed that they alone think rationally and base their beliefs on science. Either we take their statements for granted, without checking up on them, or else we challenge them. If we choose to challenge them we are compelled to dig deep into the basic foundations of science, and to build our conviction on solid ground. In doing this we will disclose the weaknesses in materialistic reasoning. But this requires a detailed analysis not only of scientific facts, but of scientific thinking. This is precisely the purpose of the present chapter.

The aim of science is to foresee, and not, as has often been said, to understand. Science describes facts, objects and phenomena minutely, and tries to join them by what we call laws, so as to be able to predict events in the future. For instance, by studying the motions of the heavenly bodies, astronomy has succeeded in establishing laws which enable us to calculate the position of these bodies with respect to the earth in an unlimited future. A wonderful machine, the planetarium, has even been constructed, which reproduces these movements and projects the past and future aspect of the nocturnal sky on the interior of a dome.

In like manner, physics and chemistry describe the behavior of solid, liquid, and gaseous bodies, the combinations of molecules and atoms, and these descriptions lead to laws which replace the amazement of ignorance by the sureness of knowledge.

But we must not confuse these human, subjective laws which our intelligence has superposed on facts, with the true, eternal laws which will, perhaps, always escape us. As we have already stated, our laws are conditioned by the structure of our brains and our sense organs and express the succession of our states of consciousness, of our sensorial impressions. It is possible that this succession corresponds to objective reality, and that the absolute laws do not differ from those we have established, but we cannot prove it. Our human laws are the expression of our confidence in the order of nature and in the identity of the reactions of all men to the same excitations. In brief, they can be described in the following manner:

When we have experimentally observed that certain definite conditions are always followed by certain phenomena which seem to be invariably linked to the first by a relation of cause to effect, we word this observation in such a way that it enables us to predict these phenomena quantitatively or qualitatively whenever the same conditions are present.

For instance, every time a stone or any other solid object falls in a vacuum at the surface of the earth, it will cover the same distance during the first second of its fall, no matter what it weighs. This is known as the law of falling bodies. Every time a volume of gas is compressed in such a way that it occupies half of its initial volume, the Boyle-Mariotte Law tells us that its pressure is doubled, or very nearly so.

Our scientific laws are always *a posteriori,* and governed by the facts to which they must submit. They are relative to man, who is the thinking-recording instrument, and merely express a relationship, or a series of relationships, between him and the external cause. They only describe the succession of psychological states determined in us by these causes. They are, therefore, essentially relative and subjective and their validity is strictly limited to man and depends on the identity of the reactions of the other individuals to the same external stimuli.

It is clear, therefore, that expressions such as "scientific truth" should only be taken in a very limited sense, and not literally, as the public so often does. There is no scientific truth in the absolute sense. The phrase *Ad veritatem per scientiam* is an absurdity. There are only certain groups of sensations which, in our experience, have always succeeded each other in the same order and which we assume will succeed each other in an identical fashion within a limited future. This is the essence of our scientific truth. As long as we do not know the relationships between a physico-chemical phenomenon and the phenomena pertaining to life and psychology which may accompany it, we shall not be able to say that we know its whole significance.

This last sentence may seem a little obscure, and the author again begs the reader for a concentrated effort. Without the presence of man—who is the receiving set, the recording instrument, and the coordinator—the phenomena which constitute his science do not exist *as isolated phenomena*. There are waves of all kinds and sizes in the universe, only a small number of which are transformed by our senses into light, heat, sound, etc. There are atoms and molecules, i.e. matter, which, when in contact with our nerve terminals, give rise in our brains to impressions termed "qualities"—hardness, softness, taste, odor, etc.— and which do not exist in objects but are the subjective result of the reaction between our nervous systems and nature. If we suppress man, the causes of our sensations remain, but they are in no way identical with the sensations. To draw a parallel: if we suppress the radio receiving sets and leave the transmitting stations, the finest melodies in the world can be broadcast but nobody will be aware of it. We will be surrounded by silent waves without knowing it. A highly complicated instrument, which detects these electromagnetic waves, changes their wave length, and transforms them into sound waves transmitted by air, is required in order to make them heard at the four corners of the earth. The *cause* is very different from the *effect*.

The same is true of nature. Man plays the part of a receiving instrument and transforms the properties of objects into properties which are perceptible on our scale of observation, either directly, or indirectly by means of admirably ingenious instruments *created* by the brain. The phenomena thus transformed, "humanized," constitute the objects of our science which is, therefore, essentially human. We can say that the great majority—if not all—of the phenomena studied are in reality derived from the combination: experimenter (man) + objective phenomenon. This observation is of the greatest importance as

far as the philosophical conclusions, which we are authorized to draw from our scientific experiments and theories,
are concerned.

That is why we said above that in order to really *understand* a phenomenon we should know, not only its objective (external) cause, but the relations which bind it to the
subjective, biological and psychological phenomena which
accompany it.

The foregoing explains in a certain measure the absence
of continuity observed in science. Indeed science is still
divided into watertight compartments. We will try to
make this clear by an example. Let us suppose that a con-
scientious and wise observer wishes to study the laws governing human societies. After having traveled through all
the countries of the world he comes to the conclusion that
it might perhaps be more useful to examine first of all the
common element in all societies, namely man. Indeed, it
seems logical to admit that the laws governing human
groups are based on the qualities and characteristics of individual man. Therefore, the observer begins to study the
individual human being. Without being aware of it, he
thus crosses a threshold which he will not be able to recross
in the opposite direction, for the psychology of crowds
cannot be deduced from individual psychology.

As he is convinced of the unity of science, that is, of the
fact that all phenomena in the universe are related and
that a complete knowledge of elementary phenomena
must automatically lead to the knowledge of more complex ones, he decides that his ignorance of the human
body is a serious handicap and that the causes for the behavior of man must necessarily be found in the study of
human anatomy and physiology. In so doing, he again

unconsciously crosses another threshold just as irreversible as the first. Physiology naturally leads him to biological chemistry: third irreversible threshold. So as to understand certain details of biological chemistry, he is forced to take up inorganic chemistry, which is its necessary foundation, and a fourth threshold is passed as easily as the others. To be consistent with himself he becomes interested not only in molecules but in the atoms which compose them, and naturally in their constitutive corpuscular elements: electrons, protons, etc. This is the last threshold. When he reaches this point *it is impossible for him by using the inverse method to retrace his steps to any of the original problems.*

He cannot retrace his steps because it so happens that the *properties* of atoms, on our scale of observation (i.e. the result of the reaction of atoms on our nervous system), have not so far been linked to the electronic structure of the atoms; because the "properties" of atoms cannot be linked to the "properties" of molecules: sodium is a metal, chlorine is a toxic gas, the combination of the two gives sodium chloride, which is harmless kitchen salt. Nothing in the properties of these atoms enables us to foresee the properties of salt. He cannot retrace his steps because the properties of life cannot be linked to those of inanimate matter; because thought and the psychology of man cannot be deduced from the physico-chemical and biological properties of living matter. In other words, by passing from one scale of observation to the other, the scientist discovers new phenomena, but wanders farther and farther away from his goal.

The method used by this observer was the true scientific method: *analysis.* This example shows its limitations. The more deeply man analyzes, the farther away he gets from the principal problem which he meant to solve. He loses sight of it and is absolutely incapable of rejoining it by means of the phenomena which he studies, although, logically, he feels that there should be a link between them.

This clearly illustrates Charles-Eugène Guye's statement: it is the scale of observation which creates the phenomenon. The scale of observation depends on man; it is he who creates it. In nature, different scales of observation do not exist. There is only one immense, harmonious phenomenon on a scale which in general escapes man because of the structure of his brain, a structure which necessitates dividing into arbitrary compartments, and cutting up into isolated pieces.

However, this is not all. Another serious obstacle greatly limits—in our day—the efficacy of theoretical science as a philosophical tool. This obstacle may be momentary. We can hope that in the future it will disappear, but today we are obliged to admit it. It can be summarily expressed in the following way:

We know that material atoms are made up of subatomic particles: protons, electrons, and neutrons. But between the realm of the atoms and that of the electrons there is today an impassable chasm; the *laws* which explain the motions and behavior of the electrons are not the same as those which govern the atoms. In other words, the birth of material atoms introduces new laws into the world, laws characterized by an *irreversibility* which does not seem to exist in the realm of electrons. Material phenomena (on our scale of observation) can only unfold *in one direction,* never in the contrary direction. Electronic phenomena, on the other hand, are not subject to this irreversibility. They are reversible according to modern physics.

For evident reasons we will not dwell on this fundamentally important question. We simply wanted to point it out, as it is important for the reader to remember that, right at the beginning, there is a break in the continuity of the history of the evolution of the universe, or rather in man's interpretation of this history. This will prepare him to accept other gaps of the same nature when we come across them, first in the study of Life and later on in that of Man.

We have seen in the preceding pages that the true aim of science is to predict and that prevision resulted from the systematic study of the succession of facts. When a certain order of succession is well established, when it is general, that is, when it does not admit exceptions (which is fairly rare), this succession is expressed stenographically in a conventional language called *mathematics,* and becomes a law.

Though a law may give us the impression that we understand the mechanism of the phenomenon it describes, this is an illusion. However, it does not matter much, for man primarily wants to think he understands and is usually satisfied by this belief. Any electrician thinks he understands how an electric battery works, but the best physicists do not share his opinion and admit that even if they can *foretell* exactly how it will function they do not fully understand, today, why it functions.

How does science succeed in foretelling, and in expressing, its laws?

The general method employed nowadays is the *statistical* method, i.e., a method based on a very great number of active elements. On a certain scale of observation, the precision obtained depends on the number of elements considered. Let us take an example.

Everybody knows that life or fire insurance companies are based on statistics which tell how many men die or how many houses burn *on an average,* per year. Experience shows that under determined conditions, in a population of several million inhabitants, the number of yearly deaths varies little, provided these conditions are not modified in a radical manner from one year to another. The same is true for fires. Supposing that out of a million policyholders there is an average annual death rate of 3 per thousand, or 3000 per year. The company will calculate its rates so as to be able, not only to meet its obligations, but to pay a dividend to its stockholders. The accuracy of this calculation is demonstrated by the fact that the company makes a profit except in the case of war, epidemics, or some other cataclysm. It can be easily understood that this accuracy, and the profits which are derived therefrom, depend on the *number* of people insured. If there were only ten policyholders, all occupying the same house, and if nine were killed by an epidemic or an accident, the company would be bankrupt. When a hundred individuals are distributed in ten different houses, the chances of the company are greater, for it is unlikely that an epidemic or an accident will destroy the whole hundred. If there are ten million policyholders, the chances of the company become almost a certitude.

Now, the analytical method led us to consider all matter as granular, that is, composed of minute elements having the same properties, and called molecules. The molecules are themselves built of smaller elements, the atoms. Beyond the atoms, analysis has revealed new individual elements, the electrons and the protons, which are grains of electricity and no longer matter, though they possess one of its qualities: mass. The bridge between matter and electricity is thus established, but cannot safely be used to pass from one realm to the other, for the laws of matter, as we have already stated, do not apply to electrons and vice versa.

As we are faced by a granular world, made up of an immense number of minute elements, we should be able to apply our methods of statistical calculation provided that, on an average, each element can be considered as obeying *solely the laws of chance.* Indeed, it is only in this case that the statistical laws, which are also called the laws of chance, are valid. This is quite obvious, for if we apply the laws of chance to the game of heads or tails, for instance, we know that if we toss our coin often enough we must ultimately obtain an equal number of heads and tails. However, this is only true if chance *alone* determines the throw and not if the coin is lopsided, if there is a *dissymetry,* which would favor either heads or tails.

Let us see, for example, how the laws of chance, or calculus of probabilities, enable us to obtain a remarkable precision in a simple physical phenomenon: the pressure of gases. A gas is constituted of free molecules in perpetual motion. These little grains moving at different speeds, haphazardly, in all directions, knock up against each other and against the sides of the vessel in which they are contained. What we call *pressure* in this vessel is nothing but the result of these impacts, the sum of the individual energies of each molecule stopped in its path by the walls of the vessel. (Kinetic theory of gases.) Per unit of surface, the number of impacts per second will be the same, *on an average,* on every part of the surface, which means that the pressure is the same everywhere. Experience has verified this fact *on our scale of observation,* which is the experimental demonstration that the collisions are really the result of chance; otherwise the pressure would be higher or lower at different points.

We know that one square inch does not receive exactly the same number of impacts per second. But the energy of each individual collision is so slight, with respect to the immense number of encounters, that the differences are too small to be detected by our instruments. Indeed we must remember that there are about 30,000,000,000,-000,000,000 molecules per cubic centimeter,[1] at 32° F., and at normal barometric pressure. This is usually written: 3×10^{19}. The grand total of all the added energy of all the molecules, acting like small cannon balls on the walls, is equal to one atmosphere.[2] It is evident that a thousand impacts more or less, per unit of surface, introduces an error much too small to be measured by our most sensitive instruments which hardly register differences millions of times greater.

It is also evident that if we did not employ a statistical method and if we tried to solve this problem rigorously, we would have to put down 3×10^{19} differential equations (3 followed by 19 zeros) each composed of 3×10^{19} terms representing the reciprocal actions of these molecules on one another. It has been calculated that it would take twenty billion human lives to solve this problem, assuming that each computer would only spend one second in dealing with each molecule. . . .

This is clearly impossible, and enables one to understand why statistical methods, based on the laws of chance, are absolutely necessary. It also explains certain facts of

[1] Less than 1/15 of a cubic inch.
[2] About 1 kilogram (1,000 grams) per square centimeter; about 14.7 lb. per square inch.

considerable importance which are called *fluctuations.* The infinitely small error, mentioned above, due to a difference of a thousand impacts on the walls, is a fluctuation. Obviously, it is too small for us to observe. However, in certain cases these fluctuations may become important. Indeed, let us consider two small vessels of one cubic centimeter each, full of the same gas, and connected by a short tube. The pressure will immediately stabilize itself and become identical in the two vessels as far as our measuring instruments are concerned. We know that the number of molecules—which determines the number of impacts on the walls—is never identically the same at all times in the two vessels, for the molecules are forced to pass from one vessel to another by the tube which unites them, and the number cannot be rigorously the same in both directions unless by an extraordinary chance. Nevertheless, *on an average,* the number of impacts per second, therefore the pressure, will be *approximately* the same. On an average, the difference will be much too small to be measured, because of the enormous number of molecules present. But, let us suppose now that we deal with smaller and smaller vessels until we come to such small volumes that instead of having 30,000,000,000,000,000,000,000 molecules in each vessel (one cubic centimeter), we only have 10. In this case, as soon as one molecule passes by chance from one vessel into another the pressure will drop 10 per cent in the first and rise 10 per cent in the second. There is a difference of 20 per cent between the two vessels. This *fluctuation* due to the passage of one single molecule is considerable.

Thus, in the first example, the excess of a *thousand* molecules in one vessel does not introduce a measurable difference. On this scale of observation, the law of the equality of pressure in communicating vessels is correct, and only an extraordinary, very improbable chance, a very rare fluctuation, could invalidate it. In the second example, on another scale of observation, the contrary takes place. On an average, the number of molecules is never the same in the two vessels, but any inequality introduces a considerable variation in the pressure. Only a slightly probable chance can maintain the same number of molecules in each vessel during a very short time. The law of equality of pressure becomes the exception and the pressure is different normally. The simple change of the scale of observation gives birth to two different phenomena with respect to the observer. Yet, with respect to nature, there is only one phenomenon. Chance is, therefore, at the same time the foundation of our scientific laws and the origin of their exceptions. The above example is important because, if it is impossible for man to construct vessels small enough to contain only one hundred or even one thousand molecules, Nature is able to do so, and living organisms contain "figured elements," i.e., structures playing an important part, which are precisely of this order of magnitude, and in which, consequently, the laws of chance no longer apply because the number of molecules present is too small. We have seen that the same observation holds true for the insurance companies, which can only function if the number of insured is considerable.

3

PROBABILITIES · AN APPLICATION OF THE LAWS OF
CHANCE · PROTEIN MOLECULES · CHANCE ALONE
CANNOT ACCOUNT FOR THE BIRTH OF LIFE

THERE are two important reasons why we have dwelt at
such length on chance and on the structure of our scientific
laws.

The first is that it was necessary for the reader to understand clearly that *all* our scientific laws at present rest on
chance, that is to say, on the hypothesis of an absolute disorder at the base. If molecules, atoms, and electrons were
not submitted to "perfectly disordered" motions, our
statistical reasoning would not lead us to definite laws.
Now, these laws of nature express a remarkable harmony
on our scale of observation. It can, therefore, be said that,
from the point of view of man, *order is born of disorder*.

It is imperative to ponder over this statement. For it is
certain that any man capable of reflection cannot help discerning in this short phrase one of the most mysterious
philosophical problems of our time. It is one of those
problems which force human reason and intelligence to
unite Nature, Man, and Cause in the same plan and impose great caution in the expression of an opinion.

The preceding chapters may seem dry and uncalled-for

if we consider the title and aim of this book, but they were partly written so as to enable the reader to understand this short sentence. We hope that he realizes its importance.

The second reason is that in the present chapter we will make use of the calculus of probabilities to demonstrate mathematically the impossibility of explaining today the birth of life by means of pure chance, that is to say, by our actual human science. The calculus of probabilities is nothing but the combination of rules which make it possible to express the laws of chance mathematically. It was, therefore, necessary that the reader become familiar with these ideas, with the mechanisms of scientific thought, with the relativity of the Universe and of the image we have built of it, and with the tremendous problems it brings up.

Our science is admirable and prodigious. Inasmuch as it is a creation of the human brain it calls forth an even greater admiration for the latter, which constructed it. But we must remember that we ignore, and probably shall always ignore, everything of the relations between the mysterious and hypothetical universe, created by our logic and genius with the help of the elements furnished by the deforming mirror of our senses, and the real, silent, colorless universe. The splendor of the world was born from the impact between it and our consciousness.

The human brain craves understanding. It cannot understand without simplifying, that is, without reducing things to a common element. However, all simplifications are arbitrary and lead us to drift insensibly away from reality. Therefore, when man tries to understand he generally loses sight of the problem he meant to study. The base from which he starts is supplied by his sensations. When he analyzes his sensations he arrives at atoms and electrons; *a sensation, atomistically conceived, loses all its significance.* The need to unify, to discover common elements in all phenomena, leads man, in spite of himself, into a different realm from the one he wanted to explore. But in this race for unity he sometimes succeeds in disengaging general laws, dynamic evolutive principles which possess great universality and an impressive amplitude. We shall encounter such laws in the course of our studies.

For the present, we will examine one specific application of the calculus of probabilities. First, however, let us define what is understood by the *probability* of an event: it is the ratio of the number of cases favorable to the event, to the total number of possibilities, *all possible cases being considered as equally probable.*

For instance, in the game of heads or tails, the number of cases possible is evidently 2 (heads *or* tails). If the coin is symmetrical, which is usual, the two cases are equally probable. Therefore, the probability that when the coin is thrown up in the air it will come down heads (or tails) is equal to 1 (number of cases favorable to each player) divided by 2, or ½ or 0.5. We will say that the probability of winning in a game of heads or tails is 0.5. In the case of dice, which have six sides, the probability will be 1/6 or 0.1666 . . .

An important point to remember is that, according to the clever phrase of the great mathematician, Joseph Bertrand, "Chance has neither consciousness nor memory." At the end of ten throws which have brought tails, the chances that the next throw will again bring tails are *the same* as after the first throw, and the same as for heads. The probability is still ½. That is why, even if it is possible to win or lose in a game of chance, it is mathematically certain that if one plays long enough the winnings and losses will balance themselves on condition that the game is honest, that chance alone intervenes.

In the same way, if a natural phenomenon is to be expressed by a law based on the calculus of probabilities, we must admit that Nature is honest, that it does not cheat. Later on we shall see that everything takes place as if this were the case as long as Life is absent, but that, as soon as Life appears, it may no longer be true.

In general the problems are less simple and the probabilities are compounded. They are then calculated by means of the following theorem:

When the event, the probability of which one seeks, consists in the successive appearance of two events, the probability is equal to the product of the probability of the first of these events multiplied by the probability that the second event will take place when the first has taken place.

Let us take a simple example, and ask ourselves what is the probability of throwing the number 5 *twice in succession,* in a game of dice? The probability of the first event is 1/6. That of the second is also 1/6. Therefore, the probability of obtaining 5 (or any other number) twice in succession will be equal to $1/6 \times 1/6 = 1/36$ or .0277, which is already much slighter. The probability of obtaining five times the same number in succession is only 1/7,776 or 0.00013 . . . The chance of obtaining it ten times running will be 1/60,466,176 (in round numbers) or about 0.000,000,016. It can be seen that the chances decrease rapidly.

Let us now discuss the real meaning of words such as possible and impossible. Ever since the idea of probability was introduced into physics these words have naturally

been stricken from our scientific language. Any event can
be highly improbable, but is always *theoretically* possible
except when, for simple, structural, logical reasons it is inconceivable, such as the impossibility of throwing 7 with
a single die. If the probability of an event is infinitely
slight it is equivalent to the *practical* impossibility of its
happening *within certain time limits*. The theoretical possibility always exists, but it can be so small that it is
equivalent to a quasi-certitude of the contrary. Here time
can intervene.

Indeed, supposing we limit the time during which a
certain phenomenon can be produced. Supposing, for
instance, that a certain event has one chance of being produced in a hundred years under certain conditions, but
that these conditions cannot be maintained for more than
twenty-four hours. For instance, let us imagine that a dice
player tries to obtain the slightly probable cast mentioned
above, namely the same number ten times in succession.
In round numbers he will have one chance in 60,000,000
(sixty million) throws. If he plays night and day (twenty-
four hours per day) and throws his die once every second,
he will throw 86,400 times per day, and he will have to
continue without interruption—without sleep or food—for
about two years to have *one chance* of casting the same
number ten times in succession. But supposing the die is
made of such fragile matter that it can only last a maximum of a few days. The player's chances will be considerably decreased, for he will not be able to play his sixty
million four hundred and sixty-six thousand throws. He
always has the chance that the lucky series will happen
almost immediately, at the end of a small number of
throws, but this chance is very slight. If he can only throw
his die ten times, it may be said that the cast is *practically*

impossible. We will shortly see why this example was chosen.

Let us imagine that we have a powder composed of 1000 white particles and 1000 black ones which only differ from each other by their coloring. At the beginning of the experiment these particles are in a glass tube, the diameter of which is only slightly larger than the particles, so that they stand in one single row next to each other and cannot mix. The 1000 white particles are at the top of the tube and the 1000 black particles at the bottom. On our scale of observation the tube is half white and half black, the dissymmetry is complete, there is no homogeneity. (Degree of dissymmetry equal to 1.)

The tube, which is closed at one end, communicates at the other with a hollow glass ball. When we turn the apparatus upside down the particles fall pell-mell into the ball and are mixed together through shaking. When we turn it up again they fall back into the tube one above the other, but they have changed their relative positions. It is extremely improbable that they will be separated in the same way as at the beginning of the experiment. At a proper distance, so that the eye cannot distinguish the individual white grains from the black ones, the tube will appear gray along its whole length.

If we shake it again and turn it up we will obtain a new arrangement of the particles, but *on our scale of observation* the tube remains gray, and the phenomenon is not modified perceptibly. Observation shows that even if we prolong the experiment for a considerable time the impression remains roughly the same. The calculus of probabilities enables us to interpret these facts precisely, for it shows that the probability that the 1000 white particles will be entirely separated from the 1000 black ones after being shaken is expressed by 0.489×10^{-600} or 489 preceded by 600 zeros to the right of the point; about twelve lines of zeros in an ordinary book. This is only true if we admit that the order in which the black particles and the white particles are placed is of no importance, namely if we admit that they are absolutely identical with the exception of color.

It is evident that exponents of over 100 lose all human significance.[1] This naturally applies to negative exponents such as —100. A negative exponent (preceded by the minus sign —) simply means that the number is divided and not multiplied: $3 \times 10^{-3} = 3 \div 10^3$ or $\dfrac{3}{1000} = 0.003$.

[1] A short explanation may be necessary to enable the reader who is not familiar with large numbers expressed by means of powers of ten to understand the significance of this method and its advantages.

It is inconvenient to write all the zeros in certain numbers, for it is difficult to read them and they take up too much space. When we spoke of the number of molecules in a cubic centimeter of gas, for instance, we dealt with 30,000,000,000,000,000,000 molecules. This is unreadable. In order to simplify, it is customary to write this number: 3×10^{19} which reads: three times 10 to the power 19, where 19, called the *exponent*, simply expresses the number of zeros after the last significant figure. Thus $10^2 = 10 \times 10 = 100$; $10^3 = 10 \times 10 \times 10 = 1000$ and $3 \times 10^3 = 3000$.

This notation is often confusing, as the powers of 10 increase with disconcerting rapidity. For instance, it is estimated that the earth is about 2,000 million years old, namely 2×10^9 years. Expressed in centuries this gives 2×10^7 centuries, and as there are less than 10^5 days (one hundred thousand days) in a century, less than 2×10^{12} days have, therefore, gone by. In one day there are less than 10^5 seconds; therefore, less than 2×10^{17} seconds have elapsed since the beginning of the world. This last figure represents *the whole history of the terrestrial globe*, namely the whole of human reality.

To reach larger figures we must turn to the age of the sun, which in all likelihood (according to modern theories) does not exceed 5×10^{12} years (5 thousand billion) or 5×10^{20} seconds. The distance from the earth to the sun expressed in 1/25,000 of an inch, 1/1000 of a millimeter or 1 micron, is only 150×10^{15} and the nearest star is 40×10^{21} microns away from us. There are 10^{19} molecules in one cubic centimeter of gas (about one thimbleful) but there are less than 10^{79} molecules in the whole universe, including the remotest stars.

Now that the reader is prepared, let us pass on to the real problem. It is impossible because of the tremendous complexity of the question to lay down the basis for a calculation which would enable one to establish the probability of the spontaneous appearance of life on earth. However, the problem can be greatly simplified and we can try to calculate the probability of the appearance, by chance alone, of certain essential elements of life, certain large molecules, proteins for instance. The elementary molecules of living organisms are all characterized by a very considerable dissymmetry. Now, we have seen that dissymmetry can be expressed by a number comprised between 0.5 and 1. The number 1 corresponds to a maximum dissymmetry (in the case of the black and white particles, all the black on one side and all the white on the other); and the number 0.5 corresponds to perfect homogeneity, the most symmetrical distribution: the white and black particles evenly mixed throughout the tube. The most probable fluctuations (slight deviations around the equal number) are grouped near the degree of dissymmetry 0.5.

These calculations were made by Professor Charles-Eugène Guye for a molecule of dissymmetrical degree 0.9, when the number of constituent atoms is equal to 2000. To simplify the problem considerably the atoms constituting this imaginary protein molecule are considered as being of *two* species only, whereas there is always a minimum of four: carbon, hydrogen, nitrogen, oxygen, plus either copper, iron or sulphur, etc. The atomic weight of these atoms being supposed equal to 10—another simplification—the molecular weight is 20,000. This figure is probably lower than that of the most simple proteins. (Egg albumin 34.500.)

The probability that a configuration of a degree of dis-symmetry 0.9 would appear under these arbitrarily simplified conditions which make it more probable, would be (if chance alone is considered) :

$$2.02 \times 10^{-321} \text{ or } 2.02 \times \frac{1}{10^{321}}$$

The volume of substance necessary for such a probability to take place is beyond all imagination. It would be that of a sphere with a radius so great that light would take 10^{82} years to cover this distance. The volume is incomparably greater than that of the whole universe including the farthest galaxies, whose light takes only 2×10^{6} (two million) years to reach us. In brief, we would have to imagine a volume more than one sextillion, sextillion, sextillion times greater than the Einsteinian universe (Charles-Eugène Guye).

The probability for *a single* molecule of high dissymmetry to be formed by the action of chance and normal thermic agitation remains practically nil. Indeed, if we suppose 500 trillion shakings per second (5×10^{14}), which corresponds to the order of magnitude of light frequencies (wave lengths comprised between 0.4 and 0.8 microns), we find that the time needed to form, on an average, one such molecule (degree of dissymmetry 0.9) in a material volume equal to that of our terrestrial globe is about 10^{243} billions of years (1 followed by 243 zeros).

BUT WE MUST NOT FORGET THAT THE EARTH HAS ONLY EXISTED FOR TWO BILLION YEARS AND THAT LIFE APPEARED ABOUT ONE BILLION YEARS AGO, AS SOON AS THE EARTH HAD COOLED $(1 \times 10^{9}$ years$)$.

We thus find ourselves in the case of the player who does not have at his disposal the time necessary to throw his die often enough to have one single chance of obtaining his series, but instead of a period three or four hundred times too short, we are faced with an interval which is more than 10^{243} times too short.

On the other hand, we can always bring out the fact that, no matter how slight the chance, it nevertheless exists, and that there is no proof that the rare configuration will only appear at the end of billions and billions of centuries. It can happen right at the start, in the first seconds. Not only is this in perfect accord with the calculus, but it can be admitted that the phenomenon occurred twice, and even three times in succession and then practically never again. However, if this happened and we maintained our confidence in the calculus of probabilities it would be equivalent to admitting a miracle, and the result would be: ONE SINGLE MOLECULE, or at most two or three.

Life itself is not even in question but merely one of the substances which constitute living beings. Now, one molecule is of no use. Hundreds of millions of *identical* ones are necessary. We would need much greater figures to "explain" the appearance of a series of similar molecules, the improbability increasing considerably, as we have seen, for each new molecule (compound probability), and for each series of identical throws. If the probability of appearance of a living cell could be expressed mathematically the preceding figures would seem negligible. The problem was deliberately simplified in order to increase the probabilities.

Events which, even when we admit very numerous experiments, reactions, or shakings per second, *need an infinitely longer time than the estimated duration of the earth in order to have one chance, on an average, to mani-*

fest themselves can, it would seem, be considered as impossible in the human sense.

Thus we are actually confronted with a dilemma. Either we have absolute confidence in our science and in the mathematical and other reasonings which enable us to give a satisfactory explanation of the phenomena surrounding us—in which case we are forced to recognize that certain fundamental problems escape us and that their explanation amounts to admitting a miracle—or else we doubt the universality of our science and the possibility of explaining all natural phenomena by chance alone; and we fall back on a miracle or a hyperscientific intervention.

In both cases we are brought to the conclusion that, actually, it is *totally impossible* to account scientifically for all phenomena pertaining to Life, its development and progressive evolution, and that, unless the foundations of modern science are overthrown, they are unexplainable.

We are faced by a hiatus in our knowledge. There is a gap between living and non-living matter which we have not been able to bridge. The reader will remember that we have already pointed out another such gap in the realm of particles, between the electrons constituting the atoms and the atoms themselves. We can hope that they will both be bridged by science some day, but at present this is nothing but wishful thinking.

The remarkable discoveries made at the Rockefeller Institute of the crystallizable viruses of rabbit Papilloma, by Wyckoff, and of the mosaic disease of tobacco, by Stanley, which were hailed as intermediaries between inorganic matter and living matter, do not alter this statement. First because their molecular weights are so high that the probabilities of their appearance as a result of chance are even slighter. (The molecular weight is of the order of

10,000,000, which means that they are built of more than 500,000 atoms). Secondly, because, in no sense of the word are these substances alive. It is true that they reproduce, but only when in contact with living matter, just like the toxins, known as ptomaines, which appear when living matter undergoes a process of decomposition.

The laws of chance have rendered, and will continue to render, immense services to science. It is inconceivable that we could do without them, but they only express an admirable, subjective interpretation of certain inorganic phenomena and of their evolution. They are not a true explanation of objective reality. What they cannot take into account or explain is the fact that *the properties of a cell are born out of the coordination of complexity* and not out of the chaotic complexity of a mixture of gases. This transmissible, hereditary, continuous coordination entirely escapes our laws of chance.

To believe that we shall ever be able to explain biological phenomena in general, and the evolution of living beings, through the use of the same calculations employed to estimate the number of houses which will burn or the pressure of a gas in a vessel, is an act of faith and not a scientific statement. Rare fluctuations do not explain qualitative facts, they only enable us to conceive that they are not impossible quantitatively.

The striking and magnificent intellectual trick which enabled the human mind to construct a pattern *practically* superposable on Nature, remains a wonderful expedient which can only be applied to non-living matter. It even had to be seriously modified in order to make it apply to the realm of electromagnetic radiation (Bose-Einstein statistics) and to electronic energy (Pauli-Fermi statistics).

To study the most interesting phenomena, namely Life and eventually Man, we are, therefore, forced to call on an anti-chance, as Eddington called it; a "cheater" who systematically violates the laws of large numbers, the statistical laws which deny any individuality to the particles considered.

To summarize the preceding chapters we can say in the first place that it has been shown that we know less about our material world than is usually believed and that our knowledge is subjective, and conditioned by the structure of our brain.

The laws we have been able to establish probably express an order of sequence, as well as quantitative variations which correspond in nature to a similar order and similar variations. But this seems to be true only when life is absent. There are gaps in the continuity of our mental image of the universe which force us to admit that the beautiful unity we are striving to demonstrate in nature is nothing more, at the present time, than a philosophical, one might almost say sentimental, conviction. Should we ever be able to demonstrate the reality of this unity, it would only prove that our human, intuitive concepts had reached truth directly, before our rational methods had enabled us to attain the same goal, and consequently that intuitive irrational concepts are not to be scorned. Should we be unable to establish this unity, it would show that our science must be rebuilt on different bases, and possibly that a dualistic concept should be envisaged. As the human mind has long ago conceived this possibility, it would, once again, teach us to respect intuitive ideas.

In the second place, it has been shown that, on the basis of our present knowledge, namely, by using the same methods which have been proved so useful for the interpretation of our inanimate world, it was impossible to explain, or to account for, not only the birth of life but even the appearance of the substances which seem to be required to build life, namely, highly dissymmetrical molecules.

Consequently, although we must keep all our confidence in our science, we must not blindly believe in its actual almightiness. We must not forget that the activities of the brain are far from being all known, and that rational thinking may very well be only one of them, conceivably not the most reliable or the fastest.

4

THE LAWS OF INORGANIC EVOLUTION CONTRADICT THOSE
OF THE EVOLUTION OF LIFE • CARNOT-CLAUSIUS LAW •
THE "POINT OF VIEW OF THE MICROBE" • FREE WILL AND
THE MATERIALISTIC ATTITUDE

WE HAVE been dealing so far with subjects which may
have led the reader to wonder why so much space was as-
signed to them, and which apparently were not logically
connected with the title of this book. Our introduction
may have sounded unconvincing.

The present chapter, however, dealing with evolution
as a whole and with human freedom—free will—would
have been almost entirely incomprehensible, had it not
been preceded by the three others. It will afford us an
opportunity to discuss the philosophical attitude known as
materialism, mechanism, rationalism, or sometimes atheism, and to demonstrate the fact that it is not as scientific
as some people believe. A whole book could be written on
the subject, but we have chosen one striking example out
of many, which we hope will suffice. Indeed the question
in our mind is not to say whether this point of view is a
good or a bad one but whether it is really supported by
facts.

We know that modern science leads us to conceive all

matter as being composed of a tremendous number of atoms and molecules, usually moving around at great speeds and with completely uncoordinated movements depending on chance alone. To describe their activity we have used the paradoxical term of "perfect disorder."

We have also pointed out that the validity of our scientific laws depends on the complete lack of organization at the base. The so-called "laws of chance" borrow their accuracy (which is considerable on our scale of observation) from the fact that no privileged atoms exist (from the particular point of view considered) and that, on an average, they all behave in the same unpredictable, disorderly manner.

One of the greatest successes of modern science was to link the fundamental Carnot-Clausius law (also called the second law of thermodynamics),[1] keystone of our actual interpretation of the inorganic world, with the calculus of probabilities. Indeed, the great physicist Boltzmann proved that the inorganic, irreversible evolution imposed by this law corresponded to an evolution toward more and more "probable" states, characterized by an ever-increasing symmetry, a leveling of energy. The universe, therefore, tends toward an equilibrium where all the dissymmetries existing today will be flattened out, where all motion will have stopped and where total obscurity and absolute cold will reign. Such will be the end of the world —theoretically.

Now, we men, at the surface of the earth, are witnesses to another kind of evolution: that of living things. We have already seen that the laws of chance, in their actual

---

[1] This law can be worded as follows: An isolated material system can never pass twice identically through the same state. Every successive state entails a definitive decrease in its available energy. Hence its irreversibility.

state, cannot account for the birth of life. But now we find that they *forbid* any evolution other than that which leads to less and less dissymmetrical states, while the history of the evolution of life reveals a systematic *increase* in dissymmetries, both structural and functional. Furthermore, this trend can hardly be attributed to a "rare fluctuation" destined to be ironed out statistically, as it has manifested itself steadily for over one thousand million years (probable age of life on this globe), and as the dissymmetries, gloriously unconcerned about the law set by man, became greater as eons passed by until they culminated in the brain of Man.

This formidable contradiction stands today as an insurmountable obstacle in the path of materialism. The only argument called upon so far, namely, that life as a whole and its evolution—including such manifestations as thought—is nothing but a negligible fluctuation, is rather pathetic, inasmuch as inorganic evolution is essentially a recent human concept hatched in man's brain, while the evolution of life is a reality supported by an immense series of observable facts such as the fossils. This does not mean that the magnificent intellectual effort which led man to conceive and to codify inorganic evolution is to be eliminated or neglected, but merely that it is to be considered as a splendid manifestation of the activities of the ultimate masterpiece of the "negligible fluctuation," namely, the human brain.

Therefore, any attempt to subordinate biological evolution to inorganic evolution cannot, *a priori,* be considered as scientific or philosophic. It is not even intelligent, if the word is used in its etymological sense (*intelligere,* Latin, to understand). The old-fashioned materialist who is honestly convinced that human life is without a cause and without a goal, that man is an irresponsible particle of matter engulfed in a maelstrom of purposeless forces, reminds us of the delightful remark made by a brilliant philosopher, Whitehead: ". . . Scientists who spend their life with the purpose of proving that it is purposeless constitute an interesting subject of study."

An explanation of the evolution of life by chance alone is untenable today. It does not permit the incorporation of man and of his psychological activities into the general pattern of things. It does not explain the progressive, ascensional development of life forms and it even denies this development. Consequently, another hypothesis must be tried. There is only one, namely finalism.

Unfortunately, finalism has been so completely misunderstood and misrepresented by such a large number of well-meaning scientists that, as a theory, it is definitely—and justly—considered out of date. The great mistake these writers generally made was to consider a finalism limited to the species. They dwelt on the prodigies of adaptation, but lost track of the more important phenomena, the transformations of great groups: the phyla, the classes, and the orders. So that, failing to explain the real problem of evolution, they were considered as unconvincing, and the finalistic hypothesis very nearly died out.

It is our belief that such a fate was deserved but that finalism can and must be rejuvenated in a different form. And this can only be done by looking at evolution from its beginning to its actual stage, that is, by covering immensely long geological periods. We must momentarily forget the details of evolution, its mechanisms, of which we know so little, and try to view the tremendous work of creation as a whole, not statically (that is, by immobilizing it), but dynamically (that is, by bearing in mind the fact that it is a succession of constant transformations). We must not allow ourselves to be smothered by particulars, no matter how interesting they are, but must keep our eyes fixed at all times on the fundamental steps of evolution, from the most elementary organism to man and the incredible manifestations of his brain.

To appreciate a cathedral, perspective is required. If we come too close to it, we shall have a better view of the statues, the portal, and the ornamentation, but we shall miss the general impression willed by the architect, which can be had only from a distance. To understand evolution, we must have perspective in time, we must cover eons, and furthermore, study it, as it were, in motion, dynamically.

A moving-picture film can be examined in two different ways: either statically, by looking at every individual photograph separately, with a magnifying glass; or cinematically, by projecting the whole film on the screen. In the first case we may discover some interesting details, which will escape us when viewing the whole, but as there is no impression of motion we miss the sequence, we do not understand the attitudes of the protagonists: their immobility kills the meaning of their expressions. Evolution presents itself to us as an incomplete film. Many parts are missing, but we know its present state and a few fairly well-preserved sections of the past which our imagination must link together as best we can.

The patient and careful accumulation of facts—the fossils—and their admirable classification, begun in the very beginning of the nineteenth century by Cuvier and by Lamarck, supply us with an abundant material which grows every day. But in trying to interpret the processes of evolution and their mechanisms, we must be careful to avoid anthropomorphic ideas, that is, ideas borrowed from our human experience or our human way of thinking.

Man is always tempted to inject his own methods of thought and his own reactions into any problem. When dealing with the psychology of animals, of insects for instance, he is inclined to compare their reactions to his own under the same conditions. He often forgets that the conditions are never identical, and that the physiological structure of animals gives birth to reactions which he is, and always will be, completely incapable of understanding.

If a microbe, living in one of the cracks of an elephant's skin, possessed our intelligence, and if his ancestors had built up and transmitted to him a science, as ours have done in less than ten generations, it is conceivable that he would not have a very clear idea of the laws governing his universe: the elephant. The microbe lives at the bottom of a valley one fifth of an inch deep, the equivalent to us of a canyon six or seven thousand feet high. There he may have created an image of his world very different from ours, and when the elephant scratches himself, or takes a bath, the microscopic dweller of the valley can be excused if he attributes these unpredictable cataclysms to an entirely different cause. Let us try to avoid the point of view of the microbe, for whom one day of twenty-four hours corresponds to a century, or four generations.

In studying the evolution to which we belong let us remember that it is only one chapter of a story which began long before. It was preceded by an inorganic evolution—governed by the above-mentioned Carnot-Clausius law—and which still goes on around us. This, in turn, was preceded by another period, when atoms and molecules did not yet exist, and of which we know very little, or nothing; for it took place perhaps ten thousand million years ago, perhaps a little less, but according to modern ideas certainly not more than ten million million years ago. This first evolution (we do not even know if we can call it that) the evolution of the particles, electrons, protons, etc., did not apparently obey the same laws as the second, while the world of atoms and molecules, as noted above, is irreversible and cannot retrace its steps.

Every event, every phenomenon wears down the original capital of energy (available power) of our universe considered as an isolated system. Obviously, if it were not isolated, some energy could be borrowed from another system. During this slow process of "degradation" of energy, the original order, namely all the dissymmetries which made energy available in the form of work, tends toward complete, absolute disorder (absence of dissymmetries). Entropy, representing the counterpart of the available energy which has disappeared in the process, can be considered as a measure of disorder.

We can, therefore, admit the existence of an Evolution of evolutions covering periods of time quite inconceivable to man. However, we are only concerned with our own evolution, with our own problems. The fact that, as we have pointed out, biological evolution does not seem to obey the fundamental key-law of inorganic evolution interests us only as an indication that human science has failed so far in its attempt to link these two evolutions together. It will make it easier for us later to accept another new departure in biological evolution itself, namely, the sudden advent of conscience in the human mind.

There is another apparent conflict which has caused

much discussion between materialists and spiritualists, namely that of freedom. It is quite obvious that the reality of free will is an absolute necessity for all religious people, all those who do not look upon man as a mere animal, an irresponsible cog in a huge and purposeless machine, all those who believe that man can shape his own destiny.

On the other hand, it is just as obvious that the pure materialist, who only believes in chance and whose efforts tend to unify science, that is, to find a common base for all phenomena (including life and thought), will never admit the existence of an element capable of playing havoc with the magnificently simple concept of a purely mechanical universe.

We are here facing two creeds seemingly opposed to each other; but the weakness of the materialist lies in the fact that, although he prides himself on being strictly rational and scientific, he often contradicts himself, so that his convictions are no less sentimental than those of the spiritualist, who, at least, is willing to admit it.

The following analogy is often used to illustrate the deterministic point of view: a stone, when thrown up in the air, may think it is free, but we men know that it is bound by the law of gravitation, and therefore, cannot be looked upon as being free. In the same way, man may believe that he is free: to an observer possessing a deeper knowledge of things, this feeling of freedom is not real and simply expresses a subjective, illusory reaction based on man's inability to reach the objective roots of reality.

We may first point out that this antiquated argument belongs to a period when the old Laplacian determinism was accepted. We know that it was replaced around 1900 by a statistical determinism in which chance alone is the *primum movens,* and which admits the theoretical possibility of fluctuations capable of eventually contradicting the law. It is, therefore, conceivable that the stone might not fall down; however, in practice, this never occurs. Furthermore, it is clear that on philosophical grounds the analogy is fallacious and unsound. The two events cannot logically be compared, one of them being evidently univocal (the motion of the stone) and the other equivocal (the actions of man). By this we mean that, no matter what the stone may "think," we, outside observers, know experimentally that it has no choice, because we have never observed a stone which did not obey the law of gravitation. Assuming that it "thinks," it must have come to the conclusion that it always chooses to fall on the ground eventually. Whether it calls this choice or obedience matters little; what matters is that it never chooses to disobey. There is, historically, only one possibility: the phenomenon is univocal.

On the other hand, let us consider man.

From his point of view, on his scale of observation, everything takes place as though he were free either to follow his animal instincts, which afford a great deal of physical satisfaction, or else to scorn these satisfactions and seek another goal, the attainment of what we call higher human and spiritual values. We know that the pursuit of this goal means a struggle against his animal self, and often entails pain, even though it is eventually conducive to the greatest joys. There can be no question that these two paths exist really, for man alone. Rationally speaking, and irrespective of man's subjective reactions, the difference between the two possible paths can easily be established, inasmuch as, if there were no difference, they would be equally probable, as in the game of heads or tails. If they were, the number of men should be very

nearly the same in both, and this is disproved experimentally. Consequently they are not equally probable;
hence there is a difference between the two. The concept
is definitely equivocal.

As a result the observer will have to make up his mind
and decide whether, according to him the evolution of
man will follow the tradition set by animals or by man.
The chances are that he will not select the path leading to
the development of man along the moral and specifically
human lines, as the majority seems to be headed in the
opposite direction. He will probably decide that the one
and only real path of evolution is the continuance of
physiological and anatomical evolution, as in the past. The
other possibility (moral evolution) will then be considered
as a mere "fluctuation" without any influence on the first.

But a "fluctuation" is not "determined"; it is, on the
basis of its very definition, entirely due to chance. Now
man knows that he is constantly confronted with this
dilemma: either yield to temptations—namely, obey the
impulses of his instinct—or else resist these temptations
and obey other impulses whose origin is not physiological
but moral, and which contradict the first. No one in his
senses will deny the existence of this dilemma. The real
question is as to whether man is free to formulate his
choice and to act accordingly, or not. As we have just
established the fact that his attitude cannot be "determined," the only other alternative is that he is free.

To say that his choice, when he faces the dual possibility, is due to chance is rationally untenable as long as we
consider the moral and spiritual trend as a mere fluctuation. Indeed, a fluctuation which persists and repeats
itself systematically over a period of at least twenty or
thirty thousand years can no longer be considered as a

fluctuation but becomes a well-characterized phenomenon.

Who can tell which one of these two groups, the animal or the spiritual, will outlive the other in the remote future? Nobody, not even our observer. The fact that the second represents today a smaller percentage of the population of the world does not mean that it is not the real evolutive element of mankind, as the story of evolution shows that its spearhead usually comprises a small number of individuals, the so-called mutant forms. The reader will find examples of this fact in the following chapters. So that the hypothesis, according to which the "fluctuation" would in reality be the main trend of evolution, is not eliminated.

Scientifically, therefore, the existence of free will cannot be brushed aside. In fact, it remains as the only acceptable hypothesis. The role of man then consists in transforming a fluctuation, which may have started as an effect of chance fifty or one hundred thousand years ago, into a law capable eventually of becoming the general law of evolution. And this can be achieved only through free will, which thus becomes the main tool of this evolution.

Humanly speaking, of course, things are much simpler. We know from experience how hard it is to follow the path of duty, how easy it is and how pleasant to follow the other. Some men are determined to bring about, at any cost, the triumph of their ideals, of their "fluctuation." They are fully aware of the reality of their struggles, as nothing is more real than the tragic story of their predecessors who bled and died for those ideals. But in spite of all their sufferings they are happier than most men and firmly believe that they shall win. Our animal ancestors fought for their lives; men fight for their faith in the higher destinies of man. Should they succeed, in the course of centuries, in filling the world with an overwhelming majority of people inspired by the same ideals, another "observer" will then decide that the so-called Christian virtues were really the consequence of the laws of evolution; and that is precisely what we believe.

The writer is not naive enough to think that this discussion will convince any materialist. People who have a faith cannot be convinced by mere words and logic. Men with an irrational faith—and we hope that we have made it clear that such is their case—do not yield to rational arguments because words do not have the same meaning for us and for them. We talk about moral and spiritual values to which we attribute a greater reality with respect to man than to the electron, while they do not even admit the existence of such values and firmly believe in a material world which we consider only as a pretext. Today, when humanity is threatened with complete destruction by the liberation of atomic forces, people begin to realize that the only efficient protection lies in a greater and higher moral development. For the first time in the history of humanity, man is afraid of what he has done with his intelligence and wonders whether he has chosen the right path.

Our aim in discussing the mechanistic attitude toward evolution and liberty, or free will, was to show that the materialist, who boasts about his strict and scientific rationalism, is not infallible in his own trade. He is not likely of course to advertise his errors or his conflicts, but it must be known that he is no longer qualified to claim strict rational thinking and scientific facts as the basic foundation of his creed.

We shall now begin the story of the evolution of life on this earth. We hope to be able to convince the reader that, unless a finalistic point of view is adopted, it completely escapes our understanding. But we shall use, as a leading light, a teleological hypothesis, that is, a finalism with a very ultimate goal, a "telefinalism," if we may be allowed to coin a new word.

BOOK II

The Evolution of Life

5

THE AGE OF THE EARTH · BIRTH OF EVOLUTION ·
ASEXUAL REPRODUCTION AND THE "INVENTION OF DEATH"
· ANIMALS EVOLVE MORE RAPIDLY THAN PLANTS · THE
PRESERVATION OF FOSSILS · TRANSITIONAL FORMS

BEFORE beginning the story of life on earth, it seems necessary to say a few words about the methods employed to
determine the age of our globe and the antiquity of geological periods. The appearance of certain animal species,
which go back hundreds of millions of years, will be discussed, and the reader is entitled to know on what authority and by means of what methods these figures were
accepted.

According to the most recent and trustworthy sources,
the birth of the earth was *almost* contemporaneous with
that of the sun and of the other planets of our system. Our
globe must be about two thousand million years old, and
can in no case be much older. As far as the sun is concerned it has been demonstrated that it cannot have
existed more than 5,000 billion (5×10^{12}) years (Milne)
and that it is probably much younger. Indeed, when we
consider the systems of stars, clusters, and galaxies, all the
evidence indicates a much shorter past. "It now seems unlikely that their birth goes back beyond 10,000 million
years" (Eddington), or 10^{10} years.

The age of the earth can be calculated fairly accurately through the study of radioactivity. Following are the broad outlines of the method:

It is known that a certain number of simple elements are subject to spontaneous disintegration. The atomic nucleus expels a part of itself, thus acquiring a new personality differing from the preceding one by its mass, or its electric charge, or both. About twenty such atoms are known in which the process is natural and it is actually possible to manufacture hundreds of them artificially. In the case of spontaneously radioactive atoms, the point of departure of these disintegrations in the three series—radium, actinium, thorium—is an almost stable element, so that the process is extremely slow and only a very slight fraction of the atoms present in a given mass of matter disintegrates in one year. The methods used to measure these radioactive phenomena (methods of Pierre Curie) are fortunately extraordinarily sensitive. It was, therefore, possible to determine the quantity of matter transmuted with considerable accuracy. In one year, heavy uranium loses spontaneously one atom out of 6,570 million; light uranium or actino-uranium one out of 1,030 million, and thorium one out of 20,000 million. The resulting atoms are much less stable than their parents, and go through a long series of transformations before finally becoming stable nuclei which are all three isotopes of lead having atomic weights of 206, 207, and 208.

Some of the intermediary bodies have a duration of life of the order of a million years. Others only exist for a fraction of a second. These phenomena follow each other in a perfectly known rhythm and are characterized by the fact that in all cases their speed cannot be changed by *any external influence* such as temperature or pressure. We thus have an absolutely faithful clock which cannot be put out of order.

If, then, a mineral containing uranium is imprisoned in a rock for a billion years (10^9), about 14 per cent of the atoms present at the origin will have disintegrated. An equal number of atoms of lead corresponding to these atoms will have replaced them. Their weight will be equivalent to 12 per cent of the weight of the original uranium, the other 2 per cent representing the weight of helium liberated in the course of the process. The older the sample, the more lead there will be. *The ratio between the quantity of lead found and the quantity of uranium present enables one to calculate the time elapsed since the rock has been formed.* We may add that no error can arise from the presence of ordinary lead of non-radioactive origin, for natural lead always contains a slight proportion of an isotope of atomic weight 204, which *never* appears in the course of the radioactive disintegration.

Only the largest figures obtained by this method interest us. It is through them that we can determine the epoch at which the earth began to solidify. The figures vary between 1,500 and 1,800 million years. The age of the fossils is obviously deduced from the age of the rocks and soil in which they are found.

Let us leave aside the problem of the origin of life, in all likelihood connected with that of the origin of proteins, and much more mysterious still, and let us only consider the evolutive point of view.

It is impossible, nowadays, to imagine how evolution began. Was there an initial cell? Or, as seems plausible to admit, did amorphous living matter precede the first cells? We do not know.

Schwann, and after him a majority of biologists, thought that all living matter was composed of cells. But a certain number of very elementary organisms—the Coenocytes—are not divided into cells; Mycetocytes, for instance, have an arborescent structure and weigh up to one pound. These organisms, which still exist in our day, display all the vital functions: nutrition, respiration, secretion, locomotion, reproduction. They are not alone, for there are also the Phycomyces, which are molds, and the Siphonales, which are algae.

It is very likely that evolution had an extremely elementary point of departure common to all living beings, animals and vegetables. But from the very beginning we observe at the same time a relationship and a profound difference between the two. The active base, the nutritive liquid of the animals, is the blood, and that of the superior animals contains a fundamental substance, the red pigment called hemoglobin, which transports oxygen to the cells so as to oxydize, or burn, the refuse. The molecule of hemoglobin is very large and highly complicated; its structure varies from one species to another (mean molecular weight: 69,000).

Chemically, this hemoglobin is fairly close to the circulatory pigment of plants and algae, chlorophyll (molecular weight: 904). There is, therefore, a relationship, but whereas hemoglobin is characterized by the presence of one atom of iron in its molecule, chlorophyll, which is much simpler, is built around an atom of magnesium. To complicate the problem further, the blood of certain arthropods and mollusks, inferior animals which preceded superior animals, contains a pigment with a molecular weight varying, according to the species, between 400,-000 and 6,700,000 and containing an atom of copper instead of iron or magnesium. (Certain snails, for instance.)

How was the chemical transition from one to the other accomplished? Honestly speaking, it is impossible to conceive it, and yet the hypothesis of a sudden appearance is not satisfactory. Some kind of transition must have taken place. We may never know how.

It is hardly probable that we will ever discover the original being, or his slightly modified descendant, amongst the elementary organisms which have persisted through millions of centuries. Nevertheless we find strange forms everywhere. They are hard to classify as either plants or animals, unless we take magnesium (from the chlorophyll) as the touchstone, for in that case they are plants. Among these elementary forms we find the dino-flagellates, algae invisible to the naked eye, abundant in stagnant waters and revealed by the microscope as being agile acrobats. They swim rapidly, leap and turn with the aid of their long supple tails. Their cellular body inflates and deflates as if it breathed, and at one point a red ocular spot sensitive to light seems to look at one. They show a remarkable diversity of aspects.

Are the dinoflagellates plants or animals? At that stage the question does not make much sense. They are monocellular organisms, containing chlorophyll, protected by a cellulose membrane often beautifully intricate. Like the more evolved plants they feed on minerals in solution in water and on the gases of the atmosphere, a thing which no animal seems able to do. Does the presence of chlorophyll already represent a long anterior evolution? It is possible, for we know some algae which are devoid of it.

On the other hand, these algae contain another pigment. The true anteriority is impossible to demonstrate.

According to certain authors, the most ancient ancestor, anterior to the algae, was a kind of bacterium (microbe having the shape of a rod) which lived in the great soft-water oceans of the remotest ages called either Pre-Cambrian, Algonkian, or Archeozoic. It seems that this bacterium has not disappeared, that certain species have not evolved and that its direct descendant can be found today in the swamps from which iron ore is extracted and in the reddish streams charged with iron oxide flowing out of them. It is the Leptothrix, and its saga was brilliantly written by Donald Culross Peattie.

In the actual state of our knowledge it is impossible to attribute a precedence to such or such an organism with respect to such another, and all the more to derive one from the other. All we can say is that a series of unknown phenomena ended in the appearance of very elementary algae which still exist today, the Cyanophyceae or blue algae. In some of these, the marvelous chlorophyll is not yet present. Their pigment is a phycocyanin. These plants resemble the bacteria by their tubular or spherical form and by their asexual reproduction. They perfect themselves (?) and one day there is a great advance: the green algae invade the waters with, at last, the hope and the possibility of a conceivable evolution. They have a nucleus—which is a kind of miracle—and it seems that they inaugurate sexual reproduction—another miracle. Do the green algae with a cellular structure and a nucleus really derive from the blue algae? We cannot affirm it. At any rate the difference between the two is tremendous and the mechanisms of transition again inconceivable. But, in the negative, what could be their origin?

In any event, the progress is considerable. For even if several methods of asexual reproduction are known in plants and in animals,[1] it is evident that these processes reproduce indefinitely the same characters. The cell or the organism separates into two individuals who live, grow, and in their turn each separate into two others (mitosis fission, budding, etc.). They never die, except accidentally. They go on untiringly doubling their number according to their specific rhythm, so that if it were not checked by a more general or dominant phenomenon, they would soon smother the earth under their mass.

It seems logical that progress and rapid evolution can only be assured by the mixture of different strains, developed in varying environments, and by the confusion of the hereditary modifications. Asexual cells do not know death as individuals. They are immortal. All of a sudden, with sexual generation we see the appearance of an entirely new and unforeseen cyclical phenomenon: the birth and death of the individual. It is clear that sexual reproduction with fecundation, which suppresses the immortality of the individual, was indispensable to make a strain progress toward complexity. It was necessary to modify, to enrich heredity by the mixture of foreign strains, by the pooling of acquired characters.

[1] Asexual reproduction is not limited to very elementary monocellular organisms, but is found in metazoa, in relatively complex animals such as Coelenterata, Platyhelminthes and Annelida (worms). These animals live today. As it is impossible to believe that they reverted to asexual reproduction, it must be admitted that they have existed without evolving for immensely long periods. However, in the Autolytus, a marine worm which reproduces by segmentation (fission) and looks very much like a centipede, the "female" bears eggs in a sac. If the original of both asexual algae and worms was the same, the animal strain must have evolved suddenly in a different way. If it was not the same, they both "discovered" the same solution, which was highly satisfactory inasmuch as both are still living today. Why, then, should *sexual* reproduction have developed?

This is an immense revolution, as important and incomprehensible as the appearance of mammals, and which has not been emphasized enough. Biological evolution could only continue, after a certain stage, by means of distinct individuals, limited both in space and in time. This notion of the role of the individual is fundamental and seems to introduce, from the very beginning, a distinct difference between inorganic matter and life, a difference which is superposed on those already existing.

Thus the birth of an already evolved individual brings about his death at the end of a time varying according to the species. After having transmitted life to one or several other individuals he disappears, he rejoins the inorganic universe from which he had miraculously emerged. And we can say that from an evolutive point of view the greatest invention of Nature is death.

From then on, progressive evolution always proceeds through transitory individuals and because of them, like a melody born of isolated notes which melt into silence leaving but a memory. It is the ephemeral individual who constitutes the primordial element of biological evolution just as in the future the psychological individual will constitute the essential element of the evolution of spirit. Until proved to the contrary, it may be said that with the advent of death natural evolution has striven to evade the statistical hold which dominates the inorganic universe and has prepared the way for the advent of human liberty.

The preceding and following pages call for an important comment whenever figures expressing periods or ages are mentioned. We must not forget that any descriptive chronological plan of evolution is extremely questionable. When we speak of the "appearance" of a species, of organisms "slowly perfecting themselves" or of "an immense stride being taken," we express ideas accepted by the best authors and scientists. However, this does not mean that either they or we affirm the existence of a definite anteriority, of a sudden appearance or of a progressive improvement. It is very important to remember that the only facts at our disposal are traces left by organisms in the ancient rocks or alluviums. It sometimes happens that very ancient imprints closely resemble those left today by certain actually living species, and we can, therefore, consider the latter as being in all likelihood practically identical to the original Pre-Cambrian species. When the imprints are numerous, it is possible to deduce, in accordance with the age of the formations in which they are found, that at such a period these organisms attained a great development. But this does not tell us the date of appearance of the first specimens of the species which may have existed in small numbers for millions of years in unexplored territories, or may have been engulfed in a catastrophe. However, as a whole, and on an average, it is permissible to outline a history of evolution based on the facts at our disposal, which, if not always rigorously exact in its details, nevertheless conveys a fairly accurate impression.

We must not forget, when we speak of the Pre-Cambrian geological level, that it covers about two-thirds of the time required for the whole of evolution, from bacteria up to man, or about 600 million years. An immense series of phenomena must, therefore, have taken place in it. This is confirmed by the study of fossils. For instance, we see that plants developed slowly and that the fauna had attained a considerable degree of perfection before they appeared on dry land. We see that the Pre-Cambrian, which painfully produced an extremely elementary aquatic vegetation, already swarmed with animals of all kinds —not only worms (Annelida) but mollusks with conical shells (resembling the barnacles now to be found on our beaches), articulated trilobites, and large crustaceans. These discoveries are really astounding, for they reveal that the Pre-Cambrian world was already a very old world.

If the worm represents an enormous progress with respect to the bacteria and the blue and green algae, the trilobite represents an even greater progress with respect to the worm. It is a highly evolved animal whose embryogeny indicates a long line of ancestors. Yet, not a trace of terrestrial vegetation has been discovered at the same epoch. We only find indications of very elementary marine flora. If, therefore, we admit that the vegetable and animal realms have the same origin, we cannot escape the conclusion that a certain primitive strain of bacteria, algae, or other organisms was differentiated soon after its appearance and replaced chlorophyll, containing magnesium, by hemocyanin, immeasurably more complicated and containing copper. The mechanism of evolution, once it had started, continued rapidly in that strain while other strains of the same species continued to live without transforming themselves. It is naturally possible that the same phenomenon took place in more than one strain, around the same period. But the others were not affected and are today, nearly one thousand million years later, very similar to what they were at that moment. This would explain the coexistence of primitive aquatic plants and of highly evolved animals and pushes back the beginning of evolution of the latter to the first ages of the earth, toward the inferior Pre-Cambrian.

It is certain that the animal realm evolved from the start much more quickly than the vegetable realm. If the vegetable preceded the animal and if the origin was the same, the passage from one to the other must have occurred rapidly, almost immediately. This is another problem to which it might be wise not to apply the calculus of probabilities.

In the primary (Silurian) epoch, the seas contained magnificent Ganoid fish, protected by a powerful bony armor; Cephalopods, the ancestors of our octopus; Nautilacea, Brachiopods, and Scorpionida possessing aerial respiration. This polymorphous fauna was already endowed with the same organs as all its descendants up to man; liver, kidney, heart, etc., essentially similar in their structure and in their functions to those of modern animals, and apparently as complicated. This was over three hundred million years ago. Not a single fern and perhaps not a single plant existed on dry earth at this period.

The first terrestrial plant was found in the Gaspé Peninsula of Canada, and dates back to the Devonian (which succeeds the Silurian) epoch. It is a poor little plant, one foot high, without leaves. Sir John William Dawson, who discovered it about eighty years ago, called it Psilophyton (naked plant). The luxuriant and elegant carboniferous flora only burst forth seventy-five or a hundred million years later. Giant ferns, over thirty feet tall, crowned by a tuft of graceful palms; Cordaites attaining a height of fifty feet, with branches and leaves, and many others. Almost all our modern industry rests on the exploitation of these immense forests which long ago stored the solar energy they now give back to us in the form of coal.

Millions of years go by. Then appear the first gymnosperms, the Cycadaccae, the Ginkgoaceae. The Cycadaceae still exist in the tropics, and a representative of the Ginkgoaceae, the Ginkgo of China, has hardly changed since the Permo-Jurassic epoch. Finally, the Coniferae developed; they occupy an important place in our forests. Ginkgo and conifers are, with the ferns, the last survivors of the period immediately preceding the age of the great reptiles. The cypress and the giants of the species, the sequoias, came later and were the contemporaries of the monstrous dinosaurs.

It is almost impossible, nowadays, not to be an evolutionist. Consequently, we must frankly face the problem of the appearance of man. Physical man can only be considered as the result of a series of organisms which go back to the most elementary forms of life. This does not authorize us to say that any particular animal of the Archeozoic, Mesozoic, or other period is an ancestor of man. We have no real proof. Nobody believes any longer that "man descends from the ape." However, the fact remains that all living beings must have a common origin, and, as evolution exists, it is infinitely probable that the original strain was slightly differentiated living matter, still very close to inorganic matter, and not an already evolved organism. Indeed, this last hypothesis would leave unanswered the question as to how such a being could have been born. We would be obliged to admit a previous evolution resulting in this being, and the same problem would reappear.

We ask paleontology to give us the experimental elements by which we try to reconstitute the filiation of man and of the animals. This science enabled us to conceive the idea of evolution, but we must not ask more than it can give. The conditions required to preserve fossil bones intact through millions of years are not frequently found. The conservation of tissues and organs in their integrity is even rarer. Exposed to the air, to light, to humidity, the bones disappear, crumble, and dissolve. Only when, by an extraordinary chance, an animal was engulfed in a sudden cataclysm, protected from air and water, or if a mineral substance could substitute itself for the organic tissues, has it been possible to reconstitute its anatomy and internal organs exactly.

It is due to a chance of this kind that we know an intermediary between the reptiles and the birds, the Archaeopteryx, whose imprint in the finely grained lithographic schists (Upper Jurassic) is preserved with such remarkable detail that the structure of the first feathers can be clearly seen.

Other equally rare cases can be found, such as petrification through the action of very calcareous water. Near Cezanne, France, flowers and insects were petrified in such a spring about forty million years ago, during the Eocene period. The phenomenon which brings about the most perfect preservation is the inclusion of insects in amber. Amber, we know, is the fossilized resin of conifers. Important beds have been found dating from forests of the Oligocene period (at least 20 million years ago). The insects trapped in this resin were not only mechanically preserved but literally embalmed, and suffered no deterioration. This naturally happened only with very small animals.

Moreover, a great part of the ancient sediment formations are actually submerged under the oceans and quite inaccessible. The exploitation of quarries and of mine pits sometimes brings about sensational discoveries like that of the twenty-three Iguanodons (dinosaurians, Lower Cretaceous) found in Belgium, several hundred yards below the surface, in the galleries of a colliery. It is easy to realize how small are the chances of discovering such beds if we compare the surface of the continents to the minute area covered by mines in the entire world. The same holds true for the imprints of feet left by animals. Splendid ones have been discovered in Wyoming, Colorado, Arizona, and Utah. Certain imprints of dinosaurs are fifty-two inches long; one can imagine the size of the animal to whom this foot belonged. Some of these tracks are amazingly impressive. When seen in full daylight under the burning sun of Arizona, near a painted desert, they give an impression of life, of reality which even mounted skeletons fail to convey. It is the very flesh of the giant which depressed the mud. One almost expects to see the shape of the monster on one of the distant mesas, outlined against the blue sky. Time contracts. Did the beast pass here one hundred million years ago, or was it yesterday?

The documents furnished by paleontology must not be interpreted lightly, especially when trying to establish the foundations and the structure of evolution. The elements are too incomplete and too disconnected. We can only hope to find, in the fossil state, those species which were very abundant and dispersed throughout large areas. New, transitional forms, necessarily rare and localized, must almost always escape us. On the other hand, chance can place us before an exceptional individual or a representative of the last specimen of an extinct line. A striking example of this is actually living today; the Hatteria or *Sphenodon punctata*. This big lizard, about two feet long, is the last representative of a *fifth* order in the class of reptiles, otherwise totally extinct since the Jurassic period (about 100 million years ago). It is found on several small islands off the north coast of New Zealand. By a prodigious chance it survived until our day, and presents some very interesting archaic characters such as the third eye on top of the head. If these rocky islands had not been explored, or if they had been recently submerged, we would have come to the conclusion that the order of Rhynchocephalia had disappeared in the Jurassic period. On the other hand, if chance wills that in a million years men should discover its well-preserved remains, not far from human bones, they will probably come to the conclusion that it was contemporaneous with our domestic animals, though probably less widespread.

6

OBVIOUSLY, to a layman, the anatomical complication of the superior animals is the most striking and puzzling phenomenon of all evolution, but it is not more surprising than the physiological complexity of monocellular microscopic beings, and, as far as evolution is concerned, the physiological transformations are more astounding and revealing than the anatomical changes.

To a biologist, who knows how to look at Nature, she is a constant source of wonder. She solved fantastic problems by means of varied solutions and after trying them for millions of years she finally chose the best, that is, the one best adapted to the end. But the problems *were the same problems* which existed independently of the solutions. Throughout the development of evolution the scientist finds himself facing this unaccountable mystery, the creation of organs destined to improve sketchy solutions so as to increase the freedom of the individual, his independence with respect to his environment.

In a single cell (the Diplodinium for instance) Nature successfully incorporated an elementary digestive system, with esophagus and tubular rectum, a nervous system which foreshadows that of multicellular organisms, inasmuch as it shows a rudimentary brain, and a circumesophageal ring. We also find a very complicated excretory system (the contractile vacuoles). The fundamental physiological problems were set and partially solved in this single cell. Later on, Nature solved the *same* problems more perfectly in animals endowed with differentiated cellular organs: the Metazoa.

When the trial was not a success, that is, when the "improved" form, after confrontation with the surrounding medium, had not demonstrated its superiority, the species disappeared or vegetated until it finally died out. It could almost be stated that the broad lines of evolution had already been realized in the Algonkian era, namely that which extends between the Archean (the earliest Pre-Cambrian) and the Paleozoic.

Almost 500 million years ago, at the end of the Cambrian period, or even earlier, the fundamental mechanisms of evolution had, in all probability, resulted in extraordinarily complex and varied beings, admirably adapted to their environment and whose physiological functions were essentially those of the animals living in our day.

Nevertheless evolution continued toward an ever greater differentiation, as though it were not satisfied with the mere creation of beings capable of living and perfectly adapted from their point of view. Innumerable attempts were made. Entire groups disappeared, as if experience had proved that they were defective and that Nature had blundered. Unfortunately, the greater part of the fundamental types in the animal realm are disconnected from a paleontological point of view. In spite of the fact that it is undeniably related to the two classes of reptiles and birds (a relation which the anatomy and physiology of actually living specimens demonstrates), we are not even authorized to consider the exceptional case of the Archaeopteryx as a true link. By link, we mean a necessary stage of transition between classes such as reptiles and birds, or between smaller groups. An animal displaying characters belonging to two different groups cannot be treated as a true link as long as the intermediary stages have not been found, and as long as the mechanisms of transition remain unknown.

The same holds true for the appearance of homoiothermism (constant temperature) in birds. This is an immense and unquestionable liberation from the servitude to the environment and has, it must be admitted, all the unsatisfactory characteristics of absolute creation, whereas we *feel* that such cannot be the case. This stands out today as one of the greatest puzzles of evolution.

Long before the appearance of mammals we are faced with just as mysterious a problem, which is all the more interesting since the first solution, the so-called arthropods (insects, arachnoids, crustaceans, etc.), had already supplied a seemingly satisfactory answer. Their muscles were inside the limbs and protected by an armor whose articulations were highly complicated and mechanically satisfactory. To realize the mechanical ingenuity of this solution one need only examine a crab or a lobster or watch an insect run. The second solution, the *internal skeleton,* seems to have required a very long time. It is not certain that this skeleton was bony right away. In fishes at least, we know that it started out by being cartilaginous. The Selachii, which still people our seas (sharks and rays, etc.), and are first found in the Silurian period, are not real bony fish. It took about 200 million years before the true fish appeared (Teleostei).

The origin of vertebrates, which, from our point of view, represent the most important group of the animal realm, has not yet been completely elucidated. It was thought for a long time that their ancestor was a very primitive fish, the Amphioxus, which exists in our day, and displays the embryo of a cartilaginous skeleton. Another theory was proposed recently, according to which the Ostracodermi (fishes with an armor of large bony plates around the head) were the starting point of the marine vertebrates. This hypothesis, which was brilliantly expounded and defended in this country by an outstanding American paleontologist, Dr. W. K. Gregory, considers the Amphioxus as a degenerate form.

Another strange thing is that, judging by fossils, and not forgetting the prudent restrictions we expressed above, the terrestrial vertebrates seem to have developed *before* the marine vertebrates. We find amphibians represented by an important group of varied and giant forms, the Stegocephalia, at the beginning of the Carboniferous period. Some of them were quadrupeds, others were serpent-like without a trace of limbs, still others had a skull three feet long. This great variety indicates a long line of ancestors. Footprints have been found in the Upper Devonian, which can be attributed to them. Amphibians, therefore, existed prior to the Carboniferous period and their skeleton developed long before that of the fishes. All we can say is that both classes, fish and batrachians, had a common ancestor. Who was he? We do not know.

Amphibians are terrestrial when they reach their full development, but aquatic until then. Reptiles, on the contrary, are completely terrestrial. The development in the aerial medium necessitates an apparatus to enable the embryo to breathe the air directly. Needless to say, the history of the development of this mechanism is entirely obscure. This is an example of a transformation *which does not confer an immediate advantage on the animals endowed with it* but which represents a necessary step to attain a still distant but superior stage: that of the mammals. We might have thought that certain forms of fish living in the Devonian period and able to breathe at the same time in the water and in the air were more perfect and more favored. Apparently this was not the case, for they are represented today only by a few species actually living in South America.

Indeed, we must not think that the complication of certain organs always represents a progress from the point of view of evolution. Nature often furnished remarkable solutions which were not maintained after having been tried out. For instance, in invertebrates, very primitive eyes are found in varying numbers, situations, and degrees of development. In arthropods, compound eyes often occur in addition to small simple eyes. Some fishes had four eyes—two for seeing under water (with the necessary optical correction) and two for seeing above water. This useless complication was abandoned. Some reptiles had a third eye (pineal eye), placed on top of the skull. We find a very clear trace of this, with the optical nerve in good condition, in the Sphenodon mentioned above; but this was also abandoned. The principle of a seeing device was retained, but the solutions changed. Everything always takes place as if a goal had to be attained, and as if this goal was the real reason, the inspiration of evolution. All the attempts which did not bring the goal nearer were forgotten or eliminated.

The amphibians present another problem, that of the

origin of the actual representatives of this class, the Anura (tailless frogs and toads) and the Caudata (salamanders). These two orders appear for the first time in the Jurassic and the Cretaceous. They are not believed to be direct descendants of the batrachians of the Carboniferous period. If they are the issue of a distant common stock, anterior to the fish, what is this stock and what became of the intermediary stages which were never discovered?

The first reptiles are found in the Upper Carboniferous. They are, therefore, contemporary with the decline of the Stegocephalia. From the Triassic on, and during the whole Secondary period, they play a preponderant part on earth, in soft waters and in the oceans. All types of reptiles belonging to the three orders (Ichthyosauria, Saurischia, Lacertae) appear "suddenly" and it is impossible to link them to any terrestrial ancestors. The same is true of the tortoises.

We have put the word "suddenly" between quotation marks so as to make the problem stand out. Nobody imagines that the carapace of the tortoises or the bony crest of certain dinosaurs was spontaneously and rapidly constituted. A long series of transitions certainly exist without which these armors would be inconceivable. But we have no precise facts to go on, and no trace of intermediaries. Yet, as early as the beginning of the Secondary period (Triassic, Mesozoic) about 200 million years ago, the first mammals "suddenly" make their appearance. Where do they come from? Apparently not from the reptiles of that epoch, still at the beginning of their evolution. Probably not from the amphibians, for the leap would be immense and inconceivable. Not from the fish either, for the same reason. But then we must look for the common ancestor in the Pre-Cambrian, and the same questions come up. Certain paleontologists believe they have found the indication of an intermediary link in the one and only Tritylodon skull which shows characteristics of both reptiles and mammals. New discoveries will have to be made before we can make a definite pronouncement.

Let us not give in to the temptation of saying: many things can happen in 100 million years. If *nothing* happens in a year there is no reason why, by multiplying *what has not happened* one million or a hundred million times, something *will* happen at the end of that time. *There must be a starting point,* no matter how humble. One starting point, due to chance alone, and even many, are quite conceivable. What is less easily comprehensible is that whenever a starting point capable of developing into a wing, for instance, was present, it finally did develop into a wing, no matter in what species, whether insect, reptile, bird, or mammal. Three different solutions were given by Nature to this problem. However, the most disconcerting event is not so much the development of one particular character in strains disconnected from the main evolution as the unceasing progress witnessed in the trunk culminating in Man.

During the whole age of the reptiles, about 100 million years, the mammals vegetated. They were small aplacental animals, a few inches long, resembling the marsupials of our day. Some of them existed on insects, others were carnivorous, and still others, rodents. The enormous dinosaurs, weighing up to eighty tons, could crush dozens of them underfoot without even being aware of it. Who could have foreseen in those days that the future belonged to these little beasts who, by their constant temperature, the proportionally greater development of their brain, and their mode of reproduction, represented an immense progress over the colossal reptiles with their rudimentary intelligence and their slavery to certain conditions of temperature and humidity. About 50 million years ago the gigantic saurians had disappeared and the mammals were beginning their reign which has been extended and consolidated up to our era.

The Upper Carboniferous period, which witnessed the appearance of reptiles and the decline of the Stegocephalia (amphibians) also gave birth to a considerable population of insects. About a thousand species have been identified, but nothing is known of their past. If they descend from the common stock we have no idea when they branched off to evolve in their own manner. Some of them were very large with a wingspread of twenty-eight inches, but they must have flown awkwardly, somewhat like butterflies. This state of things lasted for a long time, 30 or 40 million years at least throughout the Permian, up to the Secondary period.

A thick, strange vegetation covered the earth at that time. The air was saturated with humidity, the atmosphere stifling. Huge black clouds raced over the sky in layers so thick that the sun was almost never visible. Diluvial rains fell without intermission and opaque fogs charged with the smell of vegetable rot hid the landscape. Violent storms burst constantly. The earth itself spouted fire through numerous volcanoes, trembled and heaved like a monster in agony. Blazing rocks, lava falling in the marshes liberated new masses of steam. In the immense, somber forests, alive with soft, crawling beings and big dragonflies faintly outlined by the gleam of lightning and the red glow of the lava in fusion, on the plains, in the valleys, *not a flower*. This fact may have something to do with the stagnation observed amongst the insects.

A period of almost absolute calm succeeded this brutal and tragic age and lasted for more than 130 million years, during all the Mesozoic era. There were practically no earthquakes nor volcanic eruptions. The ground, however, was not still; it rose and fell in different places. The sea invaded the continents or else retreated and in so doing formed lagoons which dried out and left their trace through salt deposits. Nevertheless, these movements were slow and progressive and in no way troubled the universal calm. The climate was mild; *there were no seasons,* except in the regions near the poles. Everywhere else the temperature was almost uniform, as in the South Sea Islands nowadays.

This was probably the age during which the insects developed their prodigious instincts. Our modern trees were beginning to push back the ancient conifers in certain places. Poplars, willows, birches, beeches, oaks appeared, and with them, the flowers. The progressive change in vegetation affected the number of insects. With practically non-existent seasons their lives were not shortened by the rigors of winter. They could live long enough to acquire experience and to take care of their young. As their activity was limited to a small number of gestures, always the same and inspired by the same circumstances, these gestures ended by becoming automatic, like habits, and resulted in an organization of the brain which was transmitted hereditarily. These habits became conditioned reflexes, spontaneously accomplished at determined epochs. At any rate, it is plausible to imagine, as do certain great zoologists, that things occurred in this way.

When winters started—around the middle of the Ter-

tiary period (Oligocene, Miocene, the time when the
Rocky Mountains, the Himalayas, the Atlas and the Alps
were formed)—they separated successive generations but
did not abolish the organizations acquired in the course
of millions of years. The insects have continued to act as
in the past, and seem to know at birth the things they are
too short-lived to learn.

In brief, each group, order, or family seems to be born
suddenly and we hardly ever find the forms which link
them to the preceding strain. When we discover them they
are already completely differentiated. Not only do we find
practically no transitional forms, but in general it is impossible to authentically connect a new group with an
ancient one. Therefore, the problem remains as to whether
the passage was more or less sudden or more or less continuous. As we have seen, probability clearly indicates that
only groups which have existed long enough to multiply
and become widely dispersed can be found in the fossil
stage. There is, then, nothing astonishing in the fact that
we do not find initial forms. These observations lead to
important conclusions which do not seem to have been put
in evidence so far—namely, that the transitional forms are
not stable forms; they do not multiply in great numbers
and do not propagate. They have another role to play.
Once more, everything takes place as though there were a
goal to be attained, a higher stage of development destined
to evolve still further; as if the intermediary form lost
its importance the moment the next stage had been started.
A relationship exists between the two stages similar to
that which connects an industrial prototype with the
manufactured product, on condition that the last prototype incorporates an improvement, absent in all the pre-

ceding ones, which confers to it a superiority worthy of being tried out on a large scale. In the case of natural evolution this untried character must be hereditary.

It was necessary to ponder the main problems of evolution because in our further study of the development of man on the psychological plane, which we shall try to link with evolutionary processes in general, we shall encounter mechanisms similar to those we have just examined. In order to substantiate our hypothesis, we had to supply the reader with the facts which will enable him to understand this similarity.

7

AN ANALOGY can help one to understand evolution or, at least, to visualize its development. Let us suppose that a lake high up in the mountains gives birth to a number of streams flowing in all directions. These streams will encounter thousands of obstacles on their way, stones, trees, gullies, which will decide their course and their configuration. Drawn on by gravitation, the water will always flow toward the bottom of the valley. Some of the streams will unite with others and grow larger. Some will lose themselves in rock fissures or in marshes. Others will form small lakes and will go no farther. Rocks will create waterfalls. No stream will exactly resemble another, for none of them will have been faced by the same difficulties. Yet, all of them are actuated by the same force, the same necessity: that of reaching the foot of the mountain.

We do not mean to establish a true parallel between this schematic picture and the infinitely complex group of processes constituting evolution. What we can nevertheless bear in mind is that this example shows a force, gravitation, acting with respect to the streams as would a final cause. All the variations, all the intermediary episodes which give their shape and aspect to the streams (adaptation) depend on chance, but the apparent efforts of the water to combat and surmount these obstacles are imposed by the external conditions and the sole necessity of reaching the bottom of the valley. The goal was set, but not the means to reach it.

If, instead of studying the particular mechanisms of evolution corresponding to the individual course of each rivulet, we try to understand the *very fact* of evolution we are completely lost unless we bring in some kind of finality. Chance alone, as we said before, is radically incapable of explaining an irreversible, *evolutive* phenomenon.

If we accept the idea of evolution, we must recognize the fact that, *on an average,* since the beginning of the world it has followed an ascending path, always oriented in the same direction. The objection has been made that many transformations of animals did not constitute a progress; the exaggerated development of the antlers of certain Cervidae, for instance. This is true, and that is the reason why we suggest the hypothesis of a finality comparable to gravitation in the above analogy, that is to say, a "telefinality" directing evolution as a whole. There is no doubt that there have been trials of all sorts, sometimes successful and sometimes unsuccessful. If we imagine a goal to be attained, acting like gravitation, once the start was given, all possible combinations had to be tried and their interest or their value proved by their reaction to the environment. If the new forms were badly adapted, incapable of serving as a starting point for a new stage of evolution, if they were surpassed by other strains, they disappeared progressively, or vegetated, cut off from the principal effort. The fate of the species itself thus becomes a secondary issue. What matters is the fate of the species *considered as a link in evolution as a whole*. Prodigies of adaptation were hardly more important than extraordinary performances in the circus. Adaptation and natural selection are no longer identified with evolution. The latter is differentiated from the former by its distant goal, which dominates all the species.

In this hypothesis, and in opposition to what Darwin thought, the survival of the fittest can no longer be considered as the *origin* of the evolving strain, and the fittest of a certain line can eventually give birth to a species destined to disappear or vegetate if the external conditions (climate, etc.), are modified or if other individuals, more apt from the final teleologic point of view, displace them.

Let us make this point quite clear: the properties or qualities of living organisms are *not* attributed to special principles as was done by the old vitalist doctrines, but it is simply assumed that a goal must be attained, by means of the most varied methods, *in conformity with the physico-chemical laws and the ordinary biological laws*. Nature often has recourse to chance, to probabilities, in living beings. Fish lay hundreds of thousands of eggs, as if they knew that, owing to the conditions under which these eggs will hatch, ninety per cent of them are destined to be destroyed.

We can no more consider evolutive transformations separately than we can consider physiological functions separately, if we aim to understand the evolution of living beings or the psychology of man.

In brief, evolution should be considered as a global phenomenon, irreversibly progressive, resulting from the combined activity of elementary mechanisms such as adaptation (Lamarck), natural selection (Darwin), and sudden mutations (Naudin—de Vries). Evolution begins with amorphous living matter or beings such as the Coenocytes, still without cell structure, and ends in thinking Man, endowed with a conscience. It is concerned *only* with the principal line thus defined. It represents *only* those living beings which constitute this unique line zigzagging intelligently through the colossal number of living forms.

Evolution, we repeat, is comprehensible only if we admit that it is dominated by a finality, a precise and distant goal. If we do not accept the reality of this orienting pole, not only are we forced to recognize that evolution is rigorously incompatible with our laws of matter, as we demonstrated above, but—and this is serious—that the appearance of moral and spiritual ideas remains an absolute mystery. Mystery for mystery, it seems wiser, more logical and more intelligent to choose the one which explains, thus satisfying our need to comprehend; the one which opens the doors to hope, rather than the one which closes those doors and explains nothing.

Adaptation, natural selection, mutations are, on the contrary, mechanisms which have contributed to the slow edification of evolution *without being themselves always progressive*. Strictly speaking these mechanisms are not determining factors in general evolution, any more than the mason is a determining factor in the cathedral on which he works. The mason represents, in himself, a very complex element obeying physico-chemical, biological, human, social laws. His sole contact with the cathedral is his trowel, and from the point of view of the architect, he is only a trowel. His private life, his intimate tragedies, his illnesses are immaterial. For the bishop, who willed the cathedral, the architect himself is but a means. The same is true of the processes lumped together under the generic name of "Mechanisms of Evolution." Each one contributes materially, statistically, to evolution, but the laws which they obey are not really identical with those of evolution which dominate and correlate them. In a similar way, the laws which govern the movements of particles in an atom are special and differ from those which govern the chemical properties of the atoms themselves. The latter are, as far as our actual science is concerned, without qualitative or quantitative relation to our psychological activity. To extrapolate and predict that such a relation will be discovered some day is not substantiated by facts, and entirely hypothetical.

Indeed, man must beware more of scientific extrapolations than of moral ones, because his scientific experience has been much shorter than his psychological experience. New facts are frequently found in science which compel him to revise completely his former concepts. The history of science is made up of such revolutions: the atomic theory, the kinetic theory, the granular theories of electricity, energy, and light, radioactivity, relativity have successively transformed our point of view from top to bottom. The future of science is always at the mercy of new discoveries and new theories. The science of matter is not two hundred years old, while the science of man is over five thousand years old. Empirical psychology was highly advanced at the time of the third Egyptian dynasty, and great philosophers twenty-six hundred years ago displayed a knowledge of man which has not been surpassed, but only confirmed today. Therefore, it can be reasonably assumed that moral extrapolations are much safer than scientific ones, even though they cannot be expressed mathematically.

The laws of evolution are *teleological*, whereas those of the transformation of each species *simply tend toward a state of equilibrium with the surrounding medium.* Every-thing takes place as though adaptive transformations de-pended partly on the laws of chance and on still unknown biological laws, and as though, in all probability, they es-caped to a certain extent the fundamental physical law of Carnot-Clausius.

Adaptation, natural selection, mutations are nothing but broadly comprehensive concepts expressing the result of little known and complex mechanisms, such as those per-taining to genetics (laws of Mendel, laws of Weismann) and others. These mechanisms are, in their turn, the ex-pression, on another scale of observation, of fundamental phenomena which are at the base of evolution as a whole, such as the physico-chemical phenomena on the atomic and molecular scale. Although the results of adaptation in animals are prodigious, especially amongst the articulates, insects, arachnids, and many parasites, it is not certain that these mechanisms submit to a finality, as was thought up till now. At any rate, if they do, it is very probably an essen-tially different finality from that which dominates evolu-tion. The gravest error made by the finalists so far is that they confused the two and assimilated the marvels of adaptation, *limited to the species*, to the unlimited evolu-tive impetus which dominates all the groups.

The difference between the mechanisms of evolution and evolution itself can be compared to that which exists between the activity of cells busily cicatrizing the wound of a soldier and the motives which lead the latter to start and continue the fight.

The criterion of adaptation is USEFULNESS. It is strictly limited to the advantage of the species. But, it may happen that, once the mechanisms are started *they continue blindly* and function unintelligently, eventually giving birth not only to troublesome but even to harmful monstrosities.

The criterion of evolution is LIBERTY. Ever since the first rudiments of life this seems to have been the test which singled out the individuals destined to insure the continuity of the only branch which evolved through innumerable living forms and was finally crowned by Man. We will develop this idea further on.

Following our hypothesis, telefinality orients the march of evolution as a whole and has acted, ever since the appearance of life on earth, as a distant directing force tending to develop a being endowed with a conscience, a spiritually and morally perfect being. To attain its goal, this force acts on the laws of the inorganized world in such a way that the normal play of the second law of thermodynamics is always deflected in the same direction, a direction forbidden to inert matter and leading to ever greater dissymmetries, ever more "improbable" states.

The evolutive branch—that of Man—successively disengaged itself from all the others, first physiologically and morphologically, up to the appearance of conscious Man, then by widening increasingly, through moral ideas, the gulf which separated this man from the animal.

Outside of man, all the creatures actually living on our planet are forms which have been left behind. Some of them have been more or less stabilized for a long time, like the Annelida, dating from the Primary period, and the Sphenodon of New Zealand. Others still undergo slow transformations, or disappear gradually. All, or nearly all the forms continued to adapt themselves as best they could, when their adaptation was not perfect, or when the external conditions varied, but without hope of ever rejoining the evolving line.

A living being *always tends to adapt itself* physico-chemically and biologically. This is the manifestation of a search for equilibrium similar to that observed in the inorganic world. In the latter domain, a system always tends toward a state of equilibrium corresponding to the minimum of free energy compatible with its total energy. This tendency can be expressed mathematically and it has been demonstrated that its final state corresponds to the greatest probability (Boltzmann). We cannot as yet express verbally or symbolically the tendency of living beings toward an equilibrium with the surrounding medium. It is not certain that we shall ever be able to do so.

The individual does not often evolve but he is compelled to adapt himself. The causes which determine the necessity of adaptation act on *a whole group*. Amongst the thousands of mutant individuals forced to transform themselves so as to live, *only one*, or a small number, will evolve and *not necessarily the best adapted*. The adaptation expressing a specific internal tendency (physico-chemical and biological) is immediately "put on trial," confronted with external conditions. If the test is successful, that is, if the new individuals proliferate more because they are better fit, or less vulnerable, the species persists. The three processes, mutation, adaptation, and natural selection, function jointly and successively, in the order given.

But we know that, *when this equilibrium representing perfect adaptation has been attained, the animal naturally ceases to transform itself* as long as the external conditions are not sufficiently modified to make a new adaptation necessary, as long as the equilibrium has not been broken. This strain then constitutes one of those countless fixed branches which for thousands and thousands of centuries have dotted the history of living beings and are no longer anything but memories of a vanished past. The actual fauna of the world often represent the masterpieces of adaptation, but only the "leftovers" of evolution.

Only one strain amongst all the others never attained equilibrium and yet survived. This was the line that ended in Man. Perfect adaptation was, therefore, never a *goal*, as Lamarck and his followers believed. It seems to have been *a means* by which an immense number of infinitely varied individuals were developed, thus giving the possibility of effectuating a choice governed by teleological reasons.

The Pre-Cambrian sandworms were probably not very different from those of our shores. *Their adaptation was remarkable and very superior to that of man.* Having attained equilibrium, living under only slightly changed conditions, they had no reason to transform themselves further, and they have subsisted almost without a change for hundreds of millions of years. One of these worms, however,[1] continued to evolve because it *was less well adapted than the others,* and probably possessed a kind of instability which did not constitute an advantage at that time, but was conducive to still greater changes and could be called "creative instability." We must naturally not be taken in by this expression. Instability is not in itself creative, but expresses the aptitude to evolve. This worm, *less perfect as a worm,* may have been our ancestor.

It is, therefore, we repeat, not the being best adapted to his environment who contributes to evolution. He survives

[1] Of course, this is only meant figuratively, by contrast to the immense number existing at that time. There might have been one hundred, or a few thousand, but in any case it only represented a very small percentage of the whole. Besides, out of a number of chance mutations, only a few must have been favored with utilizable characters.

but his better adaptation eliminates him, on the contrary, from the ascendant progression and only contributes to increase the number of more or less stagnant species which people the earth.

Adaptability and the heredity of acquired characters—no longer questioned since the experiments made with colchicine—do not, therefore, necessarily constitute a means of evolution but of *transformation* and can end in blind alleys, monsters, and regressions. They are specific properties of living matter, like irritability. They tend toward a single result: equilibrium, stagnation.

Consequently, at the risk of repeating ourselves, we insist that *whereas adaptation blindly tries to attain an equilibrium which will bring about its end, evolution can only continue through unstable systems or organisms*. It only progresses from instability to instability and would perish if it only encountered perfectly adapted, stable systems.

Thus we have the first explanation of the confusing multiplicity of animal forms and of the paradoxical fact that certain of the mechanisms of evolution can eventually work against it. On the other hand it is clear that perfect equilibrium, corresponding to an ideal adaptation, is rarely realized, especially in superior organisms. That is to say that, in the species actually living, a certain latitude, a certain instability, often reduced to the extreme, persists. Otherwise it would be impossible to understand how species stabilized long ago could have adapted themselves to the variations of surrounding conditions during the last millions of years. This instability, decreasing with the complexity and age of the strain, only produces secondary adaptations and not the profound transformations required for the birth of a new species. The faculty of

creating species has been lost long ago, and their transformations have generally been toward biological specialization, *except* in the case of the line which was to end in
man.

As was indicated above, this way of interpreting the
transformations of living beings explains the contradictions for which the Darwinian and the Lamarckian
theories have been reproached, in the case when the fittest,
forced to face a change in its environment, or driven out
of it as a result of some geologic or climatic convulsion,
finds itself under such conditions that the characters which
assured it a superiority become useless, troublesome, or
even harmful. *Adaptation then works to neutralize its own
anterior efforts, and natural selection tends to eliminate
those it had heretofore protected.*

In such cases, adaptation is obviously not progressive,
but protective, defensive. We hope we have made it
clear that this is absolutely normal, inasmuch as the
"progressive" trend depends on evolution, not an adaptation.

It sometimes happened that a previous transformation
which was useful under given circumstances was too important anatomically to permit its being eradicated or corrected by a further identical process (adaptation + selection) when the change in the environment took place too
rapidly. Then the species was doomed, as there was no time
for these slow processes to rid the animal of the characters,
painstakingly acquired, which had become dangerous
under the new conditions. For instance, certain species of
reindeer, in Northern Siberia, had developed very extensive antlers. At the time of the glacial period they were
driven out of the steppes, the treeless tundras, by the advance of the polar ice fields, and found themselves sur-

rounded by the closely packed forests of the south, where their antlers became such a handicap that they finally died out.

From the telefinalistic point of view, this was nothing but a negligible accident amongst thousands of others, inasmuch as these animals *played no part in evolution* and represented only the tail end of a strain long before separated from the evolving stem. But the opponents of the evolutionary idea grabbed this fact as an unanswerable argument against it.

When the new conditions happen not to threaten the very existence of the species, and when time is lavish, the animal may progressively adapt itself by "retrograding," by losing the use of some formerly functional characters: for instance, the regression of eyesight in the burrowing mole, and the blindness of certain fish living in caverns where no light ever penetrates. Adaptation when left to itself can produce monsters; its mechanisms, when set in motion, can work unintelligently, as pointed out before. Similarly, an airplane, deprived of its pilot, may keep on flying for hours but will crash to earth eventually. The mechanisms of evolution, uncontrolled, sometimes behave like the apprentice sorcerer.

Evolution thus strikes us as being the search for a certain kind of utilizable disequilibrium materialized by "transitory" forms, monstrous at the time of their appearance, less well adapted than the others—as the rareness of their fossils shows—but often richer in future potentialities. We use the word "often," for it is evident that in certain cases the transitory form led to nothing important. That is why we can say that evolution has all the appearances of being a choice, always made in the same ascending direction toward a greater liberty, amongst hundreds of thousands of individuals, and it is amongst the mutant individuals that this choice takes place.[2] The increasing freedom of living beings is evident if one starts from the monocellular being and the mollusks: freedom of movement, liberation from the chains imposed by a strict dependence on the environment (concentration of the saline medium, temperature, food, etc.), liberation from the menace of destruction by other species, liberation from the necessity of using the hands for walking or digging, liberation from the time-consuming method of transmitting useful acquired characters and experience (through speech and tradition), and last of all, as we shall see, liberation of conscience.

The form "chosen" to evolve can be, momentarily, less favored than the others. It sometimes vegetates for hundreds of thousands of years, millions of years, while the others grow in number and in size. As we have seen in the preceding chapter, that is what happened to the first mammals which coexisted with the large reptiles of the Secondary period. But though the dinosaurians were better protected at the beginning, though the processes of mutation, selection, and adaptation multiplied them in the most varied and colossal shapes, the little mammals were better prepared *to cope with conditions which were not yet realized at the time of their appearance.* It may of course be objected that this was just a coincidence. All right; but how can we account for the fact that such coincidences succeeded each other unceasingly for more than one thou-

2 Experiments have proved (Naudin and later on de Vries) that in a collection of plants originating from identical seeds, and more rarely, amongst animals of a same line, "sudden mutations" take place, new unforeseen characters appear, probably as a consequence of accidents due to chance in the seed or the egg. A mutant individual is an individual who is not identical in every respect with the others issued from the common strain.

sand million years, so that, in the end, man and his brain appeared?

We have pointed out that adaptation can bring forth monsters. Only evolution could bring forth Man. Man has also in his experiments manufactured monsters (experiments of Morgan and his school on the *Drosophila melanogaster* flies). He can play with adaptation and acquired characters. He will certainly never be able to start an evolution.

In the history of living beings the word "link" is a dangerous word. It can never be affirmed that a certain form is a real link. That is sometimes possible. It is never sure. In any case it can be stated that no actually living form is the direct ancestor of another. Man does not descend from the monkeys. Amongst the fossils, many so-called "intermediary" forms are perhaps nothing but unsuccessful attempts at adaptation, freaks, either contemporary, anterior, or posterior to the *true* intermediary forms. The same is probably the case for those queer animals native of Australia, the monotremes (Ornithorhynchus or Platypus, and Echidna), which lay eggs and suckle their young. The Echidna, less celebrated than the Platypus, is nevertheless even more interesting because its temperature control system is not yet perfect and allows deviations of temperature attaining 23° Fahrenheit. These animals are only a trial, but through chance their direct ancestors had the luck to be born under conditions such that they could manage to live, without transforming themselves deeply. Being cut off from other continents and safe from the turmoil prevailing elsewhere they attained a state of development which enabled them to persist under relatively stable conditions. The fauna of Australia and New Zealand is still unique in that respect and rich in archaic forms. It cannot boast of a single native (autochthonous) mammal, but only marsupials. New Zealand is well known for its giant wingless birds; some of them, the moas, were twelve feet high. The Platypus and the Echidna probably underwent minor transformations but they are not the real ancestors of mammals. They are the end of a sidetrack.

The true evolutive branch was fragile and tenuous *as it could not be perfectly adapted*. It evolved rapidly and did not spread. An immense number of intermediaries were needed to pass from the poikilotherms (cold-blooded animals) to the homoiotherms (warm-blooded animals), but these transitional species, which did not differ much from one another, were probably made up of such a small number of individuals that the chances of being one day able to reconstitute the complete descendance of man are very slight.

However, in the class of mammals, we have been able to establish the lineage of the horse by means of six intermediary stages, starting with the Hyracotherium and the Eohippus of the Eocene period (about fifty million years ago) up to the modern horse. But each one of these intermediaries seems to have appeared "suddenly," and it has not yet been possible, because of the lack of fossils, to reconstitute the passage between these intermediaries. Yet it must have existed. The known forms remain separated like the piers of a ruined bridge. We know that the bridge has been built, but only vestiges of the stable props remain. The continuity we surmise may never be established by facts.

Anyhow, this is not of great importance. The real problems do not come up in the history of a genus, or of a species, but in the history of the phyla and classes. By no effort of the imagination can we actually conceive the passage from monocellular beings to Metazoa, from asexual generations to sexual generations, from the blood-pigment containing copper to the blood-pigment containing iron. As we have seen above, these transformations which have absolutely nothing to do with the ends of adaptation, and are fundamental as far as evolution is concerned, happened in the most distant epochs, during the infancy of the earth.

We have just examined one of the groups of mechanisms instrumental in the transformation of living beings. Many scientists have committed the error of thinking that they were the only ones. Once in possession of the successful hypothesis of Lamarck and Darwin, they thought that by torturing these theories and treating them like plastic sheets they would succeed in molding them into all the shapes needed to fit the different problems brought up by transformations in the course of ages. Unhappily we must recognize the fact that this group of processes alone is incapable of explaining an immense number of facts which still remain absolutely mysterious and constitute as many unsurmountable obstacles in the actual state of our knowledge.

For, assuming that we can conceive (we do not say understand) the beginning of the process of adaptation when a starting point has been given, it is obvious that this basic transformation must be sufficiently useful to confer upon the mutant organism an advantage over the other organisms of the same species. If no benefit, no momentary progress resulted therefrom, it would be difficult to understand why the new character should have been perfected or transmitted by heredity. There would only be one more monster, as in the case of Morgan's flies. Now, we are forced to admit that the eye was perfected and started to improve from the moment it enabled the animal to see, even though in a deformed and crude manner. But it only served this purpose *after* it had been optically constructed *and linked by nervous cells to a sensitive optical center in the brain.* How can we explain the simultaneous evolution of the elements necessary for vision *as long as vision did not exist?* The simple sensitivity to light of a particular region of the epiderm in no way explains the ultimate formation of the lens, of the iris, and of the retina. Likewise the membranous wing of the *pterosaurians* and the bats could act as a sustainer only after it had been perfected. The fact of falling indefinitely from a rock or a tree could not inaugurate this membrane. If its extension was progressive, and it began as a very small skin flap, it was only a hindrance at first, and had no reason to develop in size. If it occurred all of a sudden, how can the correlative growth of the fingers be accounted for? How could it, in either case, become at once hereditary? We cannot conceive this process except as the result of a long evolution: but we can only surmise, not prove it, and the whole process escapes us completely. Nature had already tried and succeeded in making animals fly. The problem had been crudely but satisfactorily solved about one hundred million years before by the Neuropteroidea, flying insects of the Devonian period. The solution was quite different, but just as remarkable. Hundreds of other examples could be found, especially in the world of insects.

If telefinalism, by postulating the intervention of an Idea, a Will, a supreme Intelligence, throws a little light on the combined transformations leading through an uninterrupted line to Man, it seems impossible not to see in the particular transformations limited to the species something more than the simple play of physico-chemical forces and chance.

Finally, several trials resulted in the Primates, and after a long series of unknown intermediary stages in the Piltdown man, the *Pithecanthropus erectus* of Java, and the Peking man. Their cranium developed more rapidly than those of the Primates. Many authors actually believe that the Peking man is really the ancestor of the Neanderthal man (?) who appeared a few hundred thousand years later in Europe. In reality the origin of the Neanderthal man is unknown. He probably came from a line which was separated from the common trunk at the same time as those which were to give birth to the orang-utan, the gibbon, and the chimpanzee. The common strain is perhaps still older. According to reliable authors, the Simiidae of the Tertiary period show a distinct tendency toward "humanization," and the morphology of the body of some extinct anthropoids (Dryopithecus, Sivapithecus) is considerably nearer that of the human species than the morphology of the anthropoid apes living today. According to others, the Eoanthropus of Piltdown (Dawn man) derives directly from the Propliopithecus of the Oligocene or Eocene (Egypt). This primate would, therefore, be the common stock from which the branches leading to the actual primates and man emerged about forty or fifty million years ago. Some other authors believe that the common ancestor is even more ancient. . . . The truth is that nothing positive is known.

In any case, the brain of Pithecanthropus is heavier than that of the large apes, even of those whose body weighs three times more than his. The ape-man (translation of the word: *pithecanthropus*) appears on the island of Java, probably later than the Piltdown man, and a little before the Peking man. Though they are still slightly bent, they walk erect. Evolution continues.

It continues through man and through him alone. However, as we shall soon see, the evolution of man does not proceed identically on the same basis as heretofore. Just as there seems to be an intellectually impassable gap between the reversible "evolution" of electrons and that of atoms (built of electrons) ; between the irreversible evolution of atoms and that of life (built of atoms) ; so there seems to be an intellectually impassable gap between the evolution of life and that of man, as such. Man is still an animal by his very structure, and has inherited a large number of instincts from his ancestors. Some of them are still necessary to protect the species. Nevertheless he has also brought into the world, from an unknown source, other instincts and ideas specifically human which have become overwhelmingly important although contradicting the first, and it is the development of these ideas, these new characters which constitutes the present phase of evolution.

Therefore, if the principle of evolution is to be maintained in his case, the modalities of its manifestation will be somewhat different, and that is why all evolutionary theories have been incapable so far of accounting for the behavior of man.

BOOK III

The Evolution of Man

8

THE NEW ORIENTATION OF EVOLUTION: MAN • THE
SECOND CHAPTER OF GENESIS

EVOLUTION goes on. The animal shape capable of sheltering the spirit, capable of allowing it to develop, is found.

From now on everything takes place as if the next step
could only be realized progressively, by abandoning on the
way the scaffolding which has become useless as a result
of the emergence of more perfect forms evolving slowly
toward ultimate and still distant perfection. Though it is
not always apparent, the "memory" of the intermediate
stages in living beings often persists, like the traces of gills
still visible in the human embryo. Not only does physical
memory persist—and by "physical memory" we mean the
anatomical structures slowly built up and transmitted
hereditarily—but also the memory of the instincts accumulated in the brain, which at a given time in evolution corresponded to conditions of existence determined by the
environment.

It is against this heredity, against this immense accumulation of memories, by now deprived of any meaning, and
dating back to epochs forever vanished, that Man must
fight to prepare the advent of the spiritual being he is
destined to become.

Evolution continues in our time, *no longer on the physiological or anatomical plane but on the spiritual and moral plane.* We are at the dawn of a new phase of evolution and the violent eddies due to this change in the order of things still conceal that fact from the eyes of the majority. The transition from the ancestral animal, still squirming within us, to Man is too recent for us to be able to understand the ensuing conflicts which often seem disconcerting and incomprehensible. We are incapable of realizing it, but we are actually living in the midst of a revolution, a revolution on the scale of evolution. In comparison, the social revolutions we witness, even if they cost hundreds of thousands of human lives, are but tragic children's games, and will leave no trace in the future.

After having for thousands of centuries blindly obeyed inexorable laws, a certain group of living beings differentiates itself biologically from the others and is confronted with new obligations. New orders are imposed, all of them contradicting the preceding ones, and restraining the realm of man's joys, of his physical pleasures. How is it possible for him not to revolt against this authority which he does not yet know but intuitively respects? Like a wild horse which reacts against the bit, but differing from the animal inasmuch as he himself imposes the check, while remaining free to reject or accept it, man finally becomes truly master of his destiny. It is from this mastery, based on the liberty to choose between the satisfaction of the appetites and the flight toward spirituality, that human dignity is born.

True human personality appeared from the moment speech was developed. Even though morphological evolution continued, animal intelligence, instincts, began to give way to a very different and specifically human form of intelligence. The still distant goal, namely the separation of man from the animal, necessitated a new phase, destined to last for millenaries.

The first indication of the new orientation of man was given by the ancient artifacts, the coarse flint implements and the traces of fires. However, other proofs of humanization were soon found and, in our opinion, these proofs were much more impressive. They were the sepultures. Not only does the Neanderthal man bury his dead, but he sometimes unites them, as in the sepulture of the Children's Grotto, near Menton (France). This is no longer a question of instinct. It is already the dawn of human thought, manifesting itself by a kind of revolt against death. And revolt against death implies lasting love of those who have gone and the hope that their departure is not final. These "ideas," the first perhaps, are seen to develop side by side with esthetic sentiments. Flat stones are piled up or propped against each other so as to protect the faces and heads of the dead. Later on, ornaments, weapons, food, pigments for coloring the body accompany the deceased. The idea of finality is unbearable. The dead will awake, and be hungry; they will have to defend themselves, they will want to adorn themselves. The dead are not dead.

The fact that they live in the memory of those who loved them, who admired them, leads in man, and in man alone, to an idea which expands beyond the sentimental realm of the individual; he projects this idea outside of himself and creates a new objective existence for the departed. This is something entirely unforeseen. He knows that he will never see the loved ones again on this earth, but he refuses to believe that they cannot live somewhere else. So he invents another life, he creates another world in which, some day, they will meet again. Thus, without too great an effort of imagination, we can conceive that the care of the dead, the combination in man of one of the oldest characteristics of living beings, memory, and of a sentiment widespread in all superior animals, love, gave birth to the specifically human notion of a beyond. Man takes advantage of all the traits inherited from his ancestors, but transforms them into new tools which hasten his own evolution.

Memory, which is the essential condition for the persistence of living beings, existed in the most rudimentary animals. Some biologists affirm that proofs of it have been found in monocellular organisms, in *Paramecium*. This much is certain: evolution could not have taken place without it. The character which first diffentiated animals from plants and gave the former an immediate superiority may have been memory. It alone is capable of building up conditioned reflexes and instincts.

However, it is probable that the mechanisms of this memory differed from those which act in individuals endowed with a centralizing brain. Irritability, a characteristic of living matter, is, one may say, the substratum of memory. The development of memory does not, therefore, any more than instinct, require localization in an evolved brain. The instincts of insects are more remarkable than those of the mammals. Yet the mammals have a more complex brain and are more intelligent, that is, more capable of *successfully facing unexpected circumstances*. The insect is a prisoner of his instinct. The intelligence of mammals expresses the greater liberty acquired through their evolution. Not only are they protected by certain hereditary instincts, but they have the ability to devise new methods of defense against numerous unforeseen events encountered in the course of migrations, or resulting from changes due to the convulsions of a world in formation, to meteors, and to dangers of all kinds.

Man, the new being, hardly freed from the ancient chrysalis, enjoyed far greater degrees of liberty than the other mammals. They were possible only in him and were sometimes the consequence of anatomical improvements closely connected with one another. The development and specialization of the hand imposed an upright position. It may have been only a trial like the others, but this trial was immediately crowned with such success that two immense gains followed: tools and fire.

Articulate speech, which depends partly on the structure of the lower jaw (protruding chin), must have come later. Thereafter the road is clear, the goal is set, man leaps ahead. Henceforth, his path separates from that of the rest of living beings, which he will always dominate. Evolution will continue through him alone and will tend increasingly to make the two roads diverge. *It is by this ever greater divergence that we must from now on measure the progress of evolution.*

However, man cannot liberate himself all at once. The weight of heredity, which goes back hundreds of millions of years, is too heavy. His own strictly human curve of evolution is only drawn progressively, and not without hesitation. Fluctuations eventually manifest themselves by individual or collective regressions which bring him back to the animal. How could it be otherwise?

The physico-chemical mechanisms at the base of his structure and of his functions are essentially the same as those of the other mammals. His body obeys the same laws.

His brain carries all the hopes of the new species but is made up of cells like those of more primitive beings. These cells are nourished like the others and their functions are ordained by the chemical products secreted by the endocrine glands which direct and maintain the harmonious equilibrium of the whole. The thyroid gland controls intelligence, and its suppression or its atrophy transforms the normal being into an idiot, but the gray cells of an idiot and those of a man of genius seem to be identical. The parathyroids partly control the nervous system. The pituitary gland controls bone growth. Its ablation brings death within a few days, just as the removal of the suprarenal glands brings death within a few hours. Finally, the interstitial glands exert an all-powerful influence over the development of certain male characters, such as the voice and the hair; when they are injured, the brain, the heart, the muscles, the skin are affected. Furthermore, moral and physical energy, the specific male qualities, are directly dependent on them.

Thus, the very foundation of the human organism is material, chemical, the same as that of the animals. It must eat, sleep, procreate. It is difficult for Man to evade this relationship, to free himself from the endocrine enslavement. By fighting against it he will affirm the difference to which he owes his human dignity, and by ceding to it he will abdicate the independence gained by hundreds of millions of years of evolution.

At a certain period of his metamorphosis, man became conscious of this fundamental dualism which is in reality the eternal theme of religions, philosophies, and arts. The awakening of this idea constitutes the most important event in all evolution. Up till then, like all the living beings before him, he did not have to intervene in the external phenomena which directed his progressive improvement. He was an irresponsible, unconscious intermediary link in a chain. He only reacted through the irritability of his tissues and obeyed the appetites inherited from the superior mammals, although he was freer than the latter. His greater intelligence, his hands capable of shaping flints and lighting fires, his larynx, apt to emit sounds that his tongue and his lips could model endlessly, enabled him to control his fate, and henceforth he had the choice between a return to animality, to slavery, and the pursuit of his role in evolution.

Up to the birth of conscience, the being who was to become man only differed from his ancestors morphologically. He was subject to the laws of nature, to the laws of evolution, he had to obey, and that was right. The moment he asked himself the question as to whether an act was "good" or whether another was "better," he acquired a liberty denied to the animals.

The more or less romanced explanation of this fact is of no importance. It matters little whether it is attributed to the family or the clan, to the reprisals of parents or of neighbors. The truth is that in man, and in man alone, the possibility of this choice has been transformed into a moral idea, whereas this is not the case in any other species. When this occurred, man took another leap and increased the gap which already separated him from the other primates; the new orientation of his evolution was clearly indicated. Henceforth, contrary to all the others, in order to evolve *he must no longer obey Nature*. He must criticize and control his desires which were previously the only Law.

The purely human conflict is born from this permanent, bitter struggle which has lost none of its violence today.

Unquestionably, when considering the majority of men, it is possible to doubt the reality of the moral idea. The examples we see daily enable the pessimist to ask himself if the chasm between the animal and man is as deep as we thought. The answer is that we are still at the dawn of human evolution, and that, if only one man out of a million were endowed with a conscience, this would suffice to prove that a new degree of liberty had appeared. Many important steps in the history of evolution started out as a mutation affecting only a very small number of individuals, perhaps only one. Similarly, the moral idea must have been sparsely distributed, and was, in fact, so fragile that instead of conferring a physical superiority upon those who harbored it, it constituted rather a hindrance. Indeed, at the time of the cave man, sentimentalism, pity, fairness, charity, all the budding qualities highly valued today in mankind, must have been a serious handicap to those who had to face the unconscious cruelty and brutality of the others. Such conflicts are not infrequent in our time. However, on an average, and in spite of their weaknesses and subjection to ancestral instincts, the masses are responsive to the great virtues which have always enjoyed a surprising prestige even though they were not practiced.

Today, when large groups of men fail to react as we think they should, when there is no collective response, there are nevertheless many individuals who, without being themselves exceptionally virtuous, without having martyr souls, spontaneously revolt and sometimes end by carrying away the crowd. The history of humanity abounds in such examples and evokes the picture of a climbing vine. If its prop is pulled up or broken, the plant creeps along the ground, unknowingly seeking a new support, another occasion to raise itself above the weeds, and as soon as it has found one it clings to it in an unconscious but untiring effort toward the light. It is sometimes mistaken; its choice may be bad; the branch it has adopted may be rotten; that is not its fault. The human flock obeys an obscure order: it must rise, and it cannot do so without a leader. Thank God, if there have been evil influences, they have been counteracted, on an average, by that of certain rare, privileged men, comparable to the transitional animals who were in advance of their time. These men attained a higher stage of evolution, and had a great part to play, a high duty to fulfill, namely, to orient the march of humanity in the path which leads away from the animal. Strange to say, in spite of their handicaps, of the fact that the doctrine they taught was less pleasant and demanded sacrifice, it is they who gained the higher prestige in history, and their teachings outlasted and outshone all the others.

This new liberty given to man was necessary in order that evolution could continue. When the physical support, the human body, reached a state of relative perfection, new trials became useless, and evolution had to continue on another plane, essentially human, the spiritual plane. Now, how can such an evolution be conceived without the constant collaboration of man himself? As we have seen, innumerable trials were made during the course of evolution. Confronted with Nature, these trials were sometimes crowned with success, in which case the new species prospered; at other times they were a failure, and the species vegetated or disappeared. But a trial on the biological plane (anatomical or physiological) *transforms itself into a test on the psychological plane.*

In the latter case it is no longer just a question of surviving; a superior level is attained. It is a question of progressing psychologically and morally. As in the past, progress can only take place by struggle, competition, and selection.

At this point it is interesting to note that telefinalism is in accord with one of the most ancient and respectable of human traditions, which inspires and directs the whole Christian world, though its origin is unknown: the Bible. This parallelism was absolutely unforeseen, and yet our conclusions are identical with those expressed in the second chapter of Genesis, provided that this chapter is interpreted in a new way and considered as the highly symbolical expression of a truth which was intuitively perceived by its redactor or by the sages who communicated it to him.

To understand this first step toward the reconciliation of science and religion, we shall be obliged to define the meaning of certain words with care. Particularly the words liberty and order, or command.

In the preceding pages we pointed out that liberty could be considered as a criterion of evolution. We showed that as we rise in the scale of living beings there is a proportional increase in liberty. It is evident that this criterion only takes on its full import with the birth of conscience and that this last liberty could only be bestowed on a being already physically freer than the others. But, in spite of this greater freedom he remains equally subject to the demands of the body, which is, as we have already pointed out, composed of elements similar to those of the other animals. Biologically, therefore, man remains an animal. Later on, we shall see that this was necessary, for it is by fighting against his instincts that he humanizes himself.

Now, in what does the liberty of an animal consist? It consists in very little. The fish is freer than the coral, or than the starfish; the mammal is freer than the reptile. But from the top to the bottom of the scale, all the animals, without exception, are the slaves of their physiological functions and of their hormonal, endocrine secretions. In no case can they liberate themselves from these any more than from their hereditary instincts, because physiological functions, endocrine secretions, and instincts are the direct and inevitable consequence of their very structure. This structure, itself a consequence of evolution, was willed, whether we place ourselves from the point of view of tele-finalism or of the Bible. Animals are, therefore, not free, and this is the symbolical meaning of Genesis when it says that God *ordered* them to live, to grow, and to multiply. It is clear that when God created animals with certain organs it was equivalent to an order to use them. They, therefore, have no choice. What they *will* do is really what they *must* do. The same command is given by God to the first human couple—male and female—on the sixth day. (This might be taken to correspond to the human form, as yet con-scienceless).

Let us try, although we may be reproached for it by many excellent scientists, to analyze the sacred text as though it were a highly symbolic and cryptic description of scientific truths. This has been done for a number of alchemistic works and has revealed that some alchemists were really much farther advanced in chemistry than was thought before. If it does not lead us anywhere, it can do no harm. So let us read Genesis very carefully.

On the eighth day,[1] God creates another living being

---

[1] The writer is aware of the orthodox exegesis of the two successive creations reported in the first and second chapters of Genesis. But the use of a prohibition, instead of a command, is so startling that he felt authorized to submit a new hypothetical interpretation. It seems indeed improbable that the same momentous event could have been reported in two such widely different ways.

having the human form also, and for the first time the sacred text uses a different language. God first breathes in the soul through man's nostrils, and then commands him *not* to eat of the fruit of the tree of the knowledge of good and evil, knowing that he will eat it. What does this mysterious language signify?

It signifies that the most important event of evolution has taken place. It signifies the appearance of a new discontinuity in nature, a discontinuity as deep as that which exists between inert matter and organized life. It signifies the birth of conscience, and of the last freedom.

Indeed, God could not have forbidden anything to the animals without contradicting himself. Having built them in a certain way, having subjected them from the very start to biological laws imposed by their structure, he could not go back on his orders without a major reason, namely, the conscience bestowed on this new animal which was required for his further evolution and which none of the preceding ones possessed. Now, this is precisely indicated by the fact that God "breathed into his nostrils the breath of life; and man became a living soul," which may be taken as signifying that He gave him—and him alone—a conscience, that is to say, the liberty of choice. From then on, God can forbid this creature to obey certain intransgressible orders given to all the others, the physiological orders, the animal instincts. He can do this because this new being is *free*, which signifies that his endocrine bondage can cease *if he wishes*. Man, henceforth, has the choice either of obeying the orders of the flesh and consequently of rejoining his animal ancestors, of regressing; or else, on the contrary, of struggling against these impulsions, these animal instincts, and of affirming the dignity he won when he acquired the last and highest liberty. If he chooses to play the part of Man, at the price of physical suffering and privations, he leaves the animal behind, he progresses as a Man, he continues evolution in the moral plane and is on the road which will eventually lead him to the spiritual plane.

The text of Genesis, extraordinarily condensed, thus becomes comprehensible and rich in meaning. Unless we interpret it in this way it is obscure. Certainly, an interdiction is also an order, a negative one; but it implies something more, namely freedom. Indeed, when a criminal is in prison, one does not forbid him to go out, nor to commit other crimes. It is *materially* impossible for him to do so. But when he leaves his prison, one can forbid him to continue his criminal activities, because now he is free to do so. The error was not to have understood that God, who created and willed living beings, does not express his orders by words, but by physical, absolute impossibility. One might as well say that an engineer who constructs a carburetor orders it to furnish the motor with explosive gases. It would be impossible to forbid the carburetor to play its part. If it is in good condition, it cannot help vaporizing gasoline as soon as the motor aspirates. But the engineer can forbid a person—if that person has free access to the car—to press on the starter.

The importance attributed by the sacred text to this event, the fact that it develops it and in reality makes it *the first human event*, the fact that, in spite of his disobedience, this guilty man is chosen as the founder of the human line, proves the henceforth preponderant importance of the liberty of choice.

In spite of the interdiction, man disobeys and commits the original sin from which humanity must eternally wash itself. This cannot signify an arbitrary punishment imposed on all the descendants of man. It signifies that the actual human being has not yet attained the degree of perfection he must reach. He did not pass the test.[2] He is still dominated by his ancestral instincts and he disobeys God by obeying them. It signifies that *every man will be confronted with the same dilemma*, that every man will have to face the same conflict and that he will only triumph by crushing the animal impulses within himself and by consecrating himself to the triumph of the spirit. Thus, he will fulfill his mission as a man, and will contribute to the divine plan which tends to produce a spiritually perfect being. Human progress, therefore, no longer depends solely on God, but on the effort made by each man individually. By giving man liberty and conscience God abdicated a part of his omnipotence in favor of his creature, and this represents the spark of God in man ("God is within you"). Liberty is real, for God Himself refused to trammel it. It is necessary, for without it man cannot progress, cannot evolve.[3]

The animal struggle against nature, against the elements, and against the enemy, the "struggle for Life," from which the human form finally emerged after ten million centuries, is transformed into a struggle of Man against the *remains* of the animal within him. But, from now on, because of his conscience, it is the individual alone who counts and no longer the species. He will prove that

[2] It is rather striking that we should find the mention of a test in the third chapter of the Book, as the whole story of evolution is based on selection through physical trials, and as we came to the conclusion that this method of testing the new forms went on after man appeared, in order to select the fittest, morally speaking. It could almost be said that the Darwinian concept was foreseen by the Bible.

[3] One of the objections which can be made consists in saying: "If God is all-powerful, why did He not create the perfect man right away?" We will answer this argument in the next chapter.

he is the forerunner of the future race, the ancestor of the spiritually perfect man, of which Christ was, in a sense, the premature example, by emerging victorious from the fight. Thus Christ can be assimilated to one of the intermediary, transitional forms, perhaps a million years in advance of evolution, Who came amongst us to keep us from despair, and to prove to us that our efforts can and must succeed. He in truth died for us, for had He not been crucified, we would not have been convinced.

Consequently, any restriction to liberty of conscience is contrary to the great law of evolution, that is, to the divine Will, and represents Evil.

If certain individuals make bad use of their freedom, so much the worse for them. The test was unfavorable. They were not evolved enough to understand. As far as they are concerned, the trial was a failure. In nature, chance favors a small number of eggs out of the hundreds of thousands laid by one fish. As it is impossible to distinguish one egg from another it does not matter which one survives. In mankind, the individual is no longer indiscernible, and each being has an equal chance to qualify as an element of moral evolution. If man does not seize this chance, if he does not understand intuitively or rationally the significance of his decision, it denotes that he was not fitted to play his part. Others will assume the responsibility of assuring the ascendant march of evolution.

We must, therefore, instruct men, and not blindfold them under the pretext that society will lead them by the hand and guide them. Nobody has the right to substitute his own conscience for that of another, for progress depends on *personal effort*, and to suppress this effort constitutes a crime.

The whole will of man must be concentrated on this

struggle in which he is upheld by the newly acquired sense of his human dignity, from which he must draw at the same time the necessary strength and the proof of his high destiny. *It is in the intensity of this effort, and not in its form nor in its result, that the true degree of humanization is revealed.*

In the telefinalist language, as well as in that of the Scriptures, liberty was given to man by God. This is true in every realm, physical as well as moral, and condemns certain doctrines on the same grounds as dictatorships. *Liberty is not only a privilege; it is a test.* No human institution has the right to exempt man from it.

The immediate conclusion is that liberty of conscience can manifest itself constructively only if the individual has access to all sources of information, if he is free to exert his judgment without hindrance. This is equivalent to the confrontation of a new animal species with its environment, the test of adaptation. He must, therefore, be equally free to gather the elements which he deems necessary for the formation of his judgment. From the strict point of view of Genesis [4] it is inexcusable for a strange will to substitute itself for his and to effectuate a preliminary choice capable of influencing him. So that his judgment may be healthy and undeformed man must be free to cultivate his faculty of reasoning and to instruct himself. Those who need to be guided are not quite free. They must be enlightened and not compelled.

If this interpretation of Genesis is adopted, it leads, therefore, to the same consequences as telefinalism. The only difference lies in the motives. For the Church, the effort of man is motivated by the redemption of the orig-

[4] And the New Testament: "Where the Spirit of the Lord is, there is liberty." (Paul, II Corinthians, 3, 17.)

inal sin which was permitted by God. Whereas for us it is made necessary by the survival in man of the ancestral memories against which he alone can fight. As the "original sin" was nothing but the animal obedience to appetites, and the disregard of human dignity, the similarity is striking.

Thus, Man bears a part of responsibility in evolution. His free choice will act very much as natural selection has done so far. It is he who must now give the fillip which will orient his individual destiny and that of the species in the direction of progress. But how can his action manifest itself? How can he contribute to evolution while resisting the natural solicitations (temptations, in the language of the Scriptures) which yesterday still were the only ones he knew, the only imperative ones? How will the fittest, who is not necessarily the strongest, nor the most agile, nor the most resistant, be able to play his part?

He will play his part with the help of a new factor of evolution which was introduced at the same time as speech—namely, tradition.

9

A NEW tool of evolution, tradition, has thus made its appearance in the human line and this tool is in the hands of the being who is to evolve. If the goal of evolution had been purely material, if the end had been simply the relative perfection of man with respect to the other animals, there would apparently be no reason for it to continue, at least by deep transformations. Man has reached a relative state of physical equilibrium and freedom which, with the help of his intelligence, enables him to adapt himself to almost any circumstances.

If, on the contrary, this relative, biological perfection was only a first stage toward a higher end transcending physical adaptation, evolution would only then enter its most significant stage.

The incomparable gift of brain, with its truly amazing powers of abstraction, has rendered obsolete the slow and sometimes clumsy mechanisms utilized by evolution so far. Thanks to the brain alone, man, in the course of three generations only, has conquered the realm of air, while it took hundreds of thousands of years for animals to achieve the same result through the processes of evolution. Thanks to the brain alone, the range of our sensory organs has been increased a millionfold, far beyond the wildest dreams; we have brought the moon within thirty miles of us, we see the infinitely small and we see the infinitely remote; we hear the inaudible; we have dwarfed distance and killed physical time. We have enslaved the forces of the universe, even before we have succeeded in understanding them thoroughly. We have put to shame the tedious and time-consuming methods of trial and error used by Nature, because Nature has finally succeeded in producing its masterpiece in the shape of the human brain. But the great laws of evolution are still active, even though adaptation has lost its importance as far as we are concerned: we are now responsible for the progress of evolution. We are free to destroy ourselves if we misunderstand the meaning and the purpose of our victories; and we are free to forge ahead, to prolong evolution, to cooperate with God if we perceive the meaning of it all, if we realize that it can only be achieved through a wholehearted effort toward moral and spiritual development. Our freedom, of which we may be justly proud, affords us the proof that we represent the spearhead of evolution: but it is up to us to demonstrate, by the way in which we use it, whether we are ready yet to assume the tremendous responsibility which has befallen us almost suddenly.

Slight changes will certainly take place in the human body. Certain authors, extrapolating without effort or fear of being contradicted, have described the man of the future bereft of hair, lacking his appendix and perhaps his teeth. . . . This is possible, but entirely without interest. What really counts is the fate of the true contributions of man, the fate of the imponderable realities he has introduced in the world: abstract ideas, moral ideas, spiritual ideas, and their harmonious coordination.

The intellectual and spiritual improvement of man is inconceivable without tradition which must now take the place of the other mechanisms. The memory of individuals, their experiences, their progress can henceforth be extended in their descendants infinitely more efficaciously and rapidly. It required hundreds of centuries for hereditary instincts to become established and only certain gestures, indispensable for the conservation of the species, could thus be perpetuated. Their development was limited, under determined conditions, by the attainment of the physical result. When conditions changed, other instincts had to develop painstakingly. This process is extremely slow when only biological mechanisms are involved. Thousands of young dogs and cats and tens of thousands of chickens and other animals have been run over on the roads since the invention of automobiles. This will continue for a long time, simply because the experience of the parents who have survived by chance cannot be transmitted to the young for lack of speech and tradition. Articulated speech alone has already considerably shortened the time necessary for certain adaptations. What we call the education of young children can be considered as an extraordinarily quick short-cut, replacing the biological process of adaptation, and obtaining in one generation results better than those which required ages amongst the animals at the cost of innumerable deaths. Speech and tradition manufacture conditioned reflexes in a few years, and these reflexes no longer need to be transformed into hereditary characters. This last transformation takes a very long time, while, with the help of speech, *everything takes place as if all the acquisitions due to experience became hereditary immediately.*

That is why we dared write that tradition constituted a new mechanism of evolution. It was thanks to this new mechanism that man could accomplish what he has accomplished in less than thirty thousand years. It is because of it that the memory of the species, recorded in the brain for millenaries, could be thrust back into our innermost depths, and replaced by a direct individual memory permitting an immediate adaptation to the changes of environment.

This conception of tradition naturally requires the adoption of our idea, namely, that evolution disinterested itself, so to speak, from the rest of organized beings, and continued on its way through the human brain as soon as the latter had appeared. The whole history of evolution demonstrates that the species which "succeeded," in other words, which persisted and evolved, did it as a consequence of the new "inventions" they introduced through the play of mutations, adaptation, natural selection, and possibly other factors. When a new character, representing a progress, an advantage, is "invented" the evolution of the species or group endowed with it is usually affected by it, and the development and improvement of this particular character can be observed (eye, ear, constant temperature, etc.). The contribution of man was unquestionably the complexity of the brain. And in this brain, the centers of speech, the intellectual, esthetic, moral, and spiritual activities. It is, therefore, evidently through the brain that man must evolve.

The purpose of our hypothesis was to give an acceptable explanation of evolution and of the appearance of man at the top of the ladder of living beings, by taking into account the least debatable results of science. It also aimed to show that one could conceive a, so to speak, indefinite prolongation of evolution which thus acquires a precise significance; that human dignity, the development of intelligence and of spiritual ideas had their place in it and really constituted the ultimate phase; and finally, that most of the myths and moral or religious principles possessed an absolute value, transcending experience, but intimately connected with evolution as a whole.

Our hypothesis takes in not only the evolution of forms but that of ideas. No one can deny the fact that mankind is governed by forces derived from ideas. The outcome of certain abstract ideas transformed our material environment (applied science, machines) and shaped our private and social life, but the incentive and inspiration of man is to be found in what might be termed "lever-ideas": superstitions, ambitions, and religious ideas. Any theory which neglects them and takes into consideration only the physical welfare of mankind, *considered as a flock*, is incomplete and inadequate. As new factors of evolution we introduce tradition and its corollary, civilization. We thus stay in permanent contact with our environment. This will necessitate giving a broader definition of civilization than that habitually used.

The first elements of a real civilization can be found in the Cro-Magnon man who flourished in France and in northern Spain. For tens of thousands of years his ancestors had learned to fashion flint into hand-axes, scrapers and arrowheads. We have seen that it is difficult to attribute an age to these artifacts. Certain authors believe that the Chellean culture, the oldest in which man's work indicates an incontestable mastery of technique, is 600,000 years old; others think it dates back only some forty or fifty thousand years, which is very doubtful. In the earlier pre-paleolithic layers, we only find flints so roughly hewn that discussions have arisen as to whether they were really carved by the hand of man. Long before this, about a million years ago (according to Osborn), a very crude civilization probably developed at Ipswich (England), and it has even been claimed that man existed as early as the Tertiary period (Pliocene and Miocene). These discoveries are still too much debated for us to dwell on them.

Everybody seems to agree, however, that the first representatives of the ancient Cro-Magnon race appeared about 30,000 years ago, in the recent Paleolithic. The first real civilization, that of the later Cro-Magnons, is about 20,000 years old. (?)

These men were tall: six foot three on an average. Those living in the Mediterranean region measured six foot five and a half. They had high foreheads, broad faces, straight noses, and protruding chins. Their cranium capacity was greater than ours. They were beautiful specimens of humanity. But the Cro-Magnon was above all a great artist. The paintings which adorn his caverns are often admirable. His sculptures, his engravings on bone and ivory are wonderfully realistic, his tools and his weapons are superbly decorated, his jewels and ornaments are remarkably ingenious and graceful. The height of the Cro-Magnon culture was probably reached 12,000 years ago.

These *useless* manifestations—this word is taken in the sense of "not absolutely necessary to maintain or defend life"—mark the most important date in all the history of mankind. They are the proof of the progress of the human spirit in the direction of evolution, that is, in the direction leading away from the animal. The primitive "useless" gestures of man are in reality the only ones that count. They carry the germ of abstract ideas, of spiritual ideas; the germ of the idea of God disengaged from pure terror, the germ of morals, of philosophy, and of science.

The other motions, the ancestral gestures, necessary for the maintenance of life and for the prolongation of the race, *which were the only important ones until then, are relegated to second place and only serve to enable the first to manifest themselves.* If we needed a proof of the fundamental, essential difference between man and the beast, the inconceivable, unpredictable birth of useless gestures would furnish it. Nothing comparable was ever produced in the course of the thousand million years which have gone by. One single, imperative preoccupation: the struggle against the pangs of hunger, the struggle against the enemy and, periodically, at imposed periods, the excretion of the immortal cells, the gametes. Then death.

Amongst the insects, an excessive specialization restrains still further the role of the individual who disappears in the impersonal personality of the society, of the hive. Each being is but a separate organ, blindly pursuing a task which derives its reason of existence from other inexorably determined gestures. They are stomachs, ovaries, jaws, independent muscles with no chance of surviving separately, when parted from the group.

Everywhere, and always, infinitely varied in form, these useful gestures are strictly directed toward the conservation of the species, even if the species is incapable of evolving and is a failure destined to disappear, or to vegetate indefinitely.

Then suddenly, liberation. The new being, Man, changes his master. He escapes from the grasp of the physico-chemical and biological laws. Esthetic desires and ideas are born in him and can be materialized by his hands. The satisfaction of his appetites no longer suffices. He looks at his universe as before, but now he *sees* it. He thinks, he copies, he invents, he learns. The sense of beauty is revealed to him. He adorns himself, he seeks and combines colors. His weapons and his tools must be something *more* than utilitarian instruments. They must be beautiful. He engraves, polishes, and sculpts them. The most current objects thus symbolize his twofold reason for existence: to perpetuate the race and to contribute to his true evolution in the exclusively human realm of ideas. The appearance of the esthetic sense, which very quickly reaches an extraordinarily high level, is the first tangible evidence of the new orientation of evolution, the real origin of pure thought. The esthetic sense is the primitive source of intelligence, of symbolism, of writing, of all the means which will condition future development.

Man hunts. He builds traps for wild animals. He creates a magic of the chase, an unreal, chimerical world, led by the sorcerers, who are capable of dominating and of advising the crowd. All these details are revealed by the paintings in French caverns. But, as we have already stated, it is much earlier, in the sepultures, which were probably the first unnecessary gestures, that we must seek the proof of the idea of another world, of a survival. The desires and needs of the dead are the same as those of the living. The living must help them, give them the objects they may lack or want when they awake. Even in those times the human being wished to endure. The primitive cult of the dead during the Paleolithic was the starting point of all the care men have taken of those who have gone. It is the origin of all the concepts that at first were superstitious, later religious and philosophical in form.

The sorcerer, at the time of the Cro-Magnon, was also the medicine man. He was called when anyone became ill or seemed about to die. He was always there, occupying an important place. He was surrounded by considerable prestige. The idea of immortality, of renewed hunting in a land rich in game—the happy hunting ground—still prevalent in our time, was probably born among the Neanderthalians, and developed and flourished in the Magdalenian caverns. These ideas, whose importance is demonstrated by the fact that they appeared later spontaneously in all parts of the world, also underwent an evolution. Though certain human groups maintained them practically unaltered, or reinvented them, others have fashioned, modeled, and complicated them into dogmas and philosophical ideas.

The role of the individual now takes on another aspect. Even in animal evolution the new characters, which appeared as a result of some kind of mechanism and were either capable, or incapable, of insuring a superiority to those who possessed them, always developed in individuals and not in the mass. A mutation can never be general and simultaneous, otherwise it would no longer be a mutation, but a distinct phenomenon having a cause. These few individuals—or this one individual—were, however, absolutely irresponsible. They were not designated; they were the anonymous tool, the tool of chance, and could only play a passive part.

On the contrary, the sorcerers, the artists, painters, or sculptors gifted with superior intelligence or talent *cultivated* their qualities and then *transmitted* them. They

chose their disciples amongst the best endowed, thus emu-
lating, without knowing it, the methods of evolution (selection). These men, therefore, unconsciously contributed to
the development of evolution, whereas the crowd hunted,
played, fought, and procreated, their only task being to
beget yearly an ever-increasing number of children, from
which the sorcerers and the artists could again select the
elite destined to assure progress. This strengthens our idea
that evolution goes on in mankind through the manifestations of the brain and with the active and willful collaboration of man himself. The same thing still takes place
nowadays, or rather should take place, but one can sometimes wonder if value, merit, and aptitude are always the
only factors in this selection.

Moral ideas, though very ancient, were probably not
numerous in the beginning, and their social sanctions were
trifling as long as no true society had been formed. It is
likely that the first rules were not to kill and not to steal.
As soon as individual or family retaliation had been superseded by a social sanction involving the clan, as soon as
"vengeance" had been transformed into "punishment," in
other words, when a true society was organized and when
the concept of sanction was born, moral ideas seem to have
developed very rapidly. Six thousand years ago they had
already reached a state of refinement such that it has
hardly been improved in our days. Of course, we only know
this to be true in a definite part of the world, in Egypt. It
may have been true in China also. The only material proof
we possess is given by one of the two most ancient books in
the world, the Instructions of Ptah-Hotep, written for the
use of Egyptian princes, at the time of the fifth dynasty,
five thousand three hundred years ago. We do not intend

to analyze this remarkable manuscript, but to show the degree of advanced wisdom displayed by the author we shall cite two passages. The first is addressed to a husband, to the head of a family.

"If thou art wise, thou wilt take care of thine own house. Thou wilt cherish thy wife, thou wilt nourish her, thou wilt clothe her, and thou wilt nurse her if she is ill. Fill her heart with joy during her whole life and be not severe . . . Be good to thy servants within the possibility of thy means. Peace and happiness are absent from the house in which the servants are unhappy . . ."

The second is addressed to the prince:

"If thou seekest responsibilities, apply thyself to being perfect. If thou takest part in a council, remember that silence is better than an excess of words . . ."

It was over five thousand years ago that a wise teacher gave this advice. How many years will it take before it is universally put into practice?

These two short extracts suffice to show that we have not progressed much, and that these precepts correspond to a state of moral civilization not very different from our own. We must, therefore, admit that the first moral code existed long before. It was purely traditional for many centuries, but so were the commandments of Moses, which are obeyed in civilized countries all over the world.

The abstract idea of good and evil has never been formulated in an absolute manner,[1] yet it has existed ever since

---

[1] Let it be understood that we use the term "absolute" as opposed to 'relative"; namely, as expressing an independence from human opinion or standards as complete as that of a scientific statement *but not more so*. To the theologian, the Absolute can only be God or anything pertaining to God; so that his definitions, absolute *a priori*, are not "absolute" by the scientist's *a posteriori* standards. The definition of Good and Evil which can be deduced from St. Thomas' writings, for example (*Summa Theologiae,* I-Iq, 5 art. 5 & 6), illustrates this difference. There is no antinomy between the two concepts; only the same word is used to describe two different sets of ideas.

the birth of human conscience. According to our hypo-thesis, this notion must have been the consequence of the newly acquired liberty. This does not contradict the words of the Bible, if our interpretation of Genesis is correct. Re-ligions have symbolized the idea of good by one or several good gods and the idea of evil by one or several evil spirits. Good attracted compensations, a happy future life. Evil brought about the worst chastisements. This duality, ma-terialized by reward and punishment, was sufficient for the majority.

Philosophers dissected these two concepts and had no difficulty in "proving" to their own satisfaction that their value was purely relative. What is good in one country is evil in another, they said. Absolute good has no sense. With very few exceptions, they did not take into account the fact that these ideas had probably been born spontaneously in the most primitive beings, and that for this reason they deserved to be studied as absolute values. The task is cer-tainly not easy, but there is so much danger in allowing the notion of the relativity of good and evil to infiltrate into the masses that it is to be regretted that only religious writers and philosophers studied the question from this point of view. Unfortunately, they did not possess the scien-tific, rational arguments necessary to convince the ag-nostics.

Indeed, there is danger. A large number of men, many of them intellectuals, behave in an approved moral way, because they deem it necessary as long as they live in society, or because they have been well trained during their childhood and have acquired conditioned reflexes. Personally they are harmless, even though they do not believe in absolute good and evil. However, they do not realize that a much larger part of mankind does not possess the same self-control, and has not had the advantage of a good elementary training. Most men need either senti-mental, spiritual, or rational barriers. The courts are filled with youngsters and grownups who are not really to blame, because they lack the proper moral training. This is an age-old problem the solution of which is made more diffi-cult if the intelligentsia is convinced of the relativity of good and evil, because the teachers throughout the world are influenced, in spite of themselves, by philosophers and writers. Some of the latter estimate themselves superior to those who blindly obey the moral rules of the Church, the antique teachings of the wise, because they themselves do not need them and because they do not believe in their absolute value. The influence of such men, of their writings, may be disastrous, and few of them realize it. They some-times base their thinking on the works of great philoso-phers, which they have read superficially, or of great scientists, which they have not read at all. Thus, Voltaire and Darwin are considered as atheists, and nothing could be farther from the truth. To substantiate this statement, let me quote a few passages extracted from Voltaire's *Philosophical Dictionary*, from the article on "Atheism":

"What conclusion can be drawn from all this? That atheism is a very pernicious monster . . .

"Some unphilosophical mathematicians have rejected final causes, but true philosophers admit them, and, as a well-known author once said: 'a catechist proclaims God to children, and Newton demonstrates Him to the wise' . . .

"Atheism is the vice of a few intelligent men; supersti-tion is the vice of fools."

It can be objected that from a scientific and philosophi-cal point of view the authority of Voltaire is obsolete, but some of the greatest living American scientists, two of whom are physicists and Nobel prize winners, are deeply religious, as was also Bergson, France's greatest modern philosopher.

Learned people who are fortunate enough to have been born intelligent, and who have had the privilege of education and instruction, should realize that a great responsibility rests on their shoulders. If they have not succeeded in convincing themselves that there is a God, and that the highest human values are moral and spiritual, let them ponder the question and ask themselves honestly whether their negative conviction is of a scientific or sentimental nature. Whatever their answer to this question, let them further ask themselves by what they are going to replace the ancient and time-tested standards of humanity—the religions. And let us hope, as there is nothing more we can do, that this pragmatical plea will find the way to their hearts if the way to their intelligence is closed.

It seems possible to formulate tentatively the criteria of good and evil by the light of the theory outlined in the preceding pages. These criteria are naturally no more absolute than the hypothesis of evolution on which they rest, but they are no less so, and if our interpretation is accepted they are absolute with respect to Man.

Good is that which contributes to the course of ascending evolution and leads us away from the animal toward freedom.

Evil is that which opposes evolution, and escapes it by regressing toward the ancestral bondage, toward the beast.

In other words, and from a strictly human point of view, good is the respect of human personality; evil is the disregard of this personality.

Indeed, the respect of human personality is based on the recognition of man's dignity as a worker for evolution, as a collaborator with God. This dignity rests on the new mechanism born with conscience which orients evolution in a spiritual direction, namely, free will. We cannot conceive of a dignity deprived of responsibility, and that which is assumed by man is considerable. Not only his own fate, but the fate of evolution is in his hands. At any moment, he can choose between progression and regression. That is the meaning, as we have seen, of the second chapter of Genesis.

Once more we repeat that there is not a single fact or a single hypothesis, today, which gives an explanation of the birth of life or of natural evolution. As far as the origin of life is concerned, we have briefly studied the problem in the first part of this book. Willy-nilly we are, therefore, obliged either to admit the idea of a transcendent intervention, which the scientist may as well call God as anti-chance, or to simply recognize that we know nothing of these questions outside of a small number of mechanisms. This is not an act of faith, but an undisputed scientific statement. It is not we, but the convinced materialist who shows a powerful, even though negative, faith, when he obstinately continues to believe, without any proof, that the beginning of life, evolution, man's brain, and the birth of moral ideas will some day be scientifically accounted for. He forgets that this would necessitate the complete transformation of modern science, and that, consequently, his conviction is based on purely sentimental reasons.

Moreover, belief in God, today as in the time of St. Paul and St. James, consists in very little. A beautiful definition was given by a great Christian writer, Miguel de Unamuno: "To believe in God is to desire His existence, and what is more, to act as though He existed."

Many men who are intelligent and of good faith imagine

they cannot believe in God because they are unable to conceive Him. An honest man, endowed with scientific curiosity, should not need to visualize God, any more than a physicist needs to visualize the electron. Any attempt at representation is necessarily crude and false, in both cases. The electron is materially inconceivable and yet, it is more perfectly known through its effects than a simple piece of wood. If we could really conceive God we could no longer believe in Him because our representation, being human, would inspire us with doubts. Of course this only applies to the man who is capable of criticizing his own intellectual mechanisms and of admitting the reality and value of intuition as well as of the irrational aspirations which, at an early stage of his development, spontaneously sprang up in the human being. These irrational aspirations are real. Man derives happiness from them and it has been wisely said that nothing which makes us happy is unreal. They are the source of our greatest virtues, of all our moral ideas, of our esthetic sense, of our thirst for ideals. Their cause must, therefore, be real also, even if it is inconceivable.

It is not the image we create of God which proves God. *It is the effort we make to create this image.*

Similarly, virtue consists in the purely subjective effort, and not in its results. A spiritual endeavor counts independently of its cause, and it is the endeavor which uplifts us. We can only find within ourselves the elements which will enable our conscience to contribute to the progress of evolution, to collaborate with the divine task.

Except for the introduction of this last idea, it can be seen that we have been rationally led to the same concepts as those of Christian morality.

Thus the progress of evolution in the spiritual realm—in

the intellectual realm it does not seem strikingly evident during the last six thousand years—demands individual, human participation; therefore, the possibility of choosing; therefore, freedom. The story of the original sin can be interpreted as the symbol of the dawn of human conscience in a still primitive being. The picture of Paradise lost by man and which man must reconquer at the cost of infinite pain is prodigiously rich in evocative power. Our entire human drama, which will last thousands of centuries, is expressed in a few lines. No philosopher ever attained such conciseness. When we try to develop this symbolism we only weaken it.

As to intelligence, symbolized by Lucifer, the Prince of Intellectuals, it will in fact almost always be opposed to moral and spiritual development, and will render the pursuit of true happiness difficult. The rationalist, who in the last forty years has had reason to doubt the all-mightiness of reason, accepts without a tremor the overthrow of physical theories considered unshakable in his youth. He admits the inconceivable space in which the electrons move (three dimensions of space for *every* electron present; thirty dimensions for ten electrons). He admits that the electron is a "wave of probability." He admits the existence of particles such as the "Neutrino," and the "Anti-neutrino" which was invented for reasons of pure mathematical symmetry. He admits, without resistance, the existence, the reality of these paradoxical entities which he is forbidden to visualize; yet he obstinately refuses to admit the possibility of a supernatural, creative power without which the greatest scientific problems are incomprehensible, simply because the models furnished by his sensorial experience do not enable him to conceive or visualize it even though he is quite aware of their limits. He knows and does not even discuss the fact that the image he has built up of the universe rests on reactions determined in him by a minute fraction (less than 1 per thousand billions, or 0.000,000,-000,001 per cent) of the vibrations surrounding him and which go through him without leaving a trace in his consciousness. There is nothing more irrational than a man who is rationally irrational.

Many centuries will be needed before any real progress becomes perceptible, in spite of the introduction of tradition which accelerates the evolutive process of the brain, and has obtained astonishing results in a few thousand years. The principal preoccupation of man until now has been the domination of his universe. In the future he will have to learn to dominate himself. To accomplish this he will have to conquer not only his lower instincts,[1] but the habits created by the rapid progress of the mechanical arts. These habits are not only "practical," not only do they decrease labor, thereby tending to make any effort more and more difficult, but they are often very agreeable. Man insensibly becomes the slave of these habits and ends by considering them as a goal. This is not surprising when we remember the sufferings and ordeals endured by the majority of men since the beginning of civilization. Consequently, it will probably take a long time before the greater part of humanity can reach a true equilibrium with the artificial conditions developed by a small number of specialists—inventors, chemists, physicists, mechanics. If this equilibrium is eventually established, which is not certain, it will still take a very long time for humanity to understand that it has another role to play which will give it higher and infinitely more complete joys of internal and not external origin.

[1] "My spirit shall not always strive with man, for that he also is flesh." (Genesis, 6, 3.)

To be sure, it is through the brain and thanks to tradition that human evolution continues, but the functions of the brain are numerous and can manifest themselves in other directions than those leading to true evolution. Pure intelligence, deprived of moral background, often ends in destructive criticism or in futile discussions, in an intricate and complicated childishness exemplified by the difficult games of medieval scholasticism. It loses its value as soon as it considers itself as an end. Esthetic sense also can lead to monstrous deformations, to absurdities, and to revolting degenerescences. No matter what his activities, man must never forget his higher destiny, and the legitimate pride derived from this knowledge should protect him throughout his life against himself and against others. His efforts must tend to raise himself. The human conflict no longer consists only in fighting the instincts inherited from the beast, but in fighting the habits created by man as a consequence of tradition itself and of the diseases of his own mind.

In other words, the human conflict, far from shrinking, is further complicated by the very development of human intelligence and its creations. The inventions of man have revolutionized the conditions of life and have become, even for those who do not yet profit by them, the false symbol of civilization and the goal of their ambition, the pagan idols of modern times. Up to the present, only deeply religious, even fanatical people, such as the Mohammedans and the Hindus, have escaped contamination.

In the course of our short study of evolution, we noted that a change in the external conditions required, and often brought about, an adaptation of living organisms to new conditions. An almost identical phenomenon exists on the psychological plane. We also showed that such an adaptation on the part of the animal did not always constitute a progress from an evolutive point of view. This is exactly what we observe today.

Man must be made to understand that the mechanical transformations he has introduced in his environment and his adaptation to them will mean either progress or ruin according to whether or not they are accompanied by a correlative improvement in his moral attitude.

The duty of man, therefore, is to rout out this false symbol of civilization and to replace it by the true one: the development of human dignity. Not by combating mechanical progress—which would actually be impossible, and might be disastrous because of the progress which must still be made in the realm of pure science and of medicine—but by instructing mankind and raising its moral standard. Surprising results would probably be observed if our rational instruction could be combined in school with a broad religious instruction conforming to ancient Christian principles, but so far this has only been tried in a small number of establishments devoted to higher education.

Intelligence, as we said before, does not seem to have increased rapidly in depth during the last ten thousand years. As much intelligence was needed to invent the bow and arrow, when starting from nothing, as to invent the machine gun, with the help of all the anterior inventions. Confucius, Lao Tse, Buddha, Democritus, Pythagoras, Archimedes, Plato were as intelligent as Bacon, Descartes, Pascal, Newton, Kepler, Bergson, and Einstein. But why should intelligence increase? It was prodigious in former times, and is just as astounding today. It is far from having said its last word. There seems no more reason for it to increase than for a bird's wing or an eye to perfect itself.

However, this is a purely personal opinion. Thanks to the accumulation of facts transmitted by written and verbal tradition it will accomplish marvels and endanger the life of civilizations. . . . That is the other side of the medal which will demand the intervention of the moral qualities of man. The struggle, to employ the symbolic language of the Scriptures, between God and Satan continues.

With the exception of a few details, the moral code has not varied for ages. It cannot be perfected; it is, or is not. It can be condensed into a small number of rules which appeared as if by miracle in the four corners of the world at different epochs, and derive from that fact a character of universality transcending experience and human intelligence. These rules must be invariable, and their progress can consist only in their diffusion. Nobody can doubt that they do diffuse slowly, and are spreading progressively on the surface. This progress cannot but be slow, as it represents, for the majority of men, their triumph in the conflict between man and the beast. It still has immense strides to make. For centuries the aim of religions has been to bring about this progress. They have not always succeeded because, in spite of the high ideals of their founders, they have sometimes been led by men who have made mistakes and spent much of their time fighting each other. The happiness of peoples depends in part on the unity of religious thought. The world will believe in peace only when the Churches will demonstrate that it can exist.

Spiritual thought, personified by Jesus, does not seem to have gained either in depth or on the surface. This was to be expected, for it can only develop in beings who have already attained an advanced degree of moral perfection. We have not yet reached such a stage. Obviously we are very far from it. Nevertheless, it represents the supreme goal of humanity.

Human evolution, therefore, still depends on the fruits of intelligence but no longer on its development which seems to have attained, long ago, such a high level, in certain individuals, that it cannot be said to have increased since that time. It depends above all on the progress of morality, that is to say, on its extension to the great majority of men, for the fundamental moral ideas are absolute and cannot be perfected. It now behooves humanity to spread these ideas and to engrave them in the hearts of men, so that they will acquire as much strength as the instincts, without, however, becoming automatic. It is a question of shaping moral generations for the future.

If humanity makes this effort, it will contribute to the advent of the superior conscience preparatory to the pure and spiritual race destined to appear one day.

We have briefly outlined the role which can and must be played by the mind in evolution. Let us now try to give a definition of civilization which will explain why it can be considered as a factor of evolution, and how it can influence the destiny of man.

10

WE have seen that tradition, considered as a new factor of evolution, enabled certain specifically human characters, such as creative, abstract intelligence and morality, to develop very rapidly in the beginning. To facilitate the expansion of these characters it was imperative to dispose of a being endowed with great physiological superiority over the preceding animals. The brain had to reach a state of structural perfection rendering future progress possible on the psychological plane.

All kinds of trials took place in the course of evolution. Certain of these failed, either because the unsuccessful strains disappeared completely, or because their evolution was stopped, at a definite stage, as a result of perfect adaptation, so that the centuries brought about only unimportant modifications. Similarly, the development of the brain did not take place with equal rapidity in the different races. Certain human groups, in particular the Australoids, the Fuegians, the Bushmen, and the Pygmies, remained stagnant and hardly progressed beyond the ancient paleolithic stage. Others, in our time, still behave like men of the recent Paleolithic. The white and yellow races frankly took the lead at the start and advanced, thanks to their civilizations. Even in these two races the development of intelligence and its practical consequences do not seem to have always gone hand in hand with moral development. I do not think that this fact is contested. As the ultimate stage, the spiritual development, must lean on the moral foundations of a people, the question arises as to whether human civilizations have always evolved in the right direction. This calls for a new definition of the word civilization.

We do not claim that this definition is any better than those given up till now. It is different because it must conform to the hypothesis which constitutes the backbone of this book. It is naturally broader because it is not based on a purely objective or subjective human criterion, but on what might be termed a cosmic concept, provided the meaning of the word "cosmic" is restricted to the history of the earth.

What has been said on the subject of "particular" evolutions, separated from general evolution by a kind of shunting due to chance, and ending either in complete disappearance, in stabilized forms, or even in regressions, is in every way applicable to civilizations. All living beings sprang from the same organisms at a very distant period of the past. Differences quickly appeared and, far from being effaced in the course of centuries, became progressively more marked. At certain epochs, the continents and the waters of the globe swarmed with animals belonging to prolific but already condemned branches. General evolution, represented by the unique line which was to culminate in man, was apparently crushed by the mass of "particular" evolutions. At times, this line almost disappeared beneath the number, and a superficial observer might not even have been able to assert that it still lived.

In spite of the invasion of the earth by these fecund but doomed branches of evolution, the chosen strain persevered untiringly in its efforts. It is possible that at certain periods it was represented only by a small number of individuals whose life was menaced every instant by innumerable dangers. Despite this precarious existence, progress continued, and each generation transmitted to the following one the advantages so painfully safeguarded which characterize the physical man of today and contribute to assure his supremacy. It is not certain that the evolutive element of humanity, that which has attained a superior degree of moral development, will not be submitted, in the future, to dangers as great, but springing, this time, from the mass of unevolved humanity. It is not inconceivable that this spearhead of spiritual progress will some day, perhaps sooner than we think, be obliged to take refuge in the desert.

Just as tentative species blossomed and vanished, so civilizations were born and died. However, in dying they never wholly disappeared. Some of them are still remembered by treasures of art and beauty which time will not always respect, but their most precious contribution was an immaterial, and therefore, we may hope, immortal heritage: our esthetic, abstract, moral, and spiritual ideas.

Thus, through ephemeral civilizations, in spite of them sometimes, perennial civilization pursued its ascendant march. It was progressively enriched and refined. It will purify itself further, but it will have to struggle against certain material forms of progress which will apparently threaten it with annihilation. These fluctuations are normal, natural; they are necessary for the development of noble, high, and pure ideals, which can only take place through strife. Without combat, evolution would stop; it would indicate that an equilibrium has been reached; man would no longer have the call to perfect himself. At our stage of evolution the struggle for morality and spirituality has replaced the struggle for life. In order to visualize morphological and physiological evolution we were forced to cover millions of centuries; similarly, in order to visualize the evolution of spirit which prolongs it, we should view the history of humanity from on high and consider very long periods. Alas, we are generally dominated by the events in which we take part. Their proximity, the fact that we are actors in the drama, warps our perspective, prevents our embracing the phenomenon as a whole, and attributing to each event its relative value. We are no more capable of casting a judgment than of appreciating a landscape when lying flat on the ground in a field, behind a molehill.

The word "civilization" evidently has two meanings: a static meaning and a dynamic one. From the static point of view it expresses a *state* defined at a given moment; for instance, the Greek civilization at the time of Pericles. From the dynamic, or kinetic, point of view, it signifies the development and history of the factors which have led to this state and which will continue their evolution beyond it.

The notion of static civilization is arbitrary. It can be compared to the extremely thin slices of tissue examined by biologists under a microscope. The cells are dead, and to get an approximate idea of the corpses one must study dozens of similar sections. The notion of dynamic civilization corresponds, on the contrary, to the cinematographic study of living cells, tissues, or organs. Two definitions are, therefore, necessary.

First, the static definition: Civilization is the descriptive inventory of all the modifications brought about, in the moral, esthetic, and material conditions of the normal life of man in society, by the brain alone.

Second, the dynamic definition: Civilization is the global outcome of the conflict between the memory of man's anterior evolution which persists in him and the moral and spiritual ideas which tend to make him forget it.

In other words, it is—or should be—the result of the struggle between what remains of the animal in us and the new aspirations which truly constitute our human personality.

The reader may object that this definition does not mention material progress as does the static definition. But there is an enormous difference between the two. The static definition should describe a state of things at a given moment. It is a photograph which should be as detailed and complete as possible. The dynamic definition, on the other hand, should seek the real sources, the profound motives which have led humanity to this point and will direct it beyond, into a very distant future. This definition cannot take into account, as does the first, the mechanical improvements which characterize an epoch, and become antiquated in the next. The bathrooms of today, the radio, the airplanes have a place in *this* civilization, but it cannot be said that these objects played a part in the development of the Egyptian culture or even in that of the 19th century. Neither have they in any way oriented or inspired human efforts. They are consequences, not prime movers; they are effects of intellectual activity, not causes of progress.

True human progress, that which can be linked to evolution, and which prolongs it, can only consist in perfecting and ameliorating man himself and not in improving the tools he employs, nor in increasing his physical well-being.

This last attitude is that of the materialists and is insulting to man, because it neglects systematically the noblest human qualities alone capable of assuring him a happiness worthy of him, and superior to that of a ruminating cow. Man can aspire to joys higher than those of his animal ancestors, and men who are convinced of the contrary— or who pretend to be convinced—are to be pitied, if they are simple citizens, and to be dreaded, if they are leaders. They work against evolution, against the divine will; they do evil.

During the period which preceded the appearance of conscience, the animal, a simple link in evolution, and even the being who represented the first stage of humanity, demanded only the satisfaction of his physiological appetites. His "duty" was dictated by the normal play of his internal secretions, and there was no possible alternative. An animal cannot do evil, "commit a sin," because he does not know. "They are naked and are not ashamed." Possessing no conscience, still enslaved by his material, ancestral contingencies, he never has to choose. His will is conditioned by his appetites except in certain rare cases (that of the dog, for instance) when his devotion to man raises him sentimentally to the level of his master, his god. But with the advent of conscience, the human being, on the verge of action, feels an unwonted anxiety welling up within him which forces him to take into account the value of his act. He must choose. He *can* choose, and immediately *he judges those who do not choose as he does*. The moral idea, forerunner of the spiritual idea, is born. This is prodigiously condensed and cryptically summarized in the little sentence of Genesis: ". . . and they knew that they were naked."

We started rationally from the critical study of evolution and were driven to admit the criterion of liberty. This led to the idea of a higher liberty, the freedom of choice, implying conscience and the sense of human dignity. The idea of God emerged progressively as an absolute necessity, *a posteriori*, from the logical correlation and concatenation of these facts; whereas, on the contrary, the Scriptures infer moral rules, identical with ours, from the postulated existence of an almighty personal God. It is interesting to note that these two diametrically opposed methods converge and meet at the center. The important point is the introduction of the concept of evolution unknown at the time the Bible was written. This tremendous epic of which Man is the crowning event was bound to become the logical basis of our belief in God and to fit into any comprehensive interpretation of man's behavior.

Men certainly exist today who, should they read the preceding pages, would find them incomprehensible. They have never heard, deep within themselves, the muffled but persistent voice which blames or encourages. They have never experienced the pride derived from a profound sense of human dignity; a costly pride, richer in sacrifices than in pleasures. These men, like all the stabilized animal forms still living today, are witnesses to an evolution which continues without them. Some of them have gone back to animality, to the gestures dictated by their hormones. Certain others, in greater numbers, behave like men, for fear of sanctions. These are the regressive and stagnant forms which we find throughout the whole history of evolution. They cannot be blamed, for only those who *choose* the road which they know to be evil are responsible. The others do not choose, they obey their instincts but they can be dangerous by their example. Still others behave naturally in a dignified manner, without exactly knowing why, and refuse to investigate the reason for their attitude which they lazily attribute to various, pragmatic motives. These last are truly evolved but no longer contribute to the progress of evolution. They lack the sense of responsibility. They accept the advantages of their role as men, but they shun its duties.

The role of civilization is precisely to decrease the size of these three groups of individuals. All the means at its disposal, intellectual, sentimental and spiritual, are indispensable for the accomplishment of this task. The intellectual means are effective only on a small number of men who are difficult to persuade, for they want to be convinced by rational arguments of the existence of profound truths which escape human logic built up for other ends.[1] Vain of their cerebral faculties, they only believe what they are capable of understanding, that is, of translating into mechanical models borrowed from a limited experience. They reason somewhat like the greyhounds who, racing after a live rabbit in a field, suddenly stop, saying: "How stupid we are; this is not a real rabbit, he has no wheel."

The sentimental means reach a greater number, but they are indirect. The spiritual means, the only direct ones, succeed only with an elite, unless a series of great physical, moral, and sentimental ordeals has prepared the ground. Comfort, welfare, and an easy life are not propitious, it seems, to spiritual development. Alas, the same is true of excessive suffering.

At any rate, it is quite clear that the real aim of civiliza-

---

[1] "There are things that intelligence alone is able to seek, but which of itself it will never find: these things instinct alone could find; but it will never seek them." (H. Bergson, *Creative Evolution*.)

tion should be to help man to improve himself in every way and not to devise contraptions destined to reduce physical effort. Only in this case will it become a mechanism of evolution. Only in this case will it endure, as its solidity will rest on the combined strength of all the individuals. It must be built from within, not from without. Any civilization which is dependent on mechanical developments and technical solutions is doomed to failure.

***

Just as innumerable trials were required to give man his definitive shape, so civilization will grope to arrive at its still far distant end, the advent of a superior conscience.

The last period will be very long, for it is probable that human societies will throw themselves into ventures which will retard real progress, as they are likely to rest on a complete incomprehension of the true nature of man and of his profound and obscure aspirations. It may take as much time to liberate man from his age-long heritage as it did to give a skeleton to mollusks, for it is by the action of man himself that this progress must take place. From now on Man will have to struggle against man, the spirit must attempt to vanquish the body. Those who are ready to wage this fight are rare. They are as rare as the mutant forms at the beginning of any transformation.

When speaking of mastering the flesh, of dominating the animal instincts, we do not in any way mean to imply that the normal satisfaction of all these instincts is forbidden or bad. What is bad is to allow oneself to be dominated by them, as this constitutes a limitation of freedom. Man must liberate himself from a bondage which is normal for animals, and, therefore, evil for him. The goal of man demands a complete mastery over the flesh. It cannot tolerate slavery in any form. But if these instincts—which are due to his physiological kinship with animals—are mastered, they are no longer to be feared.

To love, to eat, drink, and amuse oneself are not acts which are reprehensible in themselves as long as they are practiced with moderation, and the word "moderation" implies a moderator which is the conscience, the sense of human dignity. Excess indicates precisely the failure of the moderator and the victory of bestiality. A drunkard is repulsive not because he has drunk but because he has lost control of himself. A man who is intoxicated is no longer a man; he shows that his self-mastery is at the mercy of an excess which he cannot control. What confidence can we place in him? His weakness stupefies and slowly kills him.

The telefinalist morality, far from stripping life of its satisfactions and sane pleasures, enriches it on the contrary by the added satisfaction to be derived from behaving as a true man and escaping the servitude of the appetites and instincts. This sentiment of liberty, combined with the assurance of contributing to the progress of evolution, should bring to man inexhaustible sources of joy. These pleasures are deeper and more durable than the others because they are independent of his physiological aptitudes and of his state of health.

The contrary excess, asceticism and mortification, is equally harmful, not only because, by attacking the body, it can lead to warping the normal play of the brain cells and thus affect thought, but because it has been known to lead to a dangerous pride. The body and the spirit should form a harmonious whole, for only thus can man develop indulgence, tolerance, and charity needed by all.

Civilization has a double part to play. It must progress in depth, and it must extend itself to the greatest possible number of men, so as to multiply the chances of individual progression in depth.

It is through individuals that a strain progressed in the course of evolution, no matter what mechanism is invoked, even if one abides by pure chance. Indeed, the same chance could not have struck in a similar way all the members of a species, hundreds of thousands and often millions of individuals. If it had it would no longer be chance. It is through individuals that a mutation is transformed into a new hereditary character. The same holds true in post-animal evolution.

We all have our role to play individually. But we only play it well on condition of always trying to do better, of overreaching ourselves. It is this effort which constitutes our personal participation in evolution, our duty. If we fail to make it, we will not have contributed to progress, to the divine task which, according to Ernest Renan, the great French philosopher, insures immortality. If we have children, we will have collaborated in a measure, modestly, statistically, but, unless we develop our personality we will have left no trace in the true, human evolution. We will have played the part of one of the paving stones in the road, when we might have been a milestone. We will not have worked for the advent of a superior conscience.

Human progress—there is no other—depends, as we have said, on individual efforts which are at the same time its tool and its result. Its tool, because thermodynamics, which dominates inert matter, not only ignores progress but imposes an inevitable degradation against which the brain fights. Its result, because the fact that a being believes in human progress and wants to contribute to it constitutes this progress. That is the real difference which separates us from the animal. "An intelligent being," said Bergson, "carries within him the wherewithal to surpass himself." It is needful for him to know it, and it is essential for him to attempt to realize it.

Intelligence alone is dangerous if it is not subjected to the intuitive or rational perception of moral values. It has led, not only to materialism, but to monstrosities. These lines were written long before the world learned about the atomic bomb, which illustrates our meaning in a striking fashion. All of a sudden the public at large was made to realize that a wonderful triumph of science brutally challenged the security of all mankind. And at once, the so-called civilized countries understood that only a moral coalition could protect them against the threat.

Time is so short that the only possible protection had to be sought in written agreements, but every man knows that written agreements are only as good and as trustworthy as the man who signs them, and that, unless this man is honest and sincere, unless he really represents a people who will back his word of honor, they mean absolutely nothing. For the first time in the history of man, the conflict between pure intelligence and moral values has become a matter of life and death. All we can do is hope that humanity will profit by this lesson. Alas, we doubt it.

Conscience, like intelligence, is very unevenly developed amongst men. However, the sincere and sustained effort of a moderately intelligent being can have a more efficacious radiation than that of a great brain. When Christ promises the Kingdom of Heaven to the simple of spirit, he does not have in mind the infirm or the dolts, but those whose intuition dominates their intelligence and who have an implicit, subconscious faith in human dignity and in the destiny of man.

To really participate in the divine task, man must place his ideal as high as possible, out of reach if necessary. An inaccessible ideal which directs our whole life, as the stars lead the navigator, is far preferable to a mediocre goal, for once we attain the latter we are forced to choose a new one. The ultimate end is beyond our grasp. What counts is not so much local and momentary success as continuity of effort, and should we have a tendency to become discouraged, we must remember that the light is within us and that any attempt to find it outside is vain.

11

INSTINCTS • SOCIETIES OF INSECTS • INTELLIGENCE • ABSTRACT IDEAS • THE ROLE OF THE INDIVIDUAL

ONE of the most curious traits of modern thought, all the more strange in that it contrasts with the usual pride of man, manifests itself by the efforts made to prove that human intelligence is nothing but a glorified prolongation of animal instincts and animal intelligence. Instead of emphasizing the differences, which are striking, a certain number of philosophers have systematically minimized these and have written long books in which they demonstrated that the brain of higher animals functions in essentially the same way as that of man. The opposite would have been very extraordinary, considering that the brain of man is evidently the result of the long evolution of this organ throughout millions of centuries. So that it looks as though they had taken great pains to break through an open door. However, this identity of mechanism only renders the problem more mysterious, as these philosophers have never succeeded in explaining the birth of ideas which cannot be traced to endocrine glands nor to any comparable tendency in the higher animals.

Essays of that kind, deemed brilliant by some and futile by others, would in any case be harmless if they had not been used as a scientific basis for the negation of God, which is irrelevant; and as an indication that man should derive an inspiration from the example set by the "societies of insects" in order to solve his own social problems.

Apparently these writers were not struck by the profound differences existing between "societies" of insects and human societies. Human society is based on the willing association of free, autonomous beings, capable of living outside that society, while the exact opposite takes place with insects, where individual autonomy is reduced to such a point that certain of them become incapable of feeding themselves, and depend for their subsistence on other specialized individuals.

The reason is that the societies of insects are "societies" only in the sense in which the human body is a "society" of cells, and not in the sense of a social group. The human body is organized in such a way as to allow the brain cells to think, to create, to evolve, whereas the activity of an anthill is vain and frozen. The difference between them can be compared to that existing between a modern calculating machine and the man who built it in order to solve his problems. No matter how perfect and complicated the machine, it will never think; it will only answer the problems propounded by man. The suggestion that we should seek an inspiration in animal associations and in the societies of insects is abysmally stupid. Some of the writers who proposed this solution may have been sincere. That makes their attitude all the more pathetic, for it indicates a total incomprehension of human problems, an alarming absence of the sense of human dignity and of its role in evolution. It lowers man to the level of the animal and forbids all spiritual progress. It condemns all ennobling efforts, all uplifting aspirations; it tends to bring man back to the role of the stallion, and thus suppresses his basic reason for existence. It leads to a revolting regression for those who have already evolved. These writers did not ask themselves who would play the part of the productive "Queen," of the condemned male, or whether the sexless workers represented an ideal compatible with our physiological structure and our ambitions. They did not reflect that there is no leader in the anthill or the hive, and that for this reason these associations of unconscious slaves work perfectly, like a well-oiled machine. They forgot that man is not a cog but a free being.

Instinct undergoes a strange transformation in the "social" insects. Instead of being, as in other classes, a conglomeration of memories tending to protect the individual, it is replaced by other impulses imposed by the morphological and physiological structure of each group. Extremely varied forms appear in the same species through unknown influences. The instincts no longer defend individuals when they are separated from the others and abandoned to themselves. The "individual" instinct seems to forget the individual and becomes a "community" instinct, which, without conflict or struggle, combines the interest of each distinct group (workers, warriors, queens, males) with the interest of the others. Everything takes place as if we witnessed the creation of a new personality (the anthill, the termite colony) endowed with its own instinct resulting from the sum of individual instincts but outclassing them to such a degree that the interest of the individual disappears, sacrificed to the interest of the community. This seems to be in contradiction with our conception and our definition of instinct. Such a biological community is a statistical resultant without soul or future and becomes the sole reason for the existence of its members. Removed from it, they die. They are the victims of a blind adaptation resulting from the activity of prodigious mechanisms in which their author seems to have lost all interest.

In the same way, the human body is constituted of distinct beings, the cells, each endowed with totally different properties. There are the common and prolific plebeians, the fibroblasts; there are the independent chemists of the liver and of the marrow; there are the chemists who obey the orders transmitted by the brain and the nervous system, and who know how to manufacture instantaneously, at the tip of the nerves, acetylcholine which contracts the muscles and adrenalin which decontracts them. There are the noble cells, the pyramidal cells of the brain, living in proud sterility and never reproducing themselves; there are the nervous cells which transmit orders and reactions; there are those which defend, those which protect, those which heal. From the coordination of the whole emerges the autonomous personality of man.

But there is nothing of the kind in the anthill or the hive where the physico-chemical and biological properties of cells are replaced by the instincts. These "societies" are only a rough draft, a kind of caricature, an assembly of gears which apparently turn without any conceivable reason. In the bodies of living beings we find the traces of the same method: a division of work. But in man it is crowned by the birth of a real, active, creative personality which is absent from the anthill.

That is why we can see more than a quantitative difference between intelligence and instinct; more than a difference of degree between the "social" organizations of animals and in particular of insects, and those of men. One of the most striking characteristics of human intelligence, one which seems to distinguish it most clearly from that of the superior animals, is the creation of abstract ideas.

The notion of abstract ideas may not be very clear to those who are not familiar with philosophical expressions. We will, therefore, try to define it.

Let us, for instance, take a child's perfectly round ball. It is very probable that mammals, in general, see it as we do. In any case a young dog who plays with it soon learns, like a child, to know its properties. He knows that it rolls, that it usually rebounds, and that, in brief, it possesses a mobility and a sufficient personality to make it interesting, without being dangerous. The animal is quite satisfied with his "definition" of the ball, a definition which corresponds to what he expects of it, and which probably does not differ from that of a young child or of a primitive man.

But the intelligent man is not satisfied with this definition, even when he has symbolized it by a word. And this is where the fundamental difference between the two kinds of intelligence appears. Man begins by imagining, in other words creating, an ideal ball endowed with the geometrical properties of the real ball but *extended to the limit*, that is, attaining absolute perfection. He attributes to it only the properties which characterize its shape, and eliminates those which characterize its substance, i.e., color, hardness, weight, elasticity, for these qualities can be found in other bodies having a different shape. He invents another name, which no longer evokes any idea of material properties: the *sphere*. Finally, to completely "understand" this new object, he invents an invisible element, without dimensions and without mass, which does not exist, has never existed and will never exist in reality, and yet is absolutely necessary to enable him to define the sphere which he cannot conceive otherwise. This strange element is the "center."

The specifically human notion of "center" is an abstract idea.

Here we see clearly the chasm which makes the progressive transition between the intelligence of animals and that of men problematical. Man is capable of *creating* an unreal world by drawing the elements from within himself and no longer from his surroundings or from his experience. It is not a question of utilitarian adaptation, but of an absolutely new intellectual construction in which material reality is only a pretext. Behind the facts perceptible to his senses, behind his discernible universe, man invents another conceptual universe which becomes indispensable to enable him to think, to interpret his experience, and eventually *to dominate the first*. Just as he has created redoubtable, living entities behind fire, thunder, lightning; just as he has created a "magic" of the hunt, so he creates a magic of ideas and he ends by attributing a greater reality to this universe born of his brain than to that in which his animal ancestors evolved. This is the strictly human realm, the realm of pure ideas, of morals, of spiritual ideas, of esthetic ideas. Man willed by God, invested by Him, through the gift of conscience and of liberty, with a part of responsibility in the progress of evolution has, within the limits of his means, the power to emulate his Creator by himself creating an immaterial world, forbidden to animals, and which, in the future, must absorb his interests and his efforts.

Those who are slaves to their ancestral tendencies and cannot, or will not, understand what a noble and wonderful destiny is theirs, are indeed unfortunate.

We know that the following objections will be raised.

What about the primitive races? There are many human beings who live as savages or semi-savages, the Bushmen of South Africa, the Pygmies, the Australian aborigines, the Fuegians, and others, who use abstract ideas rarely and are nevertheless men. Without going to extremes, one might say with truth that more than ninety per cent of humanity make little use of abstract ideas and are just as well off.

That is true, although, if they are not intellectually developed, most of them have, like our oldest ancestors, created gods and invented crude ceremonies. But when we speak of the progress of civilization do we think of the Fuegians? When we speak of evolution do we study the stagnant forms, except to give them their place amongst those which have evolved? When we describe the artistic and cultural capital of a nation and when we evoke the part it played in the world, do we dwell on the amorphous and unproductive mass of the people? No; we choose the few rare individuals, amongst the millions of citizens of the land, who have contributed something to universal progress, those who have risen, by their talent or their genius, above their fellow-countrymen and have thus placed themselves at the head of humanity, at the extreme spearhead of civilization. It is this small group of men which alone interests us. Humanity follows them and is inspired by them, and only deserves our attention inasmuch as it strives to emulate them. We consider and study mankind as a living mass in the process of transformation. But we know that such a mass transformation can only begin through individuals who are in general very lightly scattered, if not unique, and that their contemporaries who are less well endowed only constitute the raw material which will eventually furnish other mutant individuals or will gather and transmit by tradition the progress born in a few more evolved brains. These exceptional minds are the centers of radiation around which the ripples widen as around a stone thrown into the water. They can appear anywhere in the world, in America, in Asia, or in Europe; in any class of society. They are neither Chinese, Americans, English, French, nor Hindus; they are men.

We are in the habit of extending to nations the glory won by a few of their citizens, because we live in an epoch in which "political entities" (states), in spite of their artificial nature, still have a real existence which shapes our thought. Similarly a whole university shares the glory of its athletic champion. The nation and the university derive great pride from these feats, which their average men are quite incapable of performing, and it is one of the sources of the conventional homogeneity of these groups. The truth is, we repeat, that progress depends on a very small number of individuals, and that this progress, which represents the ascending march of evolution through Man, transcends the boundaries of nations. In like manner, the root of a tree penetrates into the ground, led by a small group of cells imbued with a devouring activity, at the extreme tip. This tip is delicate and fragile, slender as a thread, but, behind it, the root swells rapidly, becomes as thick as a finger, as a wrist, as an arm, and blindly follows the path chosen and dug in the soil by the frail white hair which leads it. The whole tree grows and feeds on the sap sucked from the earth by these slender rootlets.

The chances for the appearance and development of a genius, or an unusual human intelligence, are greater in a highly civilized country, because the mind can develop in surroundings more favorable to its improvement than that of backward nations without contact with the kind of intellectual fermentation which prevails in great capitals or in university towns. Tradition is richer, and the sources of information and inspiration are more numerous.

However, we cannot affirm that the men who are today considered as the most brilliant and most profound will be the ones who, in the future, will leave a permanent trace from the point of view of evolution. For we judge the value of genius or of greatness by the standards imposed by the actual state of our civilization, of our culture. It is impossible for us to cast an absolute judgment. The man who will, in one or two thousand years, be considered as the greatest of our epoch exists perhaps today, or lived yesterday. We may have passed him in the street, we may know him, or he may be entirely unknown. We have no means of discovering him, either because we are too intelligent, or not enough so. Excessive intelligence, which creates an Archimedes or a Descartes, anesthetizes the more subtle qualities of the brain, which are not necessarily rational, and reason is not powerful enough to do without a direct knowledge of facts. Intuition disposes of a much greater field of action than does reason, and purely intuitive, religious faith is a much more efficacious human lever than science or philosophy. Action follows conviction, not knowledge.

The history of human thought furnishes a thousand proofs of our ignorance of the true value of men, and of the distant repercussions of their activities, often masked by the momentary tragedies that shake the world. Nobody can foresee how brilliant or how durable will be the trace left by those who are considered as great men today.

The Roman patricians of the year 33, the philosophers, and the intellectuals would have been highly amused if they had been told that the unknown young Jew, tried by the procurator of a distant colony, who, so as to avoid complications, handed him over against his will to the crowd, would play an infinitely greater role than Caesar, would dominate the history of the Occident, and become the purest symbol of all humanity . . .

12

SUPERSTITION · ORIGIN AND DEVELOPMENT

SUPERSTITION can be considered as the first clumsy groping of man toward religion, and from that point of view
deserves a certain respect. This does not mean that religion is based on superstition, but simply that, from the
point of view of evolution, the birth of superstitions indicated a deep transformation in animal intelligence. It was
a preparatory stage, just as the marsupials were the preparatory stage for true mammals and the light-sensitive
ocular spot of highly primitive animals might have been
the promise of the future eye.

Let us try to evoke the humanly shaped being, without
history or traditions, who lived in caverns side by side
with the most ferocious beasts. His way of life was very
similar to theirs. Both had to face the same problems. First
of all they had to eat, which meant hunt. Crude weapons,
stones, clubs, suggested to the new primate by his relative
weakness and budding imagination, were slowly perfected.
He must also defend himself; from morning till night he
was on the alert. But his brain worked, and contrary to
all the others, he was able to invent. His weapons became
more and more efficient. To obviate his physical inferiority
he improved them incessantly. Instead of leaving every-

thing to nature, his rudimentary intelligence replaced the slow natural processes of adaptation by external creations conceived by his brain and executed by his hands. He combined the properties of natural weapons. The primitive club was transformed into a lighter, harder, and more efficient stone ax. The pointed flint cleverly fastened on a staff by means of thongs cut out of the skin of slaughtered animals was made into a lance and then a javelin. Man's life became proportionately freer and less menaced as he surrounded himself with more practical and deadlier arms. He was still far from having the necessary leisure or the wish to embellish them, but he was on the way. The gradual improvement of his flint tools demonstrates this fact.

However, he was threatened by other dangers, which he did not know how to combat, and which filled him with terror. They were the meteors, thunder and lightning, volcanic eruptions, lava streams in fusion. The origin of the harnessing of fire by man has often been discussed, for it is very probable that the method which consists in rubbing two pieces of wood together came long after fire was first used. It is not inconceivable that man tried to fight the rivers of lava with his ordinary weapons, by striking this smoldering serpent with his club and ax and the wooden handle caught fire. Or he may have snatched burning brands from trees ignited by lightning. He naturally conceived the idea of preserving this dangerous element in his cave so as to use it in case of need against his other enemies. All wild animals are afraid of fire. Having thus subjugated, not the enemy itself, but a new, fearful *principle*—the flame— which could live when fed, or die when neglected, it was logical that he should surround it with a kind of frightened respect.

Primitive man differentiated himself radically from the animal by the fact that *his terror did not constitute the limit of his psychological reaction.* He alone had a brain which enabled him to go beyond. Having succeeded in mastering the flame, he invented an origin which could only be supernatural, outside the limits of his experience, and conferred upon this origin a real personality. He *created* a new being, fictitious, powerful, to whom he attributed all the human passions: anger, hate, jealousy. This was perhaps the first god. By an unconscious effort, which at one blow brought him nearer to his Creator, and thanks to his superior intellectual gifts, to this marvelous spark which later enabled him to collaborate with the Author of all things toward evolution, Man himself thus created, not a reality, but a formidable fiction. When one reflects that no appreciable difference existed at that time between the life led by the bear, the mastodon, the tiger, and man, one cannot help being profoundly impressed by this unforeseen chasm which, from then on, has deepened day by day. All attempts to make intelligence but the prolongation of animal instinct come up against insurmountable barriers that cannot be honestly overlooked at the present time.

We can say this without fear of being misunderstood, for by this time the reader knows that we will never question the reality of intermediary steps without which evolution is inconceivable. We have given many examples of the progressive edification of forms and increasingly complex characters. But we have also pointed out a few unbridgeable gaps in our knowledge which make it impossible to correlate a certain number of phenomena through a relation of cause to effect. We are sometimes incapable of accounting scientifically for the appearance of new biological characters, or functions, on the basis of our scant knowledge of the relations existing between anatomical structure, physiological functions, and psychological activity. It is undoubtedly admissible, as a hypothesis, that instinct and animal intelligence were the elementary stages which eventually developed into human intelligence. But we are not permitted to state that animal intelligence, that of mammals for instance, is a direct offshoot of instinct; or that human abstractive, creative powers of the mind are a necessary consequence either of them or of their combination. Instinct and animal intelligence may have been the results of independent trials (the amazing and quite distinct development of insect instincts would substantiate this theory), with or without any connection between the two. In any case we do not have a single proof that either of them was a simpler form of all the psychological activities of man's brain. Let us not forget that when it comes to establishing the direct descendance of any living being we are highly embarrassed. Australoids and Pygmies are men; yet their intelligence did not progress. Their origin is unknown, just as is that of the white man who is not a direct descendant of the Neanderthal man or even of the Cro-Magnon. The same holds true for the specific properties of the brain. Throughout evolution, as has been said before, we are confronted with the sudden appearance of characters which are entirely unconnected, from a paleontological point of view. The only thing we can be sure of is that, statistically speaking, there was a progressive evolution. The tremendous number of vanished species makes it almost impossible to reconstitute the detailed lineage of man, and any attempt to trace the origin of the characteristic properties of his mind to a former species is highly hypothetical and questionable.

No matter how remarkable, instinct always gives an impression of mechanical utilitarianism which strikes one as being contradictory to our conception of intelligence. Instincts imprison; intelligence frees. One can imagine a perfect instinct rigorously adapted to circumstances, but a perfect instinct would have no reason to continue to develop, no more than an organism in equilibrium with its environment has any reason for continuing to evolve. On the other hand, we cannot conceive any limit to the development of ideas, because the limits we might conceive would, obviously, be conditioned by the actual state of our mentality.

It was inevitable that the first effort of man to grasp and understand his universe should transform itself into paganism and fetishism. He was in complete ignorance and menaced on all sides not only by the dangers he could overcome by force, but by others which seemed invincible. But a creative imagination and an aptitude to give birth to abstract ideas was needed to enable him to pass from the simple terror, which maddens or paralyzes, to the invention of an imaginary being, originator of these dangers; to pass from effect to cause and to personify this cause. It would be vain to look for a similar manifestation in the most advanced animal mentality. The cult of the dead, the ceremonies and artistic creations which followed, or appeared simultaneously, confirm this point of view.

The origin of pagan rites is explainable and goes back to the very dawn of humanity. As man could not combat the elements and the meteors, as he imagined mysterious and redoubtable masters, he tried to appease them. Religions preserved this character, symbolized by bloody sacrifices, for thousands of years. Such sacrifices still existed not so long ago in different countries. The organized fight against these revolting practices, inherited from our most distant past, started nearly two thousand years ago with the advent of the gentle Christian doctrine, but victory is not complete as yet.

Superstition thus takes on two aspects. The constructive and essentially primitive form of the beginning, the first crude attempt to exteriorize the new tendency of the human spirit destined to crystallize later on in the shape of religion; and the regressive aspect which leads the unevolved, backward elements of an ethnical group to maintain archaic and often revolting practices at a time when civilizations have already outgrown them and spiritualized the old instinctive impulses based on fear. After having, through its eclosion, inaugurated a fundamental progress, superstition becomes a menace when it manifests itself at a later period.

In the psychological realm this phenomenon is analogous to that which is so often found in biological evolution and thus reinforces our thesis. It will be remembered that in certain cases (p. 91) adaptation was in conflict with evolution. The competition between two species, one which was adapted but did not constitute the evolutive branch, and another which represented this branch but was not momentarily so well adapted, could last hundreds of thousands of years, as long as conditions remained favorable to the first, until the day it was overcome by a radical change in its environment and had to cede its place to the second group. A probable and striking example of this, which we have already mentioned, is that of the great reptiles of the Secondary period, and the first mammals. Both came of a common, unknown stock, but had evolved in a different way. In the beginning, the dinosaurs had the advantage, which is demonstrated by their prodigious expansion, but toward the end of the Secondary period, about one hundred and fifty million years later, when the seasons started, the biological characters which had helped the reptiles became ineffective and harmful, and the evolutive branch, the mammals, favored in their turn, could successfully fight against the "outmoded" monsters. The dinosaurs all disappeared, killed by the arid summers and the cold winters, too weak to fight against the swarms of minute beasts, protected by their fur, who ate the enormous soft-shell eggs of the reptiles. This unequal fight lasted a long time, but the mammals, bearers of the superior characters capable of assuring the progress of evolution, finally conquered.

Superstition first appears as the manifestation of a mental reaction fundamentally important as a starting point. Like a prairie fire, it quickly gains on the surface but becomes deformed as it extends, and the less man is evolved the more it develops along monstrous lines. The majority of prehistoric men must have had a very crude psychology. Nevertheless, a few "mutant" individuals detached themselves and evolved in an ever-increasingly divergent direction, toward pure religious thinking. After a certain length of time this advanced group entered into conflict with those left behind, who had hardly progressed. It was then menaced by the anonymous power of Number, by the gross superstitions degraded during the centuries and which had thus become dangerous. In spite of their common origin, the ideas of these two human groups could not coincide. In the crowd, superstitions were dominated by the instincts of the brute and the horrible cruelties of bloody fetishisms were born of this union; in the elite—the evolving branch—they gave birth to a religious sentiment with a language unintelligible to the masses. Intellectual and spiritual weapons are without strength against fanaticism.

During the course of the centuries religions have always had to fight superstition; an enemy all the more dangerous because it seemed to be inseparable from the human mind. Even today, superstitions of all kinds spread much more easily than truth or rational doctrines, because unevolved minds still constitute a majority. The illusion that rational thought has spread extensively is often due to the fact that it has been transformed into a superstition. There is no doubt that the prestige of science amongst men is also a kind of superstition. Religions tried to sway both the intellectuals and the masses, but their main preoccupation was to win an ever greater number of adherents, and thus they found themselves in contact with the people in whom superstition was most tenacious. The enemy was so powerful that in many cases the Churches were obliged, if not actually to approve, at least to tolerate certain mild superstitions and to steer the ancestral tendencies of the crowd into less dangerous channels by adopting and transforming them. The Catholic religion, born on the shores of the Mediterranean, where imagination is fervent, accepted certain practices because it was impossible to do otherwise. It is evident that the big toe of a stone statue, worn down by the lips of the devout, the ex-votos, etc., are so many proofs of the persistent desire to adore a human god, a conceivable god, rather than an all-powerful and inaccessible entity.

It may be useful to glance back at the first period of Christianity so as to fully understand the difficulties against which the Churches had to fight. The whole Mediterranean basin was at that time highly cultured, and great civilizations had already flourished and disappeared. But they had not completely vanished, and even though their economic and military power were gone, even though their great artists, architects, philosophers, and artisans, who always blossom in triumphant periods, had followed the fate of the dynasties and governments, certain traditions which expressed a fundamental human need, the need to believe and adore, the religious sense, had penetrated the masses and solidly established themselves. In other words, the "religious complex" of the people, often manifested by superstition and idolatry, had adopted all the old legends regardless of their origin, had embellished, complicated, and adapted them to their taste, to their habits, and had cemented them into a solid whole, which resisted because of its wide diffusion amongst the people, while empires crumbled.

Only a very small proportion of the population of a country—certainly less than one per cent—makes a significant contribution to art, thought, culture, industry, everything which in our eyes constitutes the glory of a civilization. This was even more true before the Christian era than in our day. Very little time is needed to annihilate these external manifestations of human progress, because they are the result of aptitudes, of individual talents, of momentary conditions, and not the outgrowth of profound, hereditary, statistical tendencies in man. Every child, at its birth, carries the germ of superstition while those who are endowed with a creative genius or a great intelligence are very rare. Religious sentiment in its broadest sense, and in its primitive form of superstition, has, as we have seen, an origin almost as ancient as conscience. It is universally distributed and solidly rooted. No cataclysms of human or material origin can shake it; on the contrary they tend to increase it. The accidents, the tragedies, the slow degeneracy which affect the few hundred men who are responsible for a brilliant civilization, may spell its doom, but have no more effect on the ancestral tendencies of the millions of men who make up a nation than on their physiological needs.

The fact that superstitions, transmitted by tradition, the human tool of evolution, rise like barricades on the road of progress is thus explained. We once again encounter this strange phenomenon, a factor of evolution transformed by time into an obstacle that must be fought by new factors; this perennial law which seems to exact a struggle, everywhere and always.

At the time when the Christian doctrine was born, religion did not demand much of man, and no one, not even an atheist, can raise any objection to the magnificent and simple definition given by James (Epistle I, 27).

"Pure religion and undefiled before God and the Father is this, To visit the fatherless and widows in their affliction, and to keep himself unspotted from the world."

The world, alas, is not yet ripe for such teachings and the Churches are well aware of it. Guardians of an incomparable tradition, conscious of their responsibility, their first task was to endure. They wanted to survive at any price, and the cost was often so high that they sometimes hesitated a long time, only to end by compromising against their will, carried away by the irresistible flood of ancestral myths.

Christ did not come too soon, for only the example of infinite perfection and total sacrifice could inspire men with the ambition to improve themselves and with the hope of resembling Him one day. But the spark that was Jesus could light only an infinitely small part of the immense pyre which fire alone could purify, and which will illumine the world when it bursts into full blaze. In the beginning His disciples had to preserve and protect the fragile flame, while waiting for the wood to dry. His doctrine was too simple, too profound to impress a world which, two thousand years later, still has to be shown colored pictures. Humanity is far from having outgrown the stage of childhood, the stage of illustrated books. Can one blame the Church if it sometimes borrowed images belonging to another story and incorporated them in her own?

The pagan and religious legends all take their source in the same aspiration of man toward an unreal world where virtues, as well as weaknesses, are amplified and symbolized. These legends borrowed their various forms from the environment, the climate, the characters imposed on imagination by the existing conditions. In the course of several thousand years they were transformed, beautified, or disfigured. The trace of the unique inspiration which engendered them can be found without difficulty in all the different religions, at the four corners of the world. It is in this unique inspiration that the spiritual kinship of thinking men resides. The relationship is sometimes distant, but religions should tend to affirm it by disengaging the original identity smothered beneath the successive contributions of centuries. *The unity of religions must be sought in that which is divine, namely universal, in man, and not in that which is human in the doctrines.*

13

LIKE the dog in Jack London's great novel, man hesitates between "the call of the wild" and "the call of Man." The dog, in obeying the first, only abandons a sentimental servitude and follows the stronger voice of his ancestral instincts. He does not fall, he does not betray, *because he has ceased to evolve.* His destiny is to be a dog, namely, an animal sometimes passionately attached to man and capable of the highest proofs of love and loyalty for his god.

When man hesitates because the call of his body seems clear, simple, and natural, he easily convinces himself that any act characterized by these qualities cannot be evil. Some materialistic doctrines have upheld these elementary arguments without realizing that they lead man back to the slavery from which he is slowly trying to liberate himself. The other alternative often seems unnecessarily arduous. He thinks it inhuman, whereas it is simply too human for him as yet. He does not understand why he should deny himself "natural" pleasures in a cause which, outside of religion, appears neither clear, simple, nor natural. If he does not have faith, or the innate sentiment of human dignity, he does not hesitate for long. He does not even choose, he submits, he obeys his instincts, he falls, he eliminates himself from evolution. If he possesses the sense of good and evil and deliberately chooses evil, he betrays.

To be sure, we cannot be too rigorously severe at our stage of evolution. We are at the beginning of the transformations which will end in the superior race and which will require a sustained effort for hundreds of centuries. Once more, let us not forget that the perfect man is not a myth; he has existed, in the person of Jesus. Others have very nearly approached perfection—some of the prophets and martyrs—but their number is infinitely small as compared to humanity, and it is humanity that must be ameliorated. Let us remember that we assimilated these men to the rare "transitional forms" which, millions of years in advance, heralded the eclosion of the stable species eventually destined to cover the earth. Let us also remember that if, thanks to tradition, the process of evolution has been greatly shortened it still requires a long time which can only be cut down by a personal contribution to the improvement of our fellow men. If we all considered ourselves as missionaries, this last evolutive transformation would be much more rapid. One might even say that if this were the case the goal would have been reached.

In the course of these centuries of effort, man will gradually learn to appreciate the higher joys derived from his purely human faculties, until the distant day when the others will repel him.

Our attachment to sensual pleasures which recall our origin affords the proof that we are still at the beginning of human evolution. The fact that certain individuals have revolted against this physiological slavery demonstrates that something else exists within us. The presence of the superior degree of liberty which characterizes man and makes him master of his spiritual destiny is manifestly established by this will to break his chains, *which no other living being had felt up till then*. It proves the existence, the reality of his destiny. The human being ceases to obey the rigorous physico-chemical determinism which lowered him to the rank of an irresponsible, indiscernible particle, without greater individual importance than that of an ant or a microbe.

If man does not use the privilege offered him, if he does not understand the greatness of his role, he confines himself to prolonging the species, blindly, as did his inferior brothers before him. He only differs from them by his morphological characters, and fulfills but half of his task. He has not yet acquired the right to the title of true Man. He only exists statistically; he is not a progressive element so long as he has not convinced himself of the value of his effort.

This idea of the value of effort is not new. We find it in the Christian religion. The religious spirit is in us. It preceded the religions, and their task as well as that of the prophets, of the initiated, consists in releasing, directing, and developing it. This mystical aspiration is an essentially human trait. It slumbers at the bottom of our souls awaiting the event, or the man capable, in the manner of an enzyme, of transforming it into true mysticism, into faith. This explains why a false prophet, a false doctrine can electrify the masses and can arouse as much devotion, as much heroism, as many sacrifices as the true ones.

How is it possible to distinguish a false prophet from a true one? By means of the criterion we have proposed. The false prophet preaches a doctrine opposed to evolution, or which does not take it into account; a doctrine which ignores human dignity and the value of freedom.

We said before that, for the individual, the effort counts irrespective of the cause. We can only rise through what is within us. The strangest religions, those that can be the most criticized, even fetishisms, have aroused martyrs. These martyrs died for the religion which is common to all men, and it was not their fault if their enthusiasm [1] was not utilized and guided by the true prophets. They all died for the ideal rooted at the bottom of their hearts, for God, the only one, theirs, ours. That is why every religious ceremony, no matter how weird it seems to us, should be respected. It is not the rite which we honor, it is the sincerity of those who observe it. The rite is but a pretext which enables man to develop in himself this universal faculty, sometimes still obscure and confused, that separates him from the beast and brings him closer to his Creator. Independently of any rite, of any Church, there has always existed in the world a religious spirit, a desire to believe, a desire to adore without restriction, a desire to humiliate oneself in total veneration, a desire to elevate oneself by approaching a conceivable but inaccessible ideal. It is this desire which is of divine origin, because it is universal and identical in all men. Religions, doctrines, dogmas, many and varied, often intolerant, are on the contrary the product of men and bear their mark.

A great prelate, Dr. William Temple, Archbishop of Canterbury, Primate of England, dared to write: "It is a great mistake to suppose that God is only, or even chiefly, concerned with religion."

Religions are opposed to one another in their form, in the material details of the cult, and in the human interpretations of symbols. They all agree on the existence of God, on the virtues, and on moral rules. Purity, goodness,

---

[1] The word enthusiasm was chosen purposely. It is derived from the Greek *en* (in) *theos* (god) ; in other words, an inside god.

beauty, faith are venerated everywhere, and it is they which should rule. No doctrine which liberates itself from material contingencies and recognizes the necessity of disinterested effort toward a transcendant ideal can, therefore, be attacked. Men must be made to understand that the important thing is to develop what is within them, to purify themselves, to better themselves, to come closer to the perfect ideal which is Christ. The rest is secondary.

No matter what our religion, we are all like people at the bottom of a valley who seek to climb a snowy peak that dominates the others. We all have our eyes fixed on the same goal, and we agree that there is but one summit to reach. Unfortunately we differ on what road to take. Guides come forward and we follow them. Some go one way, others choose different paths. All are convinced that their trail is the best, and all are sincere. By following them we approach the one goal, but when the groups which started from different points meet, instead of uniting, they seek to convince each other mutually that it is they who have discovered the best road, and they sometimes end by throwing insults and stones at each other. Yet they know that one day, provided they never stop ascending, they must all meet at the top of the mountain and that the road to reach it matters little.

Diverse in their form, modeled by the external conditions, varying according to the climates, adapted to the soil, to the people, to the traditions, religions are all arrayed under a universal rule the source of which is supernatural and constitutes their reason for existence. Intolerance is a proof of incomprehension. The intellectual elite demands a reasonable foundation, whereas the mass is content with sentiment and turns instinctively toward those whom it believes capable of guiding it, just as a flock blindly follows the direction given by the leader. If the orientation of this group is bad or dangerous, so much the worse for the flock. Somehow the crowd must be made to understand that the important thing is, not to follow, but to make an individual effort, and it is imperative for the leaders to comprehend that their task is to obtain this effort.

Those who draw from within themselves the necessary elements to feed their faith and direct their lives are fortunate. They do not need this book, and it was not written for them. There are many others, however, whose rational ego is not in harmony with their sentimental and religious selves. Because of this they are unhappy, and it is to them that this book is dedicated.

Many intelligent men feel themselves abandoned. Their hearts are filled with disturbing and unanswered questions. They no longer even dare to ask for an explanation, or else, in their distress, they consult those who, though unqualified, inspire confidence by their moral character or simply by their professional honesty. These, in turn, vainly interrogate themselves, and all, or nearly all, advance in life filled with anguish, like children lost in a forest at night, who instinctively stretch out their hands in the hope of finding other helpful hands. Vain and unconscious men, surrounded by the halo of science, under pretense that the spiritual light which guided humanity in the past was unreal, have raised opaque veils covered with obscure symbols, in order to hide the Light. They did not understand that what mattered *was the human orientation which resulted therefrom*, and that this reality could not be denied, whereas the Light itself was not of their realm.

Adepts of an absolute determinism and causalism, which

was later considerably limited by the advancement of knowledge, they rejected without proof a Cause the effects of which could not be contested. Because this little group of scientists, drunk with their fragmentary knowledge proudly deemed that they could forego everything that was not rational, they decreed that all humanity should also go without. They never dreamed that the science in which they had put their faith would soon be completely upset.

The formulae, the equations which satisfy them have no meaning for the masses. A mathematical mysticism, even if it is indisputable, will never touch the heart of the people, no more than the chemical analysis of a painting can evoke the esthetic impression it produces. There exists a chasm between the world of quality and that of quantity which science can never bridge.

Outside of the idea of a transcendental goal which is admittedly denied by a number of perfectly sincere and honest men, there is the pragmatic side to envisage: happiness, peace of mind of those whose reactions are more sentimental than rational, hopeful resignation of those who are physically afflicted. As they constitute the majority, they cannot be overlooked, and as long as rational thinking has not succeeded in replacing spiritual ideas by a successful, constructive scheme, as long as the materialistic attitude remains a matter of taste, man has no right to turn his back on these problems.

Besides the scientific attitude, which is the privilege of a few and has led some of the greatest minds of all times to admit the necessity of God; besides religion and spiritual thinking, which have their roots in the deepest aspirations of man, there is only one mediocre and misleading approach left—an approach sadly bereft of beauty, namely, common sense.

Alas, common sense will not suffice to catalyze, to accelerate the spiritual evolution in which man is engaged. Moreover, common sense has never been a tool of evolution. It is a practical, selfish notion without value for human progress. Not only does it frequently lead us astray scientifically, as we have seen, but, as it is often based on empirical facts and superficial human logic, it suffers from the same weaknesses as the elements which serve as its foundation. It is not susceptible of development in itself, outside of experience. This is rather fortunate, for, if common sense were universal, it would mean the end of the spiritual development of man, the end of evolution. It would, indeed, prevent us from improving ourselves, from striving toward an ideal, from acting in a way opposed to our immediate interest; it would forbid our ever taking a chance. Common sense is never back of a heroic deed; if it were carried to an extreme, virtues would not have many occasions to shine. It almost looks as if God had taken care of this sad eventuality by distributing common sense parsimoniously. A certain amount of common sense is necessary, as is salt in our food, but its absence is more fruitful than its excess.

As it is impossible to direct, to help every man individually, we are obliged to fashion leaders, and, as intellectual qualities are not distributed equally, we must prepare two different methods for gaining access to consciences. The first must rest on the most plausible interpretation of scientific facts and on a precise knowledge of the goal to be attained. The second, on the knowledge of human psychology and on the preponderance of sentimental ideas. The first must be employed to prepare the teachers who will be responsible for the orientation of the coming generations. The second, less intellectual and more emotional, will enable the leaders to reach the very heart of the masses.

Religions tried to establish this distinction long ago. They created an exoteric doctrine for the people, which differed from the esoteric doctrine intended for the disciples. However, as their knowledge of the universe was extremely sketchy, a great number of their ideas were completely false and as, on the other hand, their myths were generally fanciful, they were utterly unable to build a homogeneous doctrine and resorted to tricks. Today, things have changed. We can conceive a harmonious cosmos the laws of which reinforce our intuitive, religious aspirations without ever contradicting them. Therefore, we can adapt our teachings to the state of preparedness of the audience. There is only one truth, but there are many different mentalities, and what is obvious to some may seem obscure or unacceptable to others. Religions could not always overcome the difficulties created by the immense and rapid development of science and by its ever-increasing prestige. Some of them reacted by entrenching themselves behind absolute dogmas and intransigent interpretations; they refused to evolve, and settled down in an obstinate state of stagnation which could not last forever. Others, for lack of superior leaders, and under the pretense of not losing touch with humanity, committed the error of compromising with the absolutism necessary in the moral realm. It was not in this direction that they should have evolved. Men were not deceived, and the authority of certain Churches suffered severely.

Man would accept the hardest disciplines if he could be convinced that there is no conflict between religion and science; if his intellectual, rational self did not always enter into collision with his sentimental, intuitive self.

Reason and sentiment did not have to be reconciled as long as education had not imposed on man the fallacious need to understand. But today, when a large number of men refuse to accept a truth which they do not comprehend, this fact must be taken into account. The claim that spiritual and divine truths rigorously escape reason, and must be directly perceived, will never convince everybody. In certain countries the ground has been too deeply tilled at school during the critical period, between the ages of five and fifteen. A man endowed with a critical sense, and not naturally religious, must be given a reasonable explanation, an "acceptable catechism," and above all, he must be convinced that *there can be no contradiction* between the facts of science and religion. This of course necessitates an intimate cooperation between educators and men of science.

Some spontaneously moral agnostics claim that, as the main problem is to have moral rules respected, there is no reason to bother with religions if we succeed practically in enforcing them. This attitude reveals a lack of psychology, as man will always question the validity of rules if he does not know their source, and furthermore, a complete misunderstanding of the problem, inasmuch as the aim is to improve man from within so that he will *think morally*. The goal does not consist in having man go through the gestures of morality. Unless the behavior of the individual becomes the expression of a deep inner improvement, it is nothing but an artificial, conventional, and momentary set of restrictions which will be swept away at the first provocation. If moral rules are arbitrarily imposed, no matter what their practical value is, they will never fight successfully against the brutal impulses humanity has inherited from the past.

The attitude of the wise, cultivated man who is satisfied with a modest but assured position and does not see the necessity of religion for others who are less fortunate from every point of view resembles that of an athlete who would not tolerate hurdles of less than six feet on the track under the pretext that he can jump them easily. This happy, virtuous man does not realize that he is as exceptional as an international champion, and that his moral equilibrium, his health, his freedom from care make everything easy for him. He does not know that he is almost a freak in our modern society. Neither does he understand that he has a duty to perform, the same as that of religions without whose help humanity would soon degenerate. From the point of view of human evolution, which has probably ceased on a morphological plane, this man can only play his part by contributing to the spread and, if possible, the betterment and clarification of our moral ideals by setting himself up as an example. Only he and his like can do this. He has not the right to unload this responsibility entirely on those who are administratively invested with the magnificent function of instructing children and of modeling the brain and the heart of youth. Teachers are entrusted with the transmission of tradition as it has been taught them. With a few wonderful exceptions, they rehash the standard elements which make up the actual pattern of our economic and social life without having always thoroughly digested or assimilated them. Unfortunately, this pattern often reflects a state of obsolete cultural and scientific development and, in certain countries, acknowledged errors continue to infect generations because of the invincible inertia of the teaching staff. Actually, the progress of science is measured by its practical applications and not by the evolution of philosophical thought which results therefrom, and yet the last is more important than the first: it is, or should be, the real goal of science.

The task of correcting the deformations he has observed, and of seeking the way to avoid them in the future, devolves on the educated, moral, and evolved man, *no matter what his profession*. If he fails to do this he will only leave behind him works which will probably soon be forgotten, instead of contributing to human evolution. And what is required of him? Very little in fact. If he has the ability, that he should say and write what he thinks and what he believes; that he should rise against untruth when he meets it; that he should defend the individual liberty necessary for the progress of conscience; that he expose those whose conduct seems hypocritical and evil. If he cannot write, let him reflect at length and seek the way in which he can inspire others with the moral qualities which animate him; let him spread around him the idea of human dignity and of the duties it imposes. If he believes in God, let him proclaim it and give his reasons. If he does not have faith, let him ask himself honestly what can replace religion.

None of us is, individually, indispensable, yet none of us is useless, and the degree of our usefulness depends on our will. If it is sometimes easy to be totally bad, it is always very difficult to be totally good; but let us remember that the sincere effort alone counts. They whose souls have been perfected in the course of their passage through their bodies, who have fully understood the conflict between the flesh and the spirit, of which they have been the stage, and who have triumphed over matter; they alone represent the evolutive group and are the forerunners of the superior race which is to come.

14

ANY effort to visualize God reveals a surprising childishness. We can no more conceive Him than we can conceive an electron. Yet many people do not believe in God simply because they cannot visualize Him. They forget that this incapacity is not, in itself, a proof of non-existence, considering that they firmly believe in the electron. We are in the habit of juggling nowadays with entities known to us only through their effects. These are the particles, electrons, protons, neutrons, etc. Individually, they are rigorously inconceivable and physicists who specialize in this branch of science "forbid" any attempt at visualization. This does not disturb anybody, and their existence is not doubted for an instant because the physicists, who inspire as much confidence today as did the priests in the past, affirm that without these particles our material objects, the forces we employ—in other words, our whole inorganic universe—become incoherent and unintelligible. Let us not forget that these particles move in a world where time and space do not have the same value as in ours. We have already seen that an electron moves in a three-dimensional space (like ours) but that ten electrons require a space of 30 dimensions (three per electron), which is rigorously inconceivable. Nobody questions the reality of these now familiar though elusive and strange elements.

The agnostic and the atheist do not seem to be in the least disturbed by the fact that our entire organized, living universe becomes incomprehensible without the hypothesis of God. Their belief in some physical elements, of which they know very little, has all the earmarks of an irrational faith, but they are not aware of it. Some of them have remained slaves to a naïve verbalism. I had the proof of this in a letter received after the publication of one of my books and in which the writer bitterly reproached me for having substituted the word "God" for the word "anti-chance," which according to him was entirely satisfactory whereas the word "God" should be "struck from the dictionary and forbidden." Now, the word "anti-chance" cannot be entirely satisfactory to a cultivated, scientific mind, for it simply signifies that the whole intellectual pattern which we call our science is basically wrong and, at best, but a set of artificial rules which, by a lucky chance, enables us to foresee a certain number of events. Only a superman could be satisfied with an idea which radically destroys the theory he has just built up. Indeed, as we have seen, modern science rests ultimately on statistical concepts and the calculus of probabilities. These laws postulate the completely disordered distribution of the constitutive elements of our universe. If we admit the possibility of an anti-chance in a part of this universe (the living world which has led to thought), the whole edifice crumbles unless we concede that Life obeys different laws. In either case, this is tantamount to accepting an irrational influence, foreign to our physical universe, as the determining factor in living and evolutive phenomena.

It matters little what name we give this influence; the

fact remains. Before the ideas of scientists had been crystallized into an almost homogeneous whole, at a time when the possibility of a "cheater" had only been conceived theoretically and had not imposed itself as a necessity, it was called the "demon of Maxwell" as a result of the mathematical works of this famous physicist. Later on Eddington baptized it "anti-chance." Today the study of life and evolution forces us to recognize that its action is logically required and has apparently always manifested itself in a "forbidden," ascensional direction to finally end in the thought and conscience of man. We, therefore, see no reason for not giving this cause, which perturbs our intellectual pastimes and our ideas, the name men have given since time immemorial to all the causes which escaped them, causes exacted, but not explained, by our intelligence.

The objection contained in the above-mentioned letter proves that the intolerance of the Middle Ages is not dead though it has changed sides. We must be thankful that my correspondent has not sufficient authority to impose his childish convictions on his fellow citizens in the name of reason. We can also conclude that certain "freethinkers" have an idea of freedom which oddly resembles that of the dictators.

The idea of God cannot be concretized. It is possible to have an idea of the work of God, and *to find a proof of the reality of God in the effort we make to conceive Him*, for this effort is subjective and without any material cause. It is, however, impossible to find a proof of this reality in the material result of such an effort, which can only be a human construction utilizing more or less deformed memories of sensorial origin. We will attempt to prove this last statement.

Psychological activity manifests itself in two different ways. On the one hand by subjective reactions which are the result of inherited characters and of impressions aroused by our environment; on the other hand by psychological facts the origin of which cannot be attributed, either directly or indirectly, to objective causes. The first category comprises instinct, intelligence (abstractive intelligence excepted), sentiments. Abstractive ideas, moral ideas (the notion of duty, of good and evil), and spiritual ideas (the idea of God, the aspiration toward a transcendent ideal), belong in the second category.

The first category incorporates all the ties which link us to our material universe and make us one of the units of which the living world, as a whole, is composed. Though most of the relations between organized beings and inert matter are little known or completely ignored, they might conceivably be discovered some day by a great intelligence. But even so, the contradictions which they introduce into our pattern of the universe can sometimes be imputed merely to our ignorance or to the infirmity of our brains. They are, perhaps, momentary, speculative conflicts, between the laws of inert matter and those of living matter. We referred to them at the beginning of this book (2nd law of thermodynamics, and increase in the dissymmetries of living beings). In brief, conflicts affecting the homogeneity of our concepts, *but without action on the course of the events themselves.*

The second category, on the contrary, comprises all the elements of our psychism which manifest themselves by what we termed "useless gestures," and do not link us directly with our sensorial universe but seem to surpass it and to seek, beyond, a substratum, an imaginary universe dominating the first as inspiration dominates a masterpiece.

It incorporates the world of abstract ideas, of mathematics, of geometries, as well as the world of esthetic ideas, of moral and spiritual ideas. Abstract ideas are the source of the speculative conflicts which we mentioned in the first category, but moral ideas introduce a real contradiction between our ego and its material support, the human body. Our body makes us an integral part of that colossal evolutive current of life which shrank, little by little, until it was reduced to the human strain, but by our moral and spiritual ideas we are related to the perfect being toward which evolution has tended since the beginning. On the one side we are linked to all the beings which preceded us and we bear the burden of this heredity in all its aspects. On the other side we are the ancestors of a race which will be infinitely superior to us and which will seek to liberate itself from us as a chick tries to break his shell and free himself from his calcareous prison. On the one hand we are the slaves of the past, on the other the promise of the future. Consequently, in the latter case we are dealing with a psychic activity of a different nature, for it affects not only the homogeneity of our concepts, as in the first case, but *it constitutes the very tool which will forge the future*. It not only governs our actions, but it orients evolution and prepares the definitive characters of our distant descendance.

The first group, comprising all our experiences, all our sensory impressions, is the only one, because of its objective origin, which enables us to represent something. A representation always materializes through the intermediary of memories borrowed from the reactions of the senses, and especially through visual memory. An odor, a tactile or auditive sensation, is generally accompanied by the visual representation which was associated with it or which it evokes by analogy. Any representation is, therefore, borrowed from our environment, or more exactly from the sensorial memories derived therefrom. Now, we saw (p. 4) that the information furnished by our senses is imperfect, relative, and only covers an infinitely small portion of our real universe.

The second group, constituted not by facts or impressions, but by *relations* between facts, by abstract concepts, and by moral ideas, does not lend itself directly to "visualization," but sometimes indirectly as a result of its combination with the materials of the first group (sensorial memories).

Consequently, any *representation* of God is necessarily borrowed from the first group, from the physiological reactions resulting from our contact with nature. Therefore, this representation is not only questionable but certainly false.

On the other hand, the *idea* of God is a pure idea, like the idea of force, or of energy, and does not need to be visualized; nor can it be. It develops either spontaneously through intuition, unworded and irrational, and is then called revelation; or else it emerges rationally from the contradictions observed between the homogeneous but tentative pattern proposed by science and objective reality which made the construction of this scheme possible. We have tried to emphasize these contradictions in the preceding chapters.

Their origin can be attributed either to science itself, which, at a given moment, and unawares to us, ceased to be superposable on nature (in that case science is at fault, its homogeneity no longer exists and it ceases to inspire our confidence); or else, it can be attributed to Nature, which thus reveals a heterogeneity that our homogeneous intellectual pattern can no longer account for. As a matter of fact, this last cause automatically brings about the first.

Indeed, when science declares that all phenomena of the universe must obey the principle of Carnot-Clausius, and we discover phenomena which do not seem to do so, we have a proof that the science in question does not cover all phenomena, and this restrains its universality. This is the case for natural evolution, which unfolds in a direction *forbidden* by science, i.e., toward more and more improbable states. We conclude therefrom that our science is not universal as yet and only governs inanimate matter. If we maintain our faith in science as far as inert matter is concerned—and there is no reason for us not to do so—there can be only one explanation for its failure: namely, that nature itself is not homogeneous, as we believed, and that there is a solution of continuity between inorganic matter and life which our actual science cannot account for. Thus we need not accuse science as a whole. It keeps all its value, as far as we are concerned, for everything that is not alive. Life, then, does not fit into the universal pattern we tried to build.

Should we keep our blind confidence in human reason and intelligence, we will attribute these contradictions to our momentary ignorance and will say: "In a near or distant future, new facts or new interpretations will enable us to shed light on these obscurities, due to our imperfect knowledge of reality. Science is One and there can be no realm which escapes it." But in so doing we cease to think rationally, scientifically. We simply express a hope based on a sentimental trust in science. What is more, we completely lose sight of the fact that when these contradictions deal, as in our example, not with details, but with a set of fundamental concepts, which constitute the foundations of our science, we have actually shaken the whole scientific edifice in the name of which we have condemned Faith, and have been driven, by an equally irrational faith in an unaccountable abstractive intelligence, to demonstrate its failure.

It is natural and logical that the idea of God should emerge for those who, according to the language of the Church, have not been touched by grace, not only from such logical conflicts, but also from the following contradiction: we observe the existence of an immense number of facts, which for more than a thousand million years have tended to assure the persistence of species, and all of a sudden we are confronted with tendencies leading exactly in the opposite direction. "So far, thou wast only concerned with living and procreating; thou couldst kill, steal food or mates, and go to sleep peacefully after having obeyed all the instincts put in thee to assure a numerous descendance. From this day on, thou shalt combat these instincts, thou shalt not kill, thou shalt not steal, thou shalt not covet. Thou shalt only sleep peacefully if thou hast mastered thyself. Thou shalt be ready to suffer and to give thy life, which yesterday thou wast *forced* to defend at any price, if thou art but asked to believe no longer that the ideal thou hast chosen is the only true one. To live, eat, fight, and procreate are no longer thy principal aims. Death, hunger, slavery, and chastity endured for a high ideal are nobler ends. And thou must be noble. It is the will of the new being who has risen in thee and whom thou must accept as master even though he curbs thy desires."

Alas, this new being does not yet inhabit all hearts, or if it does, its voice is still very feeble. It cannot grow unless it is clearly perceived and freely desired. It cannot blossom without effort.

According to the telefinalist hypothesis, man must continue to evolve toward spirituality. He must free himself from the domination of his animal reactions and from the crude ideas inherited from his direct ancestors, vestiges of the first conflicts between primitive conscience and adverse nature. The tenacious memories of this transitional epoch when man waged an unequal fight against instincts and meteors, when he clumsily tried to adapt himself to a new world in which unaccustomed tendencies, aspirations, and desires had just appeared, still weigh heavily on him.

All his actual efforts must be brought to bear on this fight and he must draw both the necessary strength and the proof of his high destiny from the newly acquired sense of human dignity.

When the idea of the omnipotence of God is misunderstood it becomes dangerous. It leads to a neutralizing fatalism incompatible with what we know of evolution. The Moslem concept transforms man into an impersonal living machine, only slightly superior to the insect. The Mohammedan distrusts thought so much that he renders it almost impossible by compulsory and stringent practices. It seems to us that this attitude reveals an insulting incomprehension of the Power it pretends to serve. It evokes the memory of an epoch obsessed by fear, darkened by ignorance; a period of transition impregnated with superstitions, when the purest intentions were intertwined with the most cruel instincts, when man held the same furtive, suspicious, uneasy attitude toward himself and his recently revealed spiritual realm as did his prehistoric ancestor toward the unforeseen in the material universe; when his faith was not yet liberated from the memory of bloody sacrifices nor from the perpetual fear of divine wrath; when the doctrine of love and charity still broke its wings against the bars of the ancient prison which defied the attempts of a reason disarmed by the innumerable mysteries of an inimical nature; a period of clumsy groping when man sought to liberate himself from his last chains and constantly collided, in the gloom, with the outgrown form which still clung to him as an octopus and paralyzed his efforts.

From what was said in a previous chapter it is clear that God abdicated a portion of his omnipotence when he gave man the liberty of choice. Man—according to the second chapter of Genesis, and to our hypothesis—possesses a real independence, willed by God, and which becomes, in the human species, the tool of selection. It is no longer the strongest, the most agile, the fittest physically who must survive, but the best, the most evolved morally. The new supremacy can only manifest itself if man is free to choose his path. This is, therefore, an apparent limitation of the omnipotence of the Creator, consented to by Him in order to bestow freedom upon the chosen species, so as to impose a final test. Having been endowed with conscience, man has acquired an independence of which he must show himself to be worthy, under pain of regressing toward the beast.

The omnipotence of God is manifested by the fact that man, descended from the marine worms, is today capable of conceiving the future existence of a superior being and of wanting to be his ancestor. Christ brings us the proof that this is not an unrealizable dream but an accessible ideal. The means to attain it is indicated by the secular conflict between our instincts and our conscience, the fight in which human dignity is the stake. The whole history of evolution confers a significant value on our highest, though not most apparent, aspirations, by linking them harmoniously to the most marvelous adventure conceivable.

As to the slightly naïve objection which consists in saying, "If God is all-powerful, why did He not create a perfect being right away? Why the trials, the lengthy gropings?" we can easily answer by warning the reader, as we did on page 45 against anthropomorphic reasoning, that is to say, against the tendency to adopt the "point of view of the microbe," and to reduce the events of the universe to our own scale of observation.

We have explained at length what we mean by the scale of observation (p. 10) and we have shown that it was permissible to state scientifically that it created the phenomenon.

Now, every natural event, rapid or slow, is complex. It is the result of the succession of convergent series of elementary phenomena and, from the point of view of the observer, man, its aspect depends on the *speed* at which this succession takes place. An extremely slow phenomenon would not exist in the eyes of an observer whose life was too short to cover at the same time its beginning, its evolution, and its end. For instance, a phenomenon which, instead of taking place in a few minutes or a few hours, extended over ten thousand years would not exist for an animal with a span of life of, let us say, fifty years. It nevertheless exists for man, in certain cases, because the experience of the individual is prolonged through tradition. A succession of scientists, in the course of several centuries, who carefully record the intermediary stages and confront their protocols and archives, comport themselves, as a whole, like a single man endowed with memory and capable of accumulating his observations. That is how astronomy was constructed.

On the other hand, a phenomenon accelerated to the point where direct observation is impossible escapes an observer until the moment when recording methods more delicate and quicker than his sense organs enable him to seize it, or to infer its existence by means of a reasoning based on comparable facts. The sciences of radioactivity and electronics were developed in this manner. This is but one example of the profound transformations introduced by tradition in the evolution of man. The link forged by man between successive generations is a living and growing thing, forever changing and improving, yet unwavering in its orientation.

Science struggles constantly against the imperfections of our sensorial system the rhythms of which are not always in unison with outside phenomena. Innumerable new facts revealed by slow-motion and accelerated moving pictures give an idea of our limitations. Everybody has seen films showing the blossoming of a flower, a phenomenon too slow to be followed by the naked eye. The incomparable beauty of the unfurling petal was thus revealed. In the laboratory, the mechanism of tissue-growth, of mitosis (fission of the nucleus and division of the cell), of cicatrization, much too slow to be observed directly, can be analyzed in detail by this method. Many new phenomena were thus discovered. On the other hand, accelerated cinematography (one thousand photographs per second and even more), has unveiled the mechanism of phenomena too rapid for the eye, such as the penetration of a bullet through a board or a metal plate, the motion of a fly's wings, or the explosion of a charge of powder. Here, the phenomenon was "instantaneous" and the moving picture camera was able to decompose it into a series of successive observable phenomena unknown until then.

The fundamental fact that, on our scale of observation, a phenomenon borrows its very existence, its nature, from its duration and from its speed, is not realized by the layman. For instance, the combustion of a mass of matter, such as gunpowder, will manifest itself in two totally different ways, from our point of view, according to whether it takes place in one hour or in one millionth of a second. If it lasts one hour, it is a beautiful, peaceful fire. If it lasts one millionth of a second, it is a terrible explosion. The only difference between any explosion and fire lies in their respective rapidity. The atomic bomb is fearful because a normally slow process of radioactive disintegration has been tremendously accelerated. A steel ball falling with a speed of a few yards per second can be easily stopped by the hand. The same ball, with a speed of 2500 feet per second passes through a steel plate one inch thick.

When we examine a process like evolution, which brought about such prodigies as human intelligence and conscience, we should, therefore, never take the rapidity or slowness of the event into consideration. What is "rapid" to us in relation to the rhythm of our life, of our sensorial and intellectual mechanisms, conditioned by the structure of our brains, will be "slow" for an ephemeral insect with a life span of only a few days. To an imaginary being, with a life span of ten thousand million years, evolution would seem very rapid. To God, whom we cannot even conceive in relation to time, it may well have been "instantaneous."

The omnipotence of God does not enter into the restricted pattern of our actual scientific thought. It is no more shameful to confess it than to confess our incapacity to conceive the electron which we have domesticated. By extending the concept of "power" to the limit, to use the mathematical language, namely by inventing the word "almightiness," we have deprived it of all human meaning. The resulting conflict is entirely subjective, intellectual; it is we who have created it, it does not exist outside of us.

What exists is evolution, conscience, and the sense of dignity which, were it universally diffused, would suffice to protect humanity against the return of cataclysms such as world wars which bring about so much suffering. Their immensity and tragic horror are the inevitable consequence of the subordination of moral ideas to an evil intelligence, to false gods, and to passions.

Another objection seems serious to some very distinguished minds. Why does God tolerate the presence of living beings who are apparently useless and who constitute a permanent danger to man? Why the rattlesnake, the black widow spider, the anopheles mosquito, carrier of malaria, the microbe of hideous leprosy, the spirochete of syphilis which menaces the species; all these, and many others, are incompatible with the goodness attributed to God.

An obvious answer to this objection is that it implies an idea of God based on human psychology, that it is anthropomorphic. It can also be pointed out that this criticism is valid on the individual, human scale, but loses its value on the scale of evolution. The greatness of a task reduces the importance of details. When we consider the immensity of a work such as evolution, which passes the limits of imagination, we hardly have the right to reproach its Author for the imperfections, which, though tragic for a small number of individuals, are completely lost in the radiation of the work itself. All these physical "imperfections," on the individual scale, did not keep evolution from existing, developing, and ending in moral man. Statistically speaking, evolution has succeeded.

The real answer, however, is different. When we were led to call on an external action so as to account for the birth of life and the development of evolution, when we were forced, by the contradictions observed between our intellectual pattern—our science—and Nature, to admit an anti-chance, essentially irrational, we admitted that the only possible, logical interpretation of these facts coincided with that which recognized the existence of God. For a man of science there is no difference between the meaning of the words "anti-chance" and "God." When we proposed the hypothesis of the prolongation of evolution by man, and man alone, we were once more driven, in order to explain the universe and evolution, to accept the idea of a very remote goal, of a telefinalism imposing the necessity of a force, an intelligence, a transcendent will.

However, we were careful not to define the attributes of this force, which evidently corresponds to the admitted idea of God. We, therefore, used the consecrated name, but avoided as much as possible any anthropomorphic idea.

At the beginning of this book, we wrote the following sentence: Though the goal was set, the means to attain it were not. This signifies that we are only sure of one thing, namely, the existence of laws, of rules, imposing a certain order of succession to phenomena, and governing them quantitatively. Above all the particular laws, we were forced to accept a general law, infinitely vaster than the others and covering them all. From the very beginning, life has evolved as if there were a goal to attain, and as if this goal were the advent of the human conscience. This hypothesis enabled us to understand not only the significance of man and the direction of his evolution, but a certain number of facts in evolution itself, which had been obscure and sometimes incoherent up till then.

But this general law *does not void the real, objective, particular laws,* which cannot be reached, but the shadow of which was divined by human intelligence, through the help of sense organs. This intelligence has succeeded in co-ordinating the behavior of these shadows so as to be able to foresee a certain number of facts with precision, thus proving that a correlation must exist between the real laws and those which constitute what we call our science. (Cf. Chapter 2.)

Now, if we accept the fact that a supreme power has "created" the real laws, we are led to admit that, once established, they function; in other words, this power itself cannot prevent phenomena from unrolling in the direction imposed by these laws. If this were not the case there would be no more laws, but only caprice. When a phe-nomenon is started, it continues blindly, up to the moment when the conditions are modified in such a way that other laws go into action. This explains the monsters which ap-peared in the course of evolution, the unsuccessful "trials," the extraordinary multiplicity of "useless" forms: the par-ticular laws act. Our confusion in front of the apparent "incoherence" of Nature and evolution simply derives from the fact that we sometimes seize the particular laws (or their shadow) but not the more general laws which coordinate and dominate the first. For instance, we know a small number of laws which control the germination of a seed or the development of a cell. We know the action of temperature, of the saline concentration of the culture medium, of acidity or alkalinity. This is not very much, for we ignore totally how this seed will give birth to a spe-cific plant, bearing a flower of such or such a form and such or such a color; and finally, identical seeds. We know the human body and certain biological laws, we know the different cells which compose it, but we have no idea how they become differentiated from a unique cell, the human egg, and acquire their highly specific properties and their different characters. The laws of development and the co-ordinating laws are at present inaccessible to us.

It is not Nature which is incoherent but man who is ignorant. The biological rules he has discovered, as well as many others still unknown, all depend on more simple rules, which are partially known and govern inert matter, and also on laws which escape him. This multiplicity of laws of increasing generality, this hierarchy which has not yet found its place in our science, is the source of all the difficulties man comes up against in his effort to find a unitary interpretation of Nature.

The hypothesis we have proposed admits that the particular laws continue to act as long as the conditions are favorable, because, although restricted, they are truly laws. Adaptation, a particular mechanism, sometimes works against evolution (p. 91), but it cannot, *on an average,* endanger evolution which is the expression of a more general law. The elementary laws of chance play constantly in Nature; but amongst the events due to chance, an unknown, general law seems to choose those which are more apt to obey it, owing to characters which escape us. The other events continue to be governed mainly by chance. If conflicts due to chance (fluctuations) sometimes occur, they can never, on an average, stop the unrolling of events ruled by the more general law, and this brings us at last to the point we wanted to make, namely, to supply a reason for the persistence of species considered as useless or harmful to man.

Evolution is not ended. The struggle of man against Nature goes on. Through his intelligence, he has vanquished a great number of his enemies. He continues his conquest of the world every day, and intelligence, by using its acquired knowledge, has sharpened and adapted itself to the new conditions, thus increasing the chances of the species to persist. If man had no longer been forced to struggle, through the use of his intelligence, it is possible that the latter would not have developed. But the unfolding of this intelligence, of the increased sensitivity which accompanies it and facilitates its further progress, *has not put a stop to the activity of previous mechanisms.* They are nothing more than hindrances today because they have outlived their utility, and man must still fight them occasionally. However, intelligence has succeeded in checking them partially and will do better in the future. A much greater threat lies in the expansion of the intellectual activity itself which has led man to create new dangers much more formidable and deadly than those due to nature or to the animal species forgotten by evolution. More people are killed every year by accidents due to transportation alone (automobiles, railroads, ships, airplanes) than by rattlesnakes or yellow fever, and the victims of war far outnumber those of infectious diseases. The atomic bomb may some day dwarf all records. We know now that intelligence can turn against itself and destroy man, unless it is controlled by a moral force. *The same paradox has been observed in the course of animal evolution;* but the checking factor has not appeared as yet.

The moral and spiritual evolution of man is only at its beginning. In the future it is destined to dominate his activities. However, we have not yet reached this stage, and the period of physical adaptation is far from ended.

Let us try not to transpose facts belonging to one scale of observation in our own universe onto another, and, above all, let us beware of casting human judgments on events which transcend our experience. Let us try to rise to the conception of the incomparable greatness of the work as a whole, which continues with the majestic and sometimes cruel tranquillity of cosmic phenomena. We dare hope that the reader will understand, through more profound reasons drawn from within himself, the futility and perils of criticisms tending to weaken a faith which every intelligent man should on the contrary strive to fortify.

15

THE progress and happiness of the masses can only be obtained by an improvement of the individual, and this improvement can only be based on a high and noble moral discipline, not only freely accepted but understood. That is why education and instruction can be considered as instrumental in forwarding our actual phase of evolution.

The education of children, which is so fundamental from the point of view of the moral development of a people, has always been influenced by political and social convulsions. It is possible that in certain periods of the past, education was superior to what it is today. It was evidently less general, but the problem is not so much one of quantity as of quality. A bad education, or an education based on false principles and widely extended, leads to disastrous results. The theory of universal culture is excellent, but premature as long as people do not agree on the quality and nature of the instruction and on the preparation of the ground. To give children an intellectual tincture, a smattering of "instruction," without previously constructing on firm moral foundations the base which must support it, is to build on sand; and the higher the monument the more complete will be its collapse.

This manner of procedure is, alas, much too frequent, and probably rests on the deplorable confusion between education and instruction. Education consists in preparing the moral character of a child, in teaching him the few fundamental and invariable principles accepted in all the countries of the world. It consists in giving him, from tenderest childhood, the notion of human dignity. On the other hand, instruction consists in making him absorb the accumulated knowledge of man in every realm. Education directs his actions, inspires his behavior in all his contacts with mankind, and helps him to master himself. Instruction gives him the elements of his intellectual activity and informs him of the actual state of his civilization. Education gives him the unalterable foundations of his life; instruction enables him to adapt himself to the variations of his environment and to link these variations to past and future events. Only in the past is environment immutable; it is essentially variable in the present.

An important experimental element which has not been taken into consideration up till now is the psychological value of time. Time does not have the same value in childhood as in later years. A year is much longer, physiologically and psychologically, for a child than for a man. One year for a child of ten corresponds to two years for a man of twenty. When the child is younger the discrepancy is still greater. The time elapsed between the third and seventh year probably represents a duration equivalent to fifteen or twenty years for a grown man.[1] Now, it is precisely at this age that a child builds up the framework into which all the events of his future life will fit, and in par-

---

[1] This fact was demonstrated and treated in detail in a book, *Biological Time*, Lecomte du Nouy, published in New York in 1937 (Macmillan & Co). See also: Proc. Am. Philos. Soc., Philadelphia, 1943.

ticular his moral code. This explains the considerable amount of knowledge a child can accumulate during his first years. It would be highly desirable for parents and educators to take this fact into consideration.

The moral education of a child is different from that given to a man. Indeed, for the very young it is important not to judge the gravity of a fault by its consequences. For a child a fault is serious in itself—absolutely and not relatively—because it has been decreed that it is grave. Only the absolute character of a fault can impart to the child a true moral discipline without which progress is impossible. The criterion cannot be the same for adults, except in the army.

It is impossible to model a child morally if this principle is not followed, for the faults are almost always venial by their consequences. It is only during the most tender age that the character can be formed.

When we speak of beginning education in tender childhood, we mean in the cradle. We realize that this will shock the sentiments of many parents and especially of mothers, who will object that it is exaggerated or impossible. We do not think so; they do not realize the important part played by unconscious egoism in their love. The smile, the joy of their child, gives them so much pleasure that they do not have the courage to impose at the start the disciplines which will have to intervene one day, and will become more difficult and painful to apply as the child grows older. Even though they are ready for any sacrifice, they are often weak, and the moral formation of the child is thus rendered much more painful later on, both for themselves and for him. We will not speak of the laziness of parents which unfortunately often intervenes. It is much less tiring and nerve-racking to give a child its milk as soon as it cries, or take it up in one's arms, than to let it yell. If the mother weakens only once, the child does not forget and soon becomes unbearable.

I foresee the objections of parents who will say, "It is impossible to be strict with a baby in the cradle or with a one- or two-year-old child. It is too young to learn and does not understand." That is a gross error. First of all, a child three months old can learn perfectly. It is not a question of being severe, but of being patient, stubborn, more stubborn than he. And secondly, it does not need to understand; it is even necessary that it should not understand for it is precisely at this time that one must impose habits that will have to be contracted one day, no matter what happens. Besides, without knowing it, mothers do take the trouble to form certain habits, when the child is still in the cradle. No child likes to be washed; yet all mothers—or almost all—teach their children to be clean, or at least try to do so, and everyone knows that this takes years. They keep—or should keep—their babies from sticking their fingers in their mouths. They make this effort for physical habits, but neglect the more necessary moral habits such as obedience. A child's reason and judgment should only begin to enter into play when he is of an age to use them, and when he possesses the necessary elements, thanks to his instruction—namely, when he is about fifteen years old. Let us not forget that his education should make him more able to live in a society which is largely Christian and that it is he who must adapt himself to it and not it to him.

Primary education must fashion the character of a child at the moment when his brain is still free from any imprint and infinitely plastic. This preparatory work must be accomplished before the impact of his dawning personality against his universe has created habits which will have to be vanquished some day. It is important to impress on him, from the very beginning, the simple rules, the apparent "deformations," acquired and adopted by civilization, which constitute the basis of the specifically human heritage, the tradition, faithfully preserved and slowly polished in the course of ages.

The reaction of a young child to its limited universe can only be instinctive, animal-like; it is, therefore, regressive from the standpoint of evolution, and tradition must fight against it. If the framework is patiently imposed *before* this reaction has had time to develop into a permanent attitude, the external world *must* fit into the new pattern, and when the conscience of the child awakes, it will find in itself the web on which the tapestry of its life will spread without effort and without revolt. Otherwise there will inevitably be a conflict between the ancestral heritage, which speaks out clearly, and the human tradition, which is incomprehensible for the young.

The task of the parents, or of those who assume the responsibility of the elementary formation of the child, is limited at first to the application of a small number of absolute and very simple rules. A child must learn to obey automatically. The idea that it is *possible* to disobey his parents must be eradicated. If he only succeeds in imposing his will once, he will never forget it and will always attempt to do so again with an infinite patience, much greater than that of the parents. Afterwards, he must be taught to control himself, by fighting against anger, impatience, tears, with gentle but inflexible firmness. Thus, progressively, and without his being aware of it, the authority of the parents will impose itself on him like a force of nature. His personality cannot suffer, for it is only a question of rules governing his attitude toward others in current life, and of the external manifestation of his psychological, emotive reactions.

The younger the child, the easier it is to obtain a result. The rules will impress themselves indelibly, and all the other influences resulting from his contact with his environment will never be anything but *superimpressions*, which will never efface the first impression. On the contrary, if the more complex rules of true morality, which will follow as soon as the child begins to speak, are imposed *after* he has himself already reacted, it is they which will act as superimpressions and will be incapable of completely eradicating the imprint of the first. Education must, therefore, begin by the establishment of conditioned reflexes, the reason for which can be explained later. As we said before, these habits do not affect in the least the personality of the child which is of an intellectual nature. They only contribute to make well-behaved, disciplined children who will be better prepared for life, more useful and happier.

When a child begins to speak and to think, one must not be afraid to make his brain and his memory work. The quality of a child's memory is surprising and is rapidly lost. The coordinating power between his ears and his organs of speech is prodigious and rarely persists beyond the age of ten. A child can, without effort, learn to speak two or three languages fluently, without an accent, but this becomes almost impossible when he is over ten years old, and at that time requires a great deal of work and effort which, at that age, arouses a contrary reaction, a protestation, thus handicapping the result. At the age of two or three years, this protestation does not exist.

We have mentioned the fact that the value of time is

not the same for a child as for a grownup. He can therefore absorb without effort much more knowledge than
he does at present, that is, provided the teacher remembers that ten minutes of attention correspond to more than
one hour of concentration for an adult. It is better to give
six or seven lessons of five minutes per day (equivalent to
seven lessons of one hour per week for an older person)
than one lesson of thirty minutes during which length of
time a child is physiologically incapable of fixing his attention.

*   *   *

Two principal methods are employed to bring up children. The first consists in saying: "This is forbidden; if
you do it, you will be punished. This is obligatory; if you
do not do it, you will also be punished; but if you do it,
you will have candy."

This technique, the same as that employed to train animals, and which creates conditioned reflexes, gives excellent results as long as the child has not yet come into
full possession of his personality, that is, when he is very
young. In that form, or in a less brutal form, it is at that
time absolutely necessary in order to create the rigid
framework we mentioned above. But later on, it is without
value from an educational point of view.

The second method, which is much less employed,
applies to older children and can be summarized in the
following way: "Do not do that, it is contrary to your
dignity; if you do it you lower yourself. This, on the contrary is good; it is of a nature to increase your own value
as a human being, in your eyes as well as the eyes of your
fellow men. If you do it you may be rewarded by them,
but you will derive a higher satisfaction from your own

conscience." It is clear that this method can only bear fruit in a soil of superior quality.

The same methods can be applied to grown-up men, with analogous restrictions, namely, that the first is the only one which has a chance to succeed with morally undeveloped men who have not yet attained a high degree of evolution, whereas the second will give good results only with an elite representing the spearheads of evolution. Unfortunately, the great majority of men have not gone beyond the stage of childhood from a moral point of view. They must, therefore, be considered as children, and that is the point of view of most religions. However, we must not forget that humanity is to improve, on an average, not through obedience to external rules but through a profound internal amelioration, and that its progress depends only on itself. We must, therefore, beware of excessive standardization and not discourage those who possess unusual qualities and represent the "mutant forms" which anticipate the future. We must seek them out, and help them individually.

This is a delicate point in the moral education of civilized peoples.

Intelligence, or rather the faculty of reasoning, has been cultivated by compulsory education. A certain number of individuals, gifted with brains which were apt to develop, were thus revealed. These minds learned the "tricks" which characterize civilizations, and two principal groups of unequal number and quality were formed. The first, and largest, is composed of those who have absorbed their primary or secondary instruction without digesting it. They constitute a kind of standardized mass which lives under the illusion that it knows how to use its brains and derives therefrom a pride which is sometimes dangerous.

The second is represented by those who have digested and assimilated their instruction, have gone beyond it and combined it with their intuition, with their own genius and are thus qualified to make human knowledge progress.

The existence of these two groups is practically ignored from a moral and religious point of view. Everything takes place as if moral education were a luxury, a "supplementary course" required by habit, but not worth the trouble of adapting, either to the intellectual ability of the student or to the transformations undergone by our science and our philosophy in the last fifty years. Nobody dreams of bringing it into harmony with the different degrees of culture and intelligence. In all educational centers, the strict minimum of moral principles continues to be taught with indifference, in a boring fashion, hurriedly, and without any kind of conviction. We trust social life, environment, custom to give the individual a superficial moral character. We do not seek a deep fundamental improvement.

A number of religious schools insist more on history, forms, rites, dogma, heresies, than on the profound human significance of religion. Virtually every Church, with more or less violence and intolerance, strives to demonstrate that it is the best, and dwells at greater length on the differences which separate it from the others than on the unique inspiration which unites them. Outside of a few rare exceptions, no effort is made to enliven or modernize the moral instruction derived from the Scriptures. Some Churches revolt at this idea because they think that the word "modern" is synonymous with "evil"; but they always thought so, from the time they were founded. They cannot hope to make people go back to a distant past which they themselves criticized. Which period would they select? There is no way of escaping the problems of the present. We must face them frankly.

No matter whether intelligent or stupid, whether belonging to the first amorphous group or to the second active minority, schoolboys and students absorb the same dish which the majority of them will never digest. The incomparable beauty of Christian morality, its universality, its necessity are not brought out because the old-fashioned curriculums are the same as half a century ago. The world has entirely changed its aspect in the last fifty years, but this is not yet known officially.

The whole intellectual culture of man should rest on foundations of reinforced concrete represented by an unshakeable moral education. Instead of this we build flimsily, haphazardly, and pray God that the whole may stand. Yet, it is written in the Scriptures: "Where there is no vision, the people shall perish." We would not have dared to put it so brutally. It is man who must understand and foresee. If he fails, so much the worse for him.

This phenomenon is one of the most astounding of our epoch. In far too great a number of cases, the average man is, from a religious point of view, prisoner to traditions, legends, dogmas, sometimes beautiful, impressive or touching, but almost always without relation to his rational instruction. It seems as if people were afraid to attempt the fusion which *must* take place one day. This often results in a painful and nefarious conflict in certain souls.

As long as the critical sense, resulting from the exercise of intelligence resting on science, had not developed, this state of things mattered little. Such is not the case today, and nobody has the right to neglect what little progress has been achieved intellectually. Strange to say, very few efforts have been made by religious philosophers or scientists to emphasize the fact that, as we advance, our universe becomes more marvelous, more overwhelming in the infinitely great as well as in the infinitely small, but always more mysterious in its origin and in its end.

Our rational science, as we have shown in the first part of this book, demands a cause other than chance and imposes the idea of a finalism, no matter how painful this confession may be to a sincere materialist. This is about as far as science can go; but religious educators should, on their side, understand that the notion of moral and spiritual values, or the idea of the omnipotence of God can no longer be expounded in the same way to the amorphous group, to the elite groups, and to the natives of Central Africa. Let it be well understood that the fundamental principles remain identical, but that their presentation, their development, should be adapted to the receptive ability of the student. Each of them must extract *the spirit of the teaching*. The same words will never obtain the same results with a Polynesian, a high-school boy, and a university man. By feeding them the same food, we may achieve opposite effects, and we do not foster the individual effort on which progress depends.

Evolved Man, always eager to learn, must understand the striking parallelism which exists between biological evolution and moral and psychic evolution. When he ponders over inert matter, over life, over man, he must feel the harmonious majesty of the great laws, dominating the whole, and which are today only accessible to intuition. He must remember that, even if a progression is sometimes spontaneously started by a sudden mutation, its maintenance and amplification require either other mutations in the same direction, which is incompatible with the idea of chance, or else the combined action of factors of adaptation and natural selection directed, on an average, toward more and more "improbable" forms. In the psychological realm, physical adaptation and natural selection are replaced by individual effort and free choice. In both cases, that of biological evolution and that of psychological evolution, struggle is necessary, but the mechanisms differ. Man alone must still wage a double fight; both his weapons are in his brain: intelligence which protects his body, and moral ambition which guarantees evolution.

We have seen that human evolution in the moral plane is more rapid than biological evolution because tradition has superseded the other mechanisms. But education and instruction are at the base of tradition. It is, therefore, through them that we must act, to assure the distant as well as the immediate future. And as one of the crucial problems which face us at the present time is to protect ourselves from further attack, to protect our "Christian" free civilization, our ideals, and beliefs against the threat of destruction, we are automatically led to envisage the problems set by the aggressive nations.

It is not by limiting the industrial activity of a country, admitting that this were possible, that one can hope to orient it in a progressive and pacific direction, but by establishing universal educational standards. It would be highly desirable that *all* countries should one day consent to having their school and university curriculums approved by an international committee, and that history books be replaced by others in which, for the first time, truth would be respected, responsibilities established or equitably shared, where universal, moral ideas and human dignity would be taught, and no longer merely the worship of the warrior and the tale of his prowess. This will demand a great sacrifice of vanity, and may entail a certain unfairness toward those who died for their countries, but it seems to us that only on the day when all youth has absorbed the same intellectual nourishment, the same history, only when they obey the same moral catechism will the world finally have a chance of knowing peace. Not before.

The fight to suppress future wars must be waged in the schools. If this is not done in time, the actual governments will be responsible for any conflicts that may arise; and the bravest man trembles at the thought of what they will be.

Education is the weapon of progress, one of the weapons of human evolution; but it has been turned into a personal, national, political lever. Humanity should realize that, within reasonable limits, it must be denationalized. Will the nations recognize that the peril which civilization has just escaped could only attain its gigantic proportions through the schools? Everybody agrees that propaganda has revealed itself as a powerful means of sowing distrust in all prepared minds, and of starting fissures in the populations already disrupted by internal quarrels. It stands to reason that the same methods, cynically applied to the plastic, enthusiastic, and uncritical minds of children, are bound to obtain terrible results. Nothing is easier than to exalt racial or national pride, to create a fanatical *esprit de corps* and to erect a sanguinary idol. A child's virgin mind is an ideal soil for the development of any idea, right or wrong; but he is closer to the oldest and most dangerous tendencies of humanity than the mature mind which has had time to live and to think. Up till now, only the dictators, no matter what title they choose, have availed themselves of this elementary observation, and of the power of lies. *If truth alone were taught in schools, throughout the world, there could be no totalitarian states.* Only through the schools can we undo the harm the schools have done.

The teaching of history in the whole world has, for a long time, been at fault. It invariably reflects a distinct partiality inasmuch as, in the description of conflicts with foreign powers, the facts are always presented, in each country, in such a way that the country in question will always be in the right and the enemy will always be in the wrong. One may say that this is natural. Yes, but when history is based on falsehoods or on manipulation of facts and documents it becomes dangerous because it is absorbed by all children as a gospel and because they are led to consider themselves either as victims or as supermen. Later in life they will never forget this first reaction which has become an integral part of their ego.

A more or less marked xenophobia was carefully nurtured long before the recent dictatorships. In all the textbooks historical facts are arranged, regardless of antecedents, dressed up, mutilated, and, even though events and dates correspond, the causes of the conflicts and the responsibilities are presented in a diametrically different way.

So that in the 20th century we witness the bewildering spectacle of countries whose interests and wishes are to live in peace, and in which the same subject is taught to children under such different aspects that the gentlest natures cannot help sheltering a grudge in the depth of their hearts against their neighbors, even their allies; and the grudge will be all the more active as the young brain into which this seed has been sown is more generous and noble.

A history book is a powerful weapon the importance of which was soon understood by unscrupulous leaders. How can we hope for a coordinated effort on the part of men whose brains have been systematically nourished with opposing ideas and truncated facts? Class struggles on the one hand, wars on the other, these are the only possible results of such an aberration.

The only history which makes any sense is universal history. Outside of certain purely local facts, generally without great importance, nothing takes place in a country which is not linked to the events unfolding in bordering or distant countries. The economic, political, military life of a nation is conditioned by that of its neighbors. The plant which represents its history grows its roots all around. They are sometimes strong, sometimes tenuous, and innumerable intercommunications force each country to participate unconsciously in the activity of all the others. This is truer in our day than a century ago, and will be still more marked in the future. An inextricable network of veins and arteries, invisible from the exterior, renders all nations solidary with the whole. To isolate arbitrarily the history of one country is equivalent to sectioning these veins which are thus transformed into unexplainable stumps. Yet this is the way history is taught. Only the bare, unquestionable facts are allowed to subsist, for they can be interpreted in a sense which is favorable to the maintenance of national, racial, political, and other hatreds.

Universal history, which is the only truthful one, must be propagated. It must be taught as science is taught, by putting aside all national vanity, by eliminating the sentimental element which has become dangerous and archaic in our time. A child has hundreds of other occasions to be proud of his country nowadays. There is a need for honesty and impartiality, and this need is above all felt in European countries where history, and hence hatred, have a longer past.

If this is not done, we will find ourselves in the case of a man who, having dug a hole, is forced to dig another so as to get rid of the earth which he has taken out of the first. It is a vicious circle. The best will in the world does not accomplish anything if it remains blind to the fundamental vices which paralyze its action before it can even be felt.

16

BEFORE proceeding to develop some of the practical conclusions which are the logical consequence of the ideas expounded in this book, it may be advisable to recapitulate briefly the basic points of the hypothesis which constitutes its backbone.

First of all, we observe the reality of five fundamental, undeniable facts: The beginning of life, represented by extremely simple organized beings; the evolution of life toward more and more complex forms; the actual result of this long process, namely, man and the human brain; the birth of thought, and of moral and spiritual ideas; the spontaneous and independent development of these ideas in different parts of the terrestrial globe.

None of these facts can be explained scientifically as yet. A hypothesis is, therefore, indispensable if we seek to establish a reasonable sequence between them, and the telefinalist theory of evolution makes such a correlation possible. It sets down the principle that the scientific laws established by man for matter, so far as they are coherent, correspond (we do not say "express") to an objective reality, and that any mathematical impossibility must be taken into consideration if the whole of our science is not to be discredited. It is based on the impossibility of attributing the birth of life, its evolution, and the manifestations of cerebral activity to the simple play of chance.

It states that the natural evolution of living beings is one of the least questionable and best demonstrated facts in science, even though many of its mechanisms still escape us. It observes that it is hardly probable that this progressive process which has lasted for more than twelve hundred million years should be suddenly interrupted by the appearance of man and his abstract thought, and it shows that the stem from which man has sprouted is the only one that has never ceased *to evolve*, the other strains having only undergone transformations and adaptations. Now, the greatest transformation observed in humanity since the Neanderthal man is undoubtedly that of the brain. It is, therefore, logical to assume that evolution will henceforth progress by means of the organ which alone enabled man to survive and to dominate his universe including all the other animals. This is equivalent to admitting that, henceforth, evolution develops on a different plane, a plane no longer physical but psychological, as every improvement, every new *structural* complication of the brain manifests itself, on our scale of observation, by *psychological* phenomena. And psychological evolution is expressed mainly by the improvement of abstract, moral, and spiritual ideas.

But the evolution of living beings, as a whole, is in absolute contradiction to the science of inert matter (Ch. 4). It is in disagreement with the second principle of thermodynamics, the keystone of our science, based on the laws of chance. The *reason* and even the fact of evolution are, therefore, not of the realm of our present science. No scientist on earth can deny this. To account for what has taken place since the appearance of life, we are obliged to call in an "anti-chance" which orients this immense series of phenomena in a progressive, highly "improbable" direction (incompatible with chance), resulting in the human brain. This amounts to the recognition of the existence of a goal, of an *end*, for, in at least one strain, the same orientation is always observed, on an average, and over an extremely long period. Therefore, everything has taken place as if, ever since the birth of the original cell, Man had been *willed*; not as a superior animal capable of speaking and of using his hands, but as the support of the brain, the organ of conscience, of intelligence, the seat of human dignity, and the tool of further evolution. Man, with his present brain, does not represent the end of evolution, but only an intermediary stage between the past, heavily weighed down with memories of the beast, and the future, rich in higher promise. Such is human destiny.

This Will manifests itself, therefore, through evolution, and its goal is the realization of a morally perfect being, completely liberated from human passions—egotism, greed, lust for power—hereditary chains, and physiological bondage. This does not mean the definite severing of the ties between the flesh and the spirit, which would not make sense, as we cannot conceive the latter independently of the first in the case of man, but simply the escape from the *domination* of the flesh.

Consequently, anything which opposes this evolution in the moral and spiritual realm, anything which tends to bring about a regression toward the animal, to replace man under the dictature of the body is contrary to the directing Will and represents absolute Evil. On the contrary, anything which tends to deepen the chasm between man and beast, anything which tends to make man evolve spiritually is Good.

Until man appeared, evolution strove only, from an observer's point of view, to manufacture an organ, the brain, in a body capable of assuring its protection. All the ancestors of man were but irresponsible actors playing an imposed part in a play which they did not understand, or try to understand. Man continues to play his part but wants to comprehend the play. He becomes capable of perfecting himself, and he is even the only one capable of doing this. But in order to improve himself he must be free, since *his contribution to evolution will depend on the use he makes of his liberty*.

This transformation of man into an active, responsible individual is the new event which, more than any other, characterizes man. Of course the ancient mechanism of evolution, natural selection, will again enter into play. But, instead of depending as formerly on the slow action of biological laws and of chance, natural selection now depends on *conscience*, a manifestation of cerebral activity based on freedom which becomes, in each of us, the means put at our disposal to advance. According to the degree of evolution we have reached we will choose progress or regress. Our choice will indicate precisely the state of perfection we have attained.

If man is victorious in the struggle against bestiality and against the evil deformations of his mind and ambitions, he acquires human dignity. If he is vanquished, if he succumbs to temptations, which are sometimes merely the instincts inherited from his ancestors, he eliminates himself from evolution by proving that he is not capable, not worthy, of contributing to the common effort. Natural selection has played its part. We thus understand the role of temptation which, for evolved man, replaces natural obstacles, the enemies against which the animals fought and which they had to overcome to prove their fitness.

It is, therefore, that which is rarest in man, that which characterizes him specifically and differentiates him from the beast, which seems to have been the true reason for evolution. It is still through evolution that this character must improve and attain a state of perfection hardly conceivable today, but intuitively divined, and so powerfully felt that people have preferred the martyrdom of their bodies to the defilement of their ideals. The highest duty of every man is to contribute, to the best of his ability, to this new phase of evolution. No man need worry about the results of his efforts, nor about the importance of his contribution, as long as he is sincere and devotes his attention to improving himself, since it is the effort in itself that counts. His life thus takes on a universal significance; he becomes a link in the chain; he is no longer an irresponsible toy, a cork on the water, blindly obeying uncontrollable impulses, but a conscious, autonomous element, at all times free to regress and disappear or to progress and contribute to the divine task. The whole nobility of man is derived from this liberty which has been refused to the animals. Of that alone could he be excusably proud, but he prides himself on all the rest. . . .

What are the direct consequences of this way of picturing evolution? For greater clarity they can be divided into three classes: 1st, Philosophical; 2nd, Human and Social; 3rd, Individual and Moral.

Philosophical Consequences

The first is the transformation of moral ideas into facts that can be assimilated to scientific phenomena since they are linked to evolution and represent new elements comparable to the anatomical and physiological characters which up till then constituted the only criteria of progress.

The idea of universal unity thus introduced is satisfactory because it attributes a certain homogeneity to our conceptual world. It was pointed out, at the beginning of this book, that unification, namely, the interpretation of complex phenomena by means of simple common elements, represents the general and natural tendency of rational thinking. In this way the psychic, moral, and spiritual realms become incorporated into the scientific realm and science at last is permitted to rejoin another form of intellectual activity, purely based on intuition, which culminates in religion. The ethical conclusions reached by logical thinking were attained several thousand years ago by the religions, which proves that, when they are envisaged from a certain angle, rational processes are strangely slower than others.

It now becomes imperative for the rational and intuitive efforts to blend. This imposes a broadening of science, but also a unification and clarification of religions, for they must rid their rites of the remains of superstitious pollution, which, much more than the principle of divinity, have alienated a great number of honest people from religion. This clarification, which simply means a return to the elemental teachings of the Gospel, must not be brutal, but progressive, and should closely follow the evolution of man. It is certain that the pure Christian dogma can no more be absorbed by the majority today than the theory of relativity. But the crowd can dispense with the idea of relativity, whereas it cannot dispense with religion. However, the pursuit of quantity must not overshadow the importance of quality. The desire to spread superficially and win over an immense number of faithful must not obliterate the fact that the supreme goal is the moral improvement of the individual by a sincere and enlightened personal effort, and not the more or less indifferent obedience to external rites considered as a gratuitous insurance against the eventual danger of hell.

Our period is a period of transition and, as such, painful for certain persons who suffer from having to adapt themselves. A child adapts itself instantaneously. An elderly man is sometimes incapable of doing it. This is true in every realm: biological, social, industrial, intellectual, or religious.

It is, therefore, first with children, then with students, that a beginning must be made. This naturally imposes the choice and preliminary formation of the teachers whose responsibility, as we already pointed out, is considerable. The problem is less grave in the United States than in certain European countries where revolutions, either brutal or pacific, have lessened the prestige of religion. It is evident that, in those countries, the lay instructor, proselyte of a scientifically outdated materialistic faith and consequently with few exceptions anti-religious, represents a danger which has manifested itself several times already. The teacher must have no doubts concerning the so-called conflict between science and religion if we wish to avoid a disaster. He must be honestly and sincerely convinced that this conflict does not exist in the light of modern science. This result can be obtained if his rational, scientific culture, even though superficial, is *totally* rational, that is, free of all social or political influence, in accord with the *present* state of our knowledge and not inspired by a science fifty years old. Rationalism must not be a philosophy; it is a method of work. Its prestige is borrowed from science. It does not exist without it.

If nations do not make a great effort in this direction we shall witness the reappearance, but this time in the so-called rational camp, of those old enemies of reason and liberty: intolerance and fanaticism, against which rational-ism had rightly revolted. It has already happened. The sentimental echo of ideas, either good or bad, unfortu-nately influences man more than do the ideas themselves. The idea, or rather the word which expresses it, rapidly becomes a rallying cry, a symbol bereft of all significance; and a legitimate popular reaction unleashed by excesses, which at first may obtain an excellent result, is incapable, after a short lapse of time, of preventing human nature from falling into the same rut and of committing the same excesses, in the name of principles directly opposed to the first.

It was human nature, and not religion, which bred in-tolerance and fanaticism in the ancient days. The pretext matters little. The reactions of the crowd are always the same, no matter what the instigation. They usually mani-fest themselves by anger or enthusiasm, which are easily transformed into fanaticism. The prisoner dreams of put-ting his jailer in prison, but he will do it in the name of liberty instead of doing it in the name of the law. When the average man speaks of freedom, he usually thinks of his own, and only a highly evolved man is willing to defend the liberty of others.

Such are the rules of the game, and the game will con-tinue. The same enthusiasms, the same vociferations will alternately greet law and liberty with the same momentary sincerity, as long as these two words evoke in the heart of each man only the immediate benefits which they can secure, and not the great ideas they represent or the duties they impose. In other words, as long as these ideas—and many others—are not grafted on a profound sense of human dignity.

The second philosophical consequence of telefinalism is the dissociation of the body and the spirit. This dissociation is no longer considered as an act of faith, but as a scientific fact since, even though the body can still adapt itself, it is no longer it but the spirit which evolves.

Let us have no misunderstanding. This dissociation to which we alluded in the preceding chapter is entirely different from that of the old "vitalists." The idea is not to consider the soul as an entity independent of the body and inhabiting it, which is rationally inadmissible. What we mean is this: it is necessarily the brain, made up of cells, which evolves. But this organ has reached a stage where its physico-chemical and biological activity manifests itself on a different plane, through psychological phenomena *which are perceived directly*. Their existence coincides with our perception of them, without intermediary mechanism. A psychological fact exists as such, whereas the structural or chemical modifications of the brain cells which give them birth are, up to this day, inaccessible to us. Even though they could be observed, this observation could only be indirect and would take place through the intermediary of the information supplied by our senses. In other words, this sensorial information (visual or other) concerning changes in brain cells consecutive to thought would require, in order to be understood and interpreted, the intervention of thought, i.e., of the activity of our own brain cells. It is not likely that we shall soon be able to observe the functioning of thinking brain cells and still less likely that we should be able to connect these transformations with the resulting specific idea. Anatomical study is eliminated because it would mean that the subject is dead. And the other methods would require a good deal of guesswork. On the contrary, we can play with our ideas, criticize them, improve them, without any difficulty.

The evolution of the brain is revealed by pure, abstract, or esthetic ideas, by desires and aspirations capable of completely dominating the body, and we can act systematically on this evolution *only through the intermediary of similar actions,* through psychological actions, through will. To be sure, when we talk to someone, the immaterial ideas we try to convey correspond to material modifications, structural or other, in our brain cells and determine other changes in the brain cells of the person to whom we speak; but the perceptible, controllable reaction which follows in the brain of this person is of a psychological nature and escapes physical detection and measurement. Even if we were capable, as we already pointed out (p. 10), of measuring the quantity of energy transmitted by an effort of the will, we would still be incapable of appreciating its *qualitative* result. The mechanical effort is probably the same when we say "yes" as when we say "no." We can whisper No and shout Yes. Yet the "no" can signify the despair of a man and his suicide, whereas the "yes" can bring him consolation and life. The amount of energy spent seems unconnected with the effect produced.

We can act on the mechanism of human thought chemically (by hormones, drugs), or mechanically (surgical ablation of the endocrine glands), but never in a systematic, progressive manner. We can repair accidents (cretinism checked through the injection of thyroxin or extracts of thyroid gland) ; we can put the machine out of order or repair it fairly well, but we can neither direct nor perfect it, *unless we employ processes borrowed from its specific activity*. We are faced with a peculiar phenomenon, the mechanisms of which are still tributary to the physico-chemical laws and to living matter, but the activity of which is subjected to other disciplines derived from this selfsame activity, and directly dependent, if our hypothesis is correct, on the transcendent laws of evolution.

All this complicated phraseology is expressed in a simpler but equivalent manner in the language of the Scriptures: "With the mind I myself serve the law of God; but with the flesh the law of sin." (Paul, Romans, 7,25.) However, this short cut is like a tunnel through a mountain range. The same goal is reached directly but without seeing the scenery. A great many intelligent men are never convinced that they have cleared the obstacle unless they have gone over the road themselves, by the hardest paths, and unless they can remember every stone, every effort. Man does not yet know all the resources of his intuition and still mistrusts it.

The subjective, psychical element becomes preponderant the minute we accept this dissociation in the way we have explained it or in any other way. Any man in his senses will realize that the cause of man's higher aspirations transcends our scientific concepts. Our rational activities must acknowledge this fact and give it a place in the pattern of our universe. We must recognize the reality of our unaccountable aspirations and the absolute value of the will to surpass ourselves. Our sincere desire to progress morally, the efforts made in this direction lead to the erection of an inside temple, without which the outward manifestations of faith become useless.[1]

[1] "The Temple of God is holy, which temple ye are." (Paul, I Corinthians, 3, 17.)

However, we do not pretend that this individual effort suffices by itself. We only mean that it is necessary. To affirm that this effort alone is enough would be equivalent to admitting that man can attain by his sole will the superior state toward which evolution tends. This is inconceivable, for he would then become, so to speak, the author of an evolution which existed before him. He can only collaborate with it. Just as the constant, physical intervention of "anti-chance" was necessary, in spite of the prodigies of adaptation, to assure the ever-ascendant march of evolution, so is this intervention necessary in the course of psychic evolution in order to select and to perpetuate the acquired characters.

As the mechanism is not identical and as the slow acquisition of new characters by the play of chance, by mutations, adaptation, and natural selection is replaced by individual effort and tradition, as this new process is infinitely more rapid, the supernatural intervention is of a different kind and manifests itself more "economically," that is, with less waste, one might say. During the gradual evolution of living beings, the number, at first immense, of possible solutions, namely, the number of favored forms capable of still evolving in the desired direction, decreased "on an average." The same is true in a championship where, in the course of the preliminary trials, a great number of competitors are gradually eliminated until only a few remain in the "semi-finals." The hundreds of thousands of eggs which were indispensable as long as *all* the possible forms had to be tried, are reduced in the mammals, and especially the primates, to a very limited number of offspring. As has been already stated, with speech and tradition, everything happens as though all the acquired "characters" became hereditary, since the children of man can be made to profit by his own experience. The successive generations thus gain considerable time, for each individual is warned of the dangers and instructed in the best way of dealing with them, instead of being compelled as in the past to learn anew all his universe, instead of being forced to relive the experiences of his parents and of his ancestors until finally a lucky mutation gives him a limited advantage. Time contracts for man; its value is no longer on the scale of statistical evolution depending on chance, but on the personal scale.

However, if the process of individual adaptation is accelerated, the process of global evolution, which will render the characters acquired on the moral plane hereditary, does not depend solely on conscience, but on the normal course of evolution. Man, by his conscience, his will, his sincerity, contributes to the selection, but cannot make this selection himself.

Human and Social Consequences

Every man must tend to approach, within the limits of his ability, the most perfect human ideal, not only with the selfish aim of acquiring peace of the soul, internal happiness and immortality through integration in the divine task, but for the purpose of collaborating with this task and of preparing the advent of the superior race promised by evolution.

Consequently, this theory creates a new link between all men, a profound universal solidarity, free from any personal or even national preoccupation. Men must all contribute to the common task of humanity, and *as the individual aim identifies itself with the general aim,* the effort demanded of each one no longer constitutes a sacrifice but, one might almost say, an investment. This fusion of individual and general interest can only be realized on the moral and spiritual plane. Sociologists have studied the question for a long time but have never succeeded in solving it because they have conceived and sought only a community of material interests. Socialistic ethics have always shown an appalling lack of imagination. Not only do they completely neglect human psychology and its infinite wealth, but they only advocate adaptations, modifications of existing systems. They always respect the dangerous concept of political or party groups which are artificial and which, although sometimes useful, when a wrong has to be corrected, usually end by bringing about restrictions to freedom or even dictatorships. That is the fate of any ethics tainted with materialism. The world has witnessed many experiments of the kind, not only recently, but in every period. All similar attempts are eventually doomed to failure; it is as if a chemist hoped to change the nature of a reaction by modifying the shape of the vessels in which it takes place.

The source of all evil is in the very substance of man. To extirpate this evil we must neutralize not only the instincts inherited from our animal ancestors, but the superstitions transmitted by our human ancestors, the excrescences of an uncontrolled mental activity, of misguided ambitions, and replace them with the sense of human dignity. This is not easy, for the ordinary man knows well, or guesses, that the flattering title of conscious Man is only acquired at the cost of restrictions in the activities from which he usually derives all his pleasures.

When we speak of the fight of man against himself, we think not only of the solicitations of the flesh, but also of the deformations of the mind born of life in common. They are the "excrescences" mentioned above which stand in the way of progress. There are many of them, but let us take one example: the desire to shine, to be in the first row, in the limelight. All of us are more or less afflicted with it. As long as it manifests itself by an effort to better ourselves, to outdo our fellow students in school, it is good, because it represents a wholesome spirit of competition. However, it often overshoots the mark, and becomes a goal in itself. It may assume all sorts of aspects—greed, authority, fame—all of which are detrimental to the real inner effort toward improvement, and divert our attention from our true aim. It may even turn into one of the most dangerous vices of intelligence: lust for power. A number of us are would-be dictators, in our small spheres, and ambitious men are all the more eager to play a flattering leading part when their professional abilities alone will not qualify them to outshine the others. Not only does this tendency hamper individual improvement, but it makes men drunk with power, and the world knows only too well what potential danger this represents.

It is because they were aware of this and had a profound knowledge of human nature that the religions invented a hell, which nowadays has lost most of its terror. The old Catholic religion itself did not always succeed in making *true* Christians. Philip of Spain, who was a devout and fervent Catholic, asked himself at the hour of his death if some of the reverses which accompanied the end of his life were not due to the fact that he had not burned enough heretics. What would Jesus have replied had this question been put to Him?

Another human and social consequence of telefinalism, which once again crosses the path of the Christian doctrine, is the absolute necessity of complete liberty.[2] Liberty

[2] Paul, II Corinthians, 3, 17. "Where the Spirit of the Lord *is*, there *is* liberty."

has been the criterion of evolution ever since the appearance of the original cell. It is toward liberty that the development of the personality of man tends, toward an ever-increasing independence. It is at the same time a goal and a tool. A goal, because man must one day liberate himself from the despotism of the body. A tool, because unless he is free to choose between good and evil man cannot cooperate toward his own evolution, cannot improve himself deeply, from within. In this we are in perfect agreement with a very remarkable and amazingly intelligent book, *The God of the Machine*,[3] which deals with all the problems man has to face today.

Practical and Moral Consequences

The most important, perhaps, is the necessity of revivifying religion by a return to its source, to the fundamental principles of Christianity and of fighting against the superstitions which creep into the doctrine and menace its future. It is certain that the additions to the Christian religion, and the human interpretations which started in the third century, together with the disregard for scientific truths, supplied the strongest arguments to the materialists and atheists in their fight against religion. But, as we have already pointed out, the Churches cannot be blamed for having tolerated certain ancient traditional practices. The legends, the local cults, and some touching fetishisms are but the lisping expression of the human need for an ideal, of the desire to adore a familiar God, the manifestation of that fundamental religious spirit which materializes in all kinds of different ways as soon as man is unhappy or threatened.

Without anxiety, suffering, and fear man does not really

[3] By Isabel Paterson, Putnam, New York, 1943.

humanize himself nor liberate his spiritual aspirations. It is because of this that pain is fruitful and that certain superstitions are respectable. But it is only in their simplest and most puerile form that they can be tolerated. They become dangerous when they cease to be only love, gratitude, and confidence, when they leave a wake of intolerance and fanaticism. No religion can hope to triumph if it tolerates these two cankers which are the outward form of the least noble tendencies in man; pride, hatred, hypocrisy, cruelty are thus free to manifest themselves with impunity.

The Christian religion, like all the others, has suffered from this. In Spain there were the horrors of the Holy Catholic Inquisition, in other countries of Europe and in America the trials for witchcraft. All this in the name of the same God, of the same Book, as a result of false human interpretations due to incomprehension and ignorance. Today, the Book is interpreted differently, but fanaticism and intolerance are not dead. Since a simple difference of opinion resulted in the martyrdom of thousands of innocents, would it not be wise to try and interpret as prudently and scientifically as is possible in our time? Why not confront our actual problems with a religion respectful of the Scriptures but also fully aware of the advancement of human knowledge? This seems the only way to answer successfully the attacks of the materialists who boldly claim the exclusive use of rational thinking.

It may be objected that a sincere Christian needs no book other than the Gospel. But we are not trying to convince a sincere Christian. Our ambition is to win the others, and we have learned through experience that many believers suffer profoundly from the imaginary contradictions between their intuitive or sentimental faith and their science. They must be enlightened; and as the old and symbolic language of the Bible taken literally no longer corresponds to the needs of the hour, one must employ the scientific language whenever possible to express the same ideas or reach the same conclusions. It is the only language capable today of fighting agnosticism and indifference because of its prestige which is based on the fact that it has proved its value and that it corresponds to the intellectual development and acquisitions of our epoch. Science enables us to predict the movements of the planets and to harness those of the atoms; it alleviates suffering and saves human lives; it reveals to us the infinite complexity of nature and the staggering grandeur of evolution; finally, it is independent of passions and leads us to the necessity of the idea of God.

Nature reveals itself to us as a system in a perpetual state of transformation. The Church has been obliged to recognize this by accepting successively and almost unanimously the Copernican system, the roundness of the earth, its antiquity, and evolution. It thus admitted, in the 19th century, the lack of scientific accuracy of the Bible and the possibility of its adaptation to well-established scientific facts. There is, therefore, no conflict with orthodoxy in asking that the progress due to the slow conquest of the universe by intelligence be taken into account. Happy indeed is the man who has a steadfast faith, and whose life is modeled on the precepts of the Scriptures; he who is unaware of the internal conflict, the existence of which can be felt even amongst priests. But is this pure and strong man very widespread? We do not think so. If he were, how could we explain the tragedies, the crimes, big and small, the combats, the ugliness which surround us and which some people refuse to see lest they be forced to admit failure? The spectacle offered by humanity is, on an average, with a few beautiful exceptions, heart-rending. When we try to understand the reason for this we find ourselves confronted by a dilemma.

If revealed faith is more frequent than one believes and should alone inspire confidence, then, judging from the tangible results, its value as a tool for the amelioration of the individual and of the mass is mediocre. The gestures of faith, assiduous attendance at church, outward piety, signify *nothing* if man does not conform his acts and his life to the Christian ideal.

If, on the contrary, we admit that faith is not widespread, then, when we consider the strength, the number, the prestige of the Churches, it is the proof that the catechism, the Scriptures, and the sermons have lost their power of conviction and that, consequently, other paths of access to the heart, the intelligence, and the conscience of man must be found.

We do not know which of these two hypotheses is correct. In either case, it would seem that no objection could be raised against reinforcing the highest innate or intuitive ideas by arguments based on the utilization of the intellectual capital accumulated by man in the course of centuries. It is above all important to throw down the paper barriers, camouflaged as iron, which, alas, stand between men, sterilizing their efforts at a time when it would be more than ever necessary to coordinate their forces so as to shape the future. The writer knows that there are churches which are fully convinced of all this. But there are others also, and it is they which must be won.

Everyone agrees that the moral amelioration of humanity is desirable, but certain religious minds, misunderstanding the Scriptures, rely entirely on the practice of rites and on providence, thus resembling atheists who put all their confidence in social organization and in chance. The consequences of these two attitudes, apparently so far removed, are the same, since they both relegate the individual, internal, reasoned effort to second place. The well-meaning and pious people to whom we allude condemn *a priori* any rational attempt to approach the irrational, fundamental problems dealing with God and religion, thus displaying a magnificent pride which would be admirable if it were more human, but is merely alarming in its medieval intolerance. The materialistic element relies solely on external, social solutions which suppress individual liberty and infallibly lead to dictatorships, or, what amounts to the same thing, to organizations inspired by the "societies" of insects.

It has been said that when, under the menace of death or torture, a man develops an explosive faith in God it is because his faculties of intelligence are dimmed and that in reality he only reverts to ancestral superstitions. This is not certain, and it is quite possible, on the contrary, that the intellectual faculties, liberated from any contingencies, then attain a degree of extreme acuity which is seldom encountered in normal life. But, even if we admit that the presence of danger suppresses the value of thought, even if we admit that only the men who live quietly, in a peaceful home, have the power to reason sanely, then it seems that we must take into account the judgment of the majority of great men who have built up our science and our philosophy, who were believers. The vanity of a scientist who, without being sure of leaving the slightest trace in the history of science, decides that a Newton, a Faraday, a Maxwell, an Ampère, or a Pasteur, was intellectually inferior to him strikes us as reaching the limits of paradox.

It may be argued that science has evolved, and that these men did not possess the elements which are ours to-day. In answer to this let us simply remember that a large number of our greatest modern scientists have faith, and that the first part of this book is entirely given over to demonstrating the fact that the notions acquired in the last forty years, instead of reinforcing the materialistic point of view, have made it scientifically untenable. A great astronomer and mathematician, Eddington, as well as a large number of brilliant biologists throughout the world have made no small contribution to this thesis in the past twenty years.

In the two cases, that of the religious fanatic, and that of the unbeliever, we come across the same human weakness, pride, and the same error of judgment which consists in neglecting or denying one half of the psychical activity of man. The one denies intelligence, the other intuition. The idea that the human personality emerges from the harmonious combination of the two factors does not enter their minds.

Everywhere in nature we see effort. Why should its generative or preservative action be stopped in man? Why should the new and specifically human activity of abstractive intelligence have been created if it were not meant to play a part? Any man who believes in God must realize that no scientific fact, as long as it is true, can contradict God. Otherwise, it would not be true. Therefore, any man who is afraid of science does not possess a strong faith. (This is in answer to the religious extremists.) The human conflict, as defined in this book, lies in the struggle between the irrational aspirations of man and his ancestral instincts, and requires the cooperation of all the cerebral faculties. This gives a meaning to intellectual effort, without imposing on it either an orientation or a limitation.

There is one undeniable fact: the desire for effort, the desire to fight in order to attain a superior level. Though it may not be very widespread as yet, it is nevertheless the noblest trait in human nature, the trait which above all others links man most clearly to the divine task of evolution. Who are we to decide that only one path exists toward truth and that all intellectual effort is condemned?

⁂

The only goal of man should be the attainment of human dignity with all its implications. In other words, all his intellectual acquisitions, all the facilities which society puts at his disposal—schools, universities, libraries, laboratories; all those offered by religion; all the occasions given him to develop his own aptitudes, his work, his leisure, must be considered by him as tools destined to improve his personality, his moral self and to make it progress. He commits an error if he sees in education and instruction a means of increasing the field of his intellectual activity, his power, or his prestige, or a means to enrich himself materially. He must use his science and his culture to better himself morally and to make others progress. Instruction is sterile if it is considered as a goal in itself, dangerous if it is subordinated to selfish sentiments or to the interest of one group. No matter how considerable it is, the accumulation of knowledge does not confer any superiority on man if he utilizes it only outwardly and if he reaches the end of his life without having deeply evolved as a responsible element of humanity. He must blind himself to the ugliness that surrounds him and not let himself be turned from his path by the pitfalls strewn under his feet. He must overcome his dislikes and fix his vision on the beauty he drains from within; for that beauty is perhaps an illusion today, but it is the truth of tomorrow.

Let him combat and persuade himself before trying to persuade or combat others. Let him, by all the means at his disposal, concentrate his will on the construction of an unshakeable faith even though it be only a faith in the dignity and destiny of man. The method he employs is of no importance. We have said it before: no matter what road is chosen the travelers who started from different valleys will all meet on top of the mountain, provided they keep on ascending. No one must pride himself on having chosen the best route nor force his neighbor to follow him. Everyone takes the path which suits him best, imposed by the structure of the brain, by heredity, by traditions. One can offer support, enlightenment, help. But what succeeds with one may fail with others, and every man must wage his own fight without which he cannot progress. There is no short cut to truth.

Sincere effort alone counts. It is that which affirms the spiritual kinship of men, and the link which it establishes between them is more real than any other. A day will come when, as a result of evolution, moral perfection latent in a small minority will blossom in the majority as will the universal comprehension and love radiated by Christ. In the meantime, the only way to prepare for its advent is to improve man himself. By laboring to perfect himself, by building an inner temple, by judging himself without complacency, man unconsciously shapes a soul which overflows and extends all around him, anxious to diffuse in that of others. By seeking himself he finds his brother. To progress he must fight himself; to fight himself he must know himself; if he really knows himself he learns indulgence, and the barriers which separate him from his neighbors crumble little by little. There is no other way toward human solidarity but the search and respect for individual dignity.

17

We are now close to the end of our journey in the fourth
dimension: Time. By substituting a slightly different conception of finalism for the hypotheses proposed up till now,
we were able to establish a satisfactory correlation between observed facts, thus permitting the inclusion of a
greater number of phenomena and the incorporation of
specifically human activities—in particular, moral ideas—
into a vast, unique concept of evolution. The practical consequences which logically resulted therefrom are, in general, identical with those derived from the Scriptures.

The writer never has thought that the guiding thread
which was suggested would explain everything or that it
would be definitive. It only represents, in his mind, a step
in the direction of a truth which may never be attained.
But he firmly believes that no progress will be made unless
the ultimate solution is sought in an extension of the concept of evolution to the whole of nature, including man
and his intellectual and moral development.

It is imperative that any hypothesis chosen should
respect the integrity of the scientific structure which has
been progressively built up and consolidated ever since the

246

time of Lavoisier. This edifice incorporates, in the realm of physics and of chemistry, laws so general, principles so universal, it forms such a coherent and homogeneous whole, that it very probably corresponds to an equivalent system in objective reality. Any theory of evolution which does not take into account the structure of our laws of matter, and in particular the laws of chance, namely, the current ideas on determinism, must be eliminated automatically.

It was not through any sentimental reasons that we were led to accept the idea of a finalism. It was the result of a reasoning in every respect similar to that which sometimes brings about the discovery of a new phenomenon. For several years this idea was submitted to every kind of test and to all possible criticisms. It resisted and developed. The advantage of our hypothesis over those formerly proposed was that it did not contradict any of the results acquired by the sciences of inorganic matter, that it respected the mechanisms of natural phenomena and made them participate statistically in evolution. However, this theory may hurt the unscientific feelings of a certain number of excellent scientists who refuse to admit that the Carnot-Clausius law does not apply to living organisms. It is up to them to prove, experimentally, that this is untrue. The writer, an old biologist, is not in the least worried over the results of their experiments, but fears they will take a long time to materialize.

Some readers may have been surprised and even shocked by the fact that this hypothesis has been extended to the moral and spiritual realm. But this was entirely logical. Indeed, as we were led to accept the necessity of a finalism or, in other words, to recognize our inability to account for evolution without the intervention of a para-scientific "anti-chance," we did not have to restrict ourselves to scientifically known and measurable phenomena in attempting to supply an explanation. Our theory is not fundamentally different from those which have been advanced up till now, as far as the play of physico-chemical laws is concerned. It differs only because it is frankly finalistic, and admits that even in the most simple living organisms, these physico-chemical laws are controlled and dominated by more general laws, different from those of inorganic matter and unknown to us.

Similar restrictions are found in the inorganic world, as for instance, when crystals develop in a homogeneous mother-solution and thus introduce dissymmetries which destroy the statistical homogeneity imposed by the Brownian movement, or when surface-active molecules are "adsorbed," i.e., separate from the others and come to the surface in accordance with the Gibbs-Thomson law. In both cases, the "particular" laws of solutions are limited by others which apply to these special molecules. Life confers specific properties upon certain solutions (protoplasm) which render them subject to new laws.

Evidently, the hypothesis we propose is based on a postulate. But so is Euclid's geometry, and there are more than a dozen of them in Einstein's theory. The same is true of many other modern theories. This postulate, however, seems to be the only one which gives man a reason for existence and attributes a definite significance to his life. It is scientifically useful, and it throws light on many hitherto obscure problems. Finally, it has the further advantage of linking man's inner activities to evolution as a whole, thus rationalizing the spiritual support so badly needed by all.

If we were bold enough to extrapolate at long range on the basis of the ideas expounded in the first chapters of this book, we might say that, in the prudent wording of Sir Isaac Newton, everything takes place as if the descent of the material universe toward an inert chaos and toward annihilation were compensated by the simultaneous ascent of an imponderable universe, that of the spirit, whose harmony and perfection would rise from the ashes of the inorganic world.

Without going so far, and with more verisimilitude, it is possible to extrapolate at short range, and to ask oneself if the activity of the brain is destined to continue in the moral and spiritual realm or in the purely intellectual realm. This is an important question which is worth thinking over.

Intelligence, in the etymological sense, makes of mankind a student who learns continuously (Pascal). In relation to his universe, man is, therefore, in a constant state of inferiority. Let us, however, admit that one day he will know all. What will he do with his science? And what will be the consequences of his success? If he has nothing more to learn he will no longer devote his time to intellectual endeavors, which will have no more secrets for him, nor will he be interested in material things, which constitute the object of his science. Life in common will be unbearable, for a man of genius or of great learning, whose sole quality is intelligence, becomes odious. Egoism, all the basest passions, will develop without restraint; hardness of heart, which economizes sentimental suffering, will necessarily flourish and logic alone will be honored. Thirst for power, bolstered by destructive inventions, of which modern war has given us an idea, will bring about horrible conflicts and reduce the majority of men to slavery. Or else, if his intelligence has shorn him of all ambition, man will be bored in a world without mystery, from which he will have chased even beauty. For it is not certain that the esthetic sense, totally independent of intelligence, could survive. It is then conceivable that the race would rapidly die out unless a return to animality brought about an abundant procreation, not very probable if we take into account the supposed material progress and the absence of religious and moral rules.

Besides, it will never be possible to manufacture a race of men completely and equally intelligent, no more than to create a nation in which all the citizens will beat all the athletic records. There will always be individuals more intelligent than the average and who will not consider themselves bound by the social laws imposed on others. They will be so intelligent that, not being restrained by any moral brake, they will end by developing a civilization similar to that imagined by Aldous Huxley,[1] which is tragically plausible and truly represents the acme of intelligence.

Somehow, such a world seems inhuman. After all, man seeks happiness, and the joys he derives from the exercise of his sentimental, affective, and esthetic qualities are deeper than those based on strictly speculative and intellectual activity. Moreover, a careful analysis of intellectual satisfaction usually reveals the presence of a personal, sentimental element, which is as a rule the real source of pleasure. Intelligence, one might say, would strive to multiply joys; but why should it seek those which are not strictly egotistical? Why should it seek those which are accompanied by pain and sacrifice? It would fight against them and try to replace them by others, strictly rational. The inevitable result would be a deterioration of man which would work against evolution. From the tele-

[1] *Brave New World.*

finalistic point of view, it would be evil. From the human viewpoint it would be contradictory with what we know of man. For, this much is certain: moral values have always held a great prestige, and are universally respected even by those who are morally inferior. The martyrs represent one of the most powerful levers of humanity, and can transform a bloodthirsty mob into a group of men ready to die for an ideal of justice or freedom. That is why, in the course of revolutions, governments are usually careful not to "make martyrs," so as not to arouse an unmanageable fanaticism in the crowd.

Real recognized disinterestedness carries within itself an invincible force which will always have the advantage over the most subtle philosophies. Men are sensitive to it, intuitively, without any explanations, as if they all knew that it symbolizes an incontestable ideal from which they are separated only by their passions, their cowardice, and their vices.

Who knows if Christianity would have developed had Jesus not been crucified?

Moral law imposes disinterestedness; it orders that which is disagreeable, hard, and painful. Its requirements often revolt the flesh whose sole ambition is to persist and to enjoy. It demands the throttling of selfish sentiments for the sake of something which is still obscure to those who do not have faith, but which is even more powerful than the instinct of self-preservation: human dignity. The profound awareness of this dignity imposes a highly moral existence and paves the way to spirituality. And the greatest miracle is that this cruel law has won the universal respect of man who sometimes uses his intelligence to combat it, thus affirming its reality.

The joys it procures compensate for the sacrifices it demands. The sentiment of duty accomplished is accompanied by a kind of total satisfaction which alone gives true peace of soul. The moral man—in olden days one would have said the virtuous man—spreads happiness and goodwill around him or, if happiness is impossible, the resignation which takes its place. Such perfection is rarely found, but are we not justified in thinking that it is toward this ideal that evolution tends, rather than toward a dry, personal, and inhuman intellectualism?

Intelligence, which helped man to adapt himself, to survive and conquer, has played an important part and will continue to do so. It should lead to the ultimate reconciliation of religion and science, on condition that religion realizes the desirability of this aim and lends a helping hand. But like all other adaptive processes, intelligence, left to itself, can work against evolution. Rational thinking has definitely contributed to evolution by discovering the scientific laws which, through their application to industry, enabled man to dominate his environment, to liberate himself. By making wars more and more deadly, by fighting the idea of God, the notion of absolute good and evil, by denying the existence of a goal and suppressing all significance to life and to the efforts of man, intelligence struggles against evolution and against itself. It ceases to be a marvelous tool of progress when it fails to lift itself above the consideration of immediate interests, when blinders prevent its perception of such realities as evolution. It then becomes a freak, a kind of monstrosity. Intelligence, at that moment, ceases to be intelligent.

Today we are faced with the question of whether intelligence or morality will win. The fate of humanity, its happiness, depend on the answer chosen by man. Intellectualism can only lead to a utilitarian morality, apparently practical, but deprived of the mysterious and imperative character which is felt if not understood, and to which the moral law owes its prestige and its strength. Admitting that the rules set by purely intellectual ethics coincided with religious rules, they would only have the cold authority of civil laws, the respect for which is maintained only through sanctions. The human being who does not kill, or does not steal, simply because he will be executed or thrown into jail if he is caught, is not a very interesting specimen. If intelligence alone should rule, all the human traits of which we are proudest, the sense of duty, of liberty, of dignity, of the beauty of disinterested effort, would disappear little by little and fade out into oblivion, until civilization would vanish without even an afterglow.

On the other hand, if the moral law dominates, it will not oppose itself in any way to the free development of the mind. It will progressively gain ground and will allow all the human, intuitive, and intellectual characters to develop in perfect freedom. It will allow the human spirit to blossom and to perfect itself without limit. It does not matter how the spirit evolves; we repeat that what matters is the individual effort; true progress is internal and depends solely on the sincere, passionate desire to improve in the strictly human sense of moral and spiritual values. It is the will to surpass oneself, the conviction that it can be done, and the certitude that such is the role of man in evolution which constitutes human law.

The destiny of Man is not limited to his existence on earth and he must never forget that fact. He exists less by the actions performed during his life than by the wake he leaves behind him like a shooting star. He may be unaware of it himself. He may think that his death is the end of his reality in this world. It may be the beginning of a greater and more significant reality.

We cannot but be struck by the disproportion between the duration of a man's life and the duration of his influence on future generations. Every one of us leaves a trail either modest or brilliant, and this conviction should make itself felt in all the acts of our lives. Consider the case of the father of a family who by his character, example, and opinions has won the admiration of his children and associates. His memory will persist long after his death, his words and behavior will inspire people whom he has not known. That which was best in him, which he gave sometimes unconsciously to his circle of friends and relations, will never die completely. An impressive trail is that left by the thinkers, the prophets, those to whom we owe the unalterable framework of our moral life. Their names are forgotten after a period of five or six thousand years. We only know those who inherited the most ancient oral tradition and created the written tradition that perpetuates the memory of their personalities, the memory of their brief passage on earth. But the immortality of the unknown ones, the pioneers, is just as real, even though it only manifests itself amongst men by an anonymous tradition.

Figuratively, one might say that the sparkling trail of the evolution of spirit is blazed on the dark background of eternity by the combined individual wakes. Every man can, if he wishes, leave a more or less brilliant trace behind him, which widens or prolongs the existing path and contributes to its fanlike expansion.

This is a kind of impersonal immortality of which we are sure. True, individual immortality escapes rational conception, but is hardly questionable if we admit the reality of the wake.

The wake of the first man who buried his dead and protected their faces with two tilted stones; the wake of the first man who forbade his children to kill their fellow men; the wake of the first man who decided that the wounded and impotent, incapable of hunting, should be fed and not left to die; all these wakes are real today, more real perhaps than when they originated. We have forgotten the gratitude we owe these trail blazers. They are with us at all times; modern man is a tributary of the most distant past, and linked to his remotest ancestors by an immaterial but unbroken thread more durable and more impressive than the pyramids of Egypt.

The wakes of Moses, of Buddha, of Confucius, of Lao Tse, of Christ, probably exert a greater influence over humanity today than when these men were pondering over its fate and happiness. No man ever disappears completely if he strives to do good and expects no reward outside of the joy of having contributed to the progress of mankind. Our intellectual endeavors, our whole science will be of no avail if they do not lead man to a better comprehension of himself, of the meaning of his life, and of the resources buried in his inner self.

The immortality of protozoa can in no way satisfy our ambition. The fossilized traces of the great reptiles of the Mesozoic era are not a monument which can inspire man. The trace he must leave behind him is of a higher order; it must bring the proof of his real superiority, manifested by a will bent toward an ideal, by an untiring effort to draw nearer to God.

Who knows what will remain of our civilization? We may be certain that in a distant future, ten or twenty thousand years hence, nothing will be left of its material endeavors. Our proudest buildings are far from possessing the stability and majesty of the Egyptian temples, protected as they are by the dryness of the climate. Metals become oxydized and reinforced concrete disintegrates. Our great works of art, our books, will crumble into dust even if they survive the fury of wars. Some of the ideas they contain may persist if man's mentality has not been too deeply transformed. It is conceivable, however, that the imponderable fluidity of moral ideas will take its revenge on matter and that, like the clear water of a stream winding its perennial path through the indestructible granite of the temples in ruins, they will be the only witnesses of a dazzling past.

The extraordinary strides made in the conquest of nature will not bring to man the happiness he has a right to expect, unless there is a corresponding moral development. This development can only be based, in our actual society, on a unification, a reconciliation of the rational—science—with the irrational—faith; of the ponderable with the imponderable; on an explanation of the relation between matter and spirit; on the distinction between the role of the animal, prisoner of his instincts, and that of free man, in natural evolution. That is what we have attempted to do by showing that the future of this evolution is in our hands and identifies itself with the future of spirit.

As we have said before, these considerations may help a few, but will never suffice to satisfy the majority which unconsciously seek fundamental, absolute, superhuman truths. For a long time, man will be, on an average, incapable of reconciling the acts of his everyday life with his task as a responsible actor in evolution. He cannot be expected at present to understand fully that the way in which he behaves, discharges his humblest or highest duties and solves his sentimental problems can make him either a co-worker with God or a dreg of evolution. He needs enlightenment, encouragement, advice, consolation, and hope. Efficient, disinterested help can only come to him from the wise, inspired human traditions represented by the Christian religion, heir to all the spiritual treasures of mankind and keeper of the eternal flame which the greatest and purest men have passed on to one another, from time immemorial, over the bodies of dying civilizations.

18

IT IS too early to ask all men to think "universally," to consider themselves as elements of humanity as a whole. Many attempts have been made to arouse "world-consciousness." The idea was noble, but the arguments invoked were too nebulous, too sentimental, not rational enough to correspond to the present psychological resources of the majority, or even of the greater part of the minority. This universal psychology depends in a great measure on the environment and on the degree of advancement in every realm. If the caveman had been asked to think "nationally" he would not have understood. His ancestors thought in terms of "family"; he himself, at the end of several millenaries, had extended the notion of family to the descendants of his brothers, as well as his own, and then to the family clan which became the village. But the realm of his interests did not go beyond the area covered by his hunting activities: a few square miles.

Mankind slowly covered the earth. Warrior races born on poorer soil spread abroad, divided, penetrated amongst the others, pillaging and killing on their way. Those which had advanced far enough settled themselves by force without meeting any resistance but local combats. This infiltration of nomadic races into sedentary tribes established relations between different groups which had been without contact up till then and this resulted in a kind of symbiosis which, much later, when personal grudges had been forgotten, engendered the idea of a community enlarged to an ever-increasing territory. Natural barriers, streams and mountains, became the bulwarks against new invaders. The spirit of solidarity born of common interests spread to more and more distant groups; the leaders became ever more powerful and the idea of Nation, cemented by local wars, slowly emerged. The new "moral person," the idea of Fatherland, grew. Men thought "nationally." We live today in this period which has lasted for several thousand years.

During all these centuries, nothing very much happened to change the attitude of man toward the rest of humanity. The invariability of the distances, the rigidity of the material structure, assured as long as the horse represented the most rapid means of transport, imposed on life a kind of noble rhythm favorable to the development of great civilizations and to the sumptuous blossoming of the arts.

About one hundred years ago, very slowly at first, the earth began to contract. The railroad had come, scorning distances, shrinking continents, drawing men together and increasing their ambitions. It was as if the doors of a prison had been opened; as if a real meaning had been given to words which until then had only evoked differently colored spots on maps, or uncontrollable legends about beings who were sometimes monstrous or else strangely garbed and who followed extraordinary customs. Steam navigation gradually killed the myths brought back by the navigators of the 15th century.

Progressively the white race invaded the earth, generally destroying traditions and picturesque local customs without bringing anything in exchange but cotton goods, weapons, and vices. This is the process ordinarily called "civilization."

Finally, at the beginning of the 20th century, the airplane and the radio appeared, reducing the entire earth to the dimensions of Switzerland as seen by the lake dwellers. Today we live in a big park which grows smaller every day. Time is no longer respected, neither are the works it has helped to create, because it has been beaten in the race. This erstwhile invincible enemy has ceased to be a serious hindrance to enterprise, for a merciless war is being waged on it. By eliminating distances, man has learned to know his domain and the beings which inhabit it. He has familiarized himself with his fellow men, and the mystery which surrounded them no longer exists. He still judges according to his own standards, but he is free to judge personally and no longer by hearsay. He is rapidly informed of events which take place in the remotest countries of the world, and a severe fire in Sydney or in Brooklyn, an inundation in the valley of the Ganges, or in the valley of the Mississippi, have an equivalent value in his eyes because he hears about them a few moments, or at most a few hours, after they have started and because they continue their havoc at the very time when his receiving set brings him the news. The grimness of an event is minimized by time much more than by distance. There is a violence in actuality only surpassed by personal participation. There is a great difference between these two sentences: "A terrible famine ravaged India in 1840," and, "A terrible famine now rages in India. More than a thousand people died yesterday." Those who died of hunger a hundred years ago would in any case be dead today. Those who died yesterday, this morning, could have been saved if . . . A kind of vague responsibility invades the soul. "At the very moment when *I* am eating, they fall extenuated, incapable of picking themselves up." Imagination is fed by painful photographs taken the day before. "I could doubtless save several poor children if I could give them the food on the table in front of me." The guilt of the authorities arouses indignation; a new solidarity, unaware of distance, of mountains, of oceans, wiped out by the instantaneity of waves, begins to develop. Thus, a strong human link is being progressively forged between men on earth that could not have been established without the marvelous invention which suppresses time.

The radio, amazing fruit of intelligence, has thus powerfully contributed to one of the tasks pursued by religion: the *rapprochement* and mutual understanding of men.

Man will at last be able to think "universally." His mechanical intelligence has come to the rescue of his moral intuition. He has gained centuries by eliminating space and time which separated him from the suffering of his brothers and erected isolating barriers all around him. His horizon is closer, his vision is enlarged, his heart is softened. His wonderful ingenuity will perhaps contribute to his true, cosmic evolution, the profound meaning of which he will someday grasp when he understands that he is at the same time its artisan and its beneficiary. For he now possesses the external means which will facilitate the internal effort required to tighten the bonds which make him one of the cells in that giant organism called humanity.

Mechanical progress unfortunately had other consequences: it also resulted in "bigger and better" wars. The

enemy need not be the man next door; he may live anywhere in the world since it takes less time to fly half way
around the earth than it does to go from New York to
California by train. Wars, which bring man back to the
archaic social state of insects by rendering a part of the
population unable to feed itself because all its time is given
over to the handling of arms, will not cease until the
majority of men think universally, until the same ideal
orients all wills, and until governments, under the same inspiration, limit their activities to the administration of the
common patrimony and the defense of individual liberties.
Without being pessimistic, it can be stated that we have
not yet reached this stage. But in a few thousand years
great changes should take place. . . .

Our confidence in human destiny and in the future of
the spirit is great, but it is to be feared that the immediate
future—by immediate we mean the coming century—will
not bring to the world the happiness, the *joie de vivre,*
the tranquillity, and the satisfactory feeling of being finally
engaged in the period of progress promised by evolution.
All these dreams, all these legitimate hopes which will
infallibly materialize someday, depend on the individual
development of man's conscience, on the deep penetration
of the virtues of the Scriptures, on the comprehension of
human dignity.

For want of concentrating his efforts on the *true* problem, the internal problem, man will scatter his strength
in vain endeavors which will end by restricting his liberty
through the creation of collective entities whose artificial
personality will smother the individual. New ethics based
on the necessity of protecting these collectivities at the cost
of the interests of their members will threaten individual

morality which alone has any real meaning; or else will relegate it to second place, under the domination of the first, and keep it from developing. An artificial, entirely external solidarity will be imposed. It will never replace that which should spring from what is best in the heart of man and radiate around him. To impart a real cohesion to separate elements, it is not sufficient to seal them in a box; every element must be welded to the others. An imposed solidarity, entirely based on the material interests of a group, is contradictory to real human solidarity and impedes its development.

Alas, the convulsions which the world has just undergone will leave the people in such a state of exhaustion that individualism will be endangered. Ambitions, especially in Europe, will for a long time be restricted to security: security against aggression, against hunger, against cold. Men will be too tired of suffering. They have rediscovered the fears of their prehistoric ancestors, and the need to aggregate, the spirit of the herd, the elementary instinct of the horde may reappear in the masses. Premonitory signs can already be seen. They will probably materialize through the multiplication of professional or other defense organisms which begin by protecting private interests and, in general, end by annihilating the individual and suppressing his liberty. The subjugation of man to things, the disindividualization of man, his submission to soulless social or political machines, in which he will seek refuge in the vain hope of a material protection, will lead to his exploitation by unscrupulous leaders; the disaffection from a spiritual power, which, for lack of energy and clear vision, has sometimes disappointed those who asked only to be guided, may lead to the lulling of conscience. It will perhaps be a somber period in human evolution, a period of anonymous, underhanded strife, of distrust against all initiative, a period of regression for true civilization.

God grant that we are mistaken. But if we have read the signs of the times correctly, or even if we have exaggerated some of the symptoms, the only salvation for mankind will be found in religion. However, it must be a sound Christian religion, vitalized by its own primitive ideals; aware of the progress of science, rid of prejudice against fair speculative intelligence, and soaring high above frontiers. Never in her two thousand years has the Church had a more urgent call and a nobler opportunity to fulfill her obligation as the comforter and guide of humanity.

This point of interrogation, which only concerns the near future, in no way weakens our faith in the ascendant evolution of man. Indeed, the study of living beings constantly reveals particular mechanisms dominated by much more general laws the existence of which can only be inferred from certain concatenations which do not find their place in any of the groups of laws governing our universe. Thus we observe series of phenomena, on a higher scale of observation, which manifest themselves by discontinuous events but show a regular progression indicating that they are a part of a homogeneous whole. Likewise, when we enter a long winding tunnel, through mountain country, we sometimes have brief glimpses of the scenery through windows cut in the rock. These brilliant pictures are discontinuous, the scenes and the background change each time, and seem detached from the others. Yet we know that they belong to the same valley and that only the walls of the tunnel prevent us from seeing the whole.

The work of numerous scientists has enabled us to draw a sketch of the history of evolution revealed to us by similar vistas opened up by the findings of paleontology. They are windows on time and not on space. We observe the slow progress of living forms during the course of more than ten million centuries, but we also observe that this progress is not independent of the environment nor of the laws which govern it. Evolution has been moulded in its details by the surrounding medium and every transformation of the medium brought about new forms adapted to the new conditions. The resulting global phenomenon presents all the characters of continuity in time and is the resultant of two groups of activities dominated by seemingly contradictory laws. Those which govern the global phenomenon and finally resulted in man are inaccessible at present.

Thus, we men are the last evolving branch of this tremendous adventure. We denote a gigantic progress since, in opposition to all animals, the acquisition of conscience has made us craftsmen of our own evolution. We are, nevertheless, linked by a thousand chains to our material universe, inorganic as well as living. The unknown laws, the existence of which we infer from the slow and laborious rise of the human flood toward its distant destiny, come up against unforeseen accidents and must circumvent them, just as the general laws of inert matter must envelop the "particular" laws of nature. Everything takes place as though there were a hierarchy of order and as though the harmony of the great general scheme were hardly troubled by the momentary perturbations on an inferior plane. On the scale of the evolution of life, the significant unit of time was of the order of a thousand centuries. On the scale of human evolution it is perhaps of a thousand years. But the intelligence of man lacks the power to embrace dynamically the global phenomenon which spreads over hundreds of thousands of years and, wounded by physical pain and sentimental suffering, cannot help being alarmed by what seems unexplainable and revolted by what seems undeserved.

Humanity under the influence of such events as wars, or as a result of the necessity to adapt itself to the changes brought about by mechanical progress and the ensuing social problems, reacts violently by twists of the helm which seem to carry it far from its course. But the transscendent laws it unknowingly obeys have brought it in less than a thousand centuries to its present state and scorn these ephemeral digressions which become imperceptible on the scale of evolution. Like the ship constantly kept on its course by the pilot who corrects its deviations, humanity may seem to hesitate and waver; however, it will infallibly reach the port which is at the same time its goal and its reason of existence.

In current life, in his relations with his fellowmen, man must use his reason, but he will perpetrate fewer errors if he listens to his heart. Indeed, the sanest judgment is always questionable because it is impossible to assemble all the elements required to give it an absolute value. Causes of error, therefore, exist in all decisions which seem purely rational, first of all because they are never as rational as we believe and always contain a certain amount of sentiment, and secondly, because they are based on incomplete information. As one is obliged in any event to take sentiment into account, it is preferable to frankly concede its share in doubtful cases. It is better to be generous than just. It is sometimes better to sympathize instead of trying to understand. Nevertheless, though individual indulgence should be cultivated as long as the fate of spiritual development is not involved, this indulgence should not be inspired by indifference, weakness, or cowardice and one must not forget the words of Aristotle: "There is no worse injustice than to treat unequal causes equally." The strength of nations of prey and of fundamentally bad men is drawn in part from the relative immunity derived from the humanitarian sentiments of their victims. They know pertinently that a civilized being will never dare to apply torture, for instance, nor practice massive systematic destructions nor deportations of civilians on a large scale. Men and peoples in whom the voice of the brute covers that of man should be deprived of their power to harm.

The time has come for nations, as well as individuals, to know what they want. If civilized countries *want* peace, they must understand that the problem must be approached basically. The old scaffolding willed to us by past generations cracks on every side. It cannot be consolidated by makeshifts, by bits of string, by pots of glue and treaties gravely signed by Highly-Dignified-Gentlemen. Moreover, consolidation does not suffice. Peace must be established by transforming man from the interior and not by erecting external structures. We have already said it: the source of all wars, the source of all evil, lies in us. No outside protection will be efficient if the enemy cowering at the bottom of our hearts is authorized to live. He will only be annihilated with the help of time, and if we seek him out with the firm intention of reaching him. To attain this result there is only one method. First, to reestablish the cult of historic truth, by feeding the youth of the entire world with *the same* substance, thus establishing a basis for mutual understanding. This is a preliminary step and it can be taken immediately. Next, to strive to establish the cult of individual human dignity and to improve man by stifling his archaic instincts. This will be the work of the centuries to come.

It is only by direct action on youth that a better society can be successfully moulded. All pseudo-mysticisms—social, philosophical or political—must be replaced by the Christian mysticism, the only one based on liberty and the respect of human dignity. When people have received the same education, when they obey the same moral rules and think universally, they do not easily accept the idea of fighting each other and are very near an understanding. Today the nations constituted by individuals but possessing their own independent life want to exist and concentrate all their efforts toward this goal, sometimes sincerely in the interest of their members, sometimes solely in the interest of their leaders or of what the latter believe is an ideal superior to that of the individual. Governments, evidently, have the duty to protect their countries against enemies, for in so doing they protect the individual which they are supposed to represent. But they also have the duty to prepare the future by spreading the light and by attacking the roots of the evil. Unless this is done the game can last indefinitely and it is never by changes in the social architecture that the soul of the institutions themselves can be modified. As long as they remain what they are, the progress of civilization, of evolution, will be slow, because the activity and efforts of some countries are oriented toward aggression and those of others toward defense. The unanimity of individuals can only emerge from the identity of moral, spiritual, and intellectual instruction, and can alone furnish the concrete base on which to build a stable and permanent society. The state should be the servant of Man, protect him in his free individual expansion and be worthy of him. It should not dominate him. The value of a country is the sum of the values of its children. Any government which seeks to substitute its interests to the pursuit of individual development is regressive and threatens human dignity.

Some people may say that we are still far removed from the time when man will be sufficiently evolved to be fully conscious of himself, and to be worthy of being treated in any way but as a child. This may be true, but all the more reason to help him to develop and to organize society toward this goal. For, as long as the state pursues an end different from that which should be the aim of its members no real progress is conceivable.

These simple ideas, this general logical principle, which consists in viewing the solution of all human problems *through the individual,* by considering him as an active, fundamental factor in the improvement of the organisms to which he is incorporated, be it a factory or a state; this principle which consists in remembering that in nature, in evolution, it is man alone who counts and that the social events *follow* his psychological evolution; that *nothing* permanent is built which is not the consequence of a deep previous transformation in the individual soul, and that this transformation must be the goal of all his efforts; these ideas, which are the logical result of the telefinalist hypothesis of evolution, which was developed in this book, are essentially those of Christian morality. Yet they are still far from having penetrated into the brain of even the most sincere, responsible leaders, those most worthy of confidence.

At present, everybody is preoccupied by the organization of peace. All are agreed that this is the crucial problem which dominates all the others. But we hear only of "external" solutions affecting the surrounding medium and not the thinking being, whose personality vanishes like that of an animal in a herd. The writer does not question the immediate necessity of these measures, but nothing is foreseen for the future. We only hear of treaties, signatures, understandings, conventions, international police, courts of arbitration, but we never hear anything about the *respect* of these treaties and signatures, the *integrity* of the commissions, the *impartiality* of the judges, the *good faith* of all, without which these instruments lose all their value. Yet we should know by this time that their effectiveness depends entirely on the moral character of the men who have draughted them or participated in them. We know that papers destined to settle for ten, twenty, or thirty years the relations between countries and the fate of their peoples, and signed in great pomp, often only engage the momentary responsibility of the signers and are sometimes nothing but shortlived "scraps of paper."

As long as there is no collective conscience, rendering the nations—that is, the citizens, not the governments—jointly liable for the engagements taken by their representatives, treaties will constitute a tragic comedy and it is surprising that anyone can still be their dupe. Yet the game continues and the above-mentioned gentlemen-who-take-themselves-very-seriously dictate and sign acts which are supposed to assure the peace of the world. For how long?

The problem of peace is far too grave and complex to be solved by such superficial methods. It will only be settled by systematic action on the minds of children and by imposing rigid moral structures which, in the absence of real conscience, slower to erect, will render certain acts odious. Were the sense of human dignity spread universally, it would suffice to guarantee the respect of the given word, of the signed engagement, and consequently would confer a real value to all acts and treaties. Peace would be assured without effort, since every citizen would feel morally responsible for the fulfillment of the terms agreed upon. In the meantime, it is permissible to think that a strong moral education, centered on the absolute obligation of respecting an engagement, no matter what it is, would prepare the ground in which the seed could be sown with the hope of seeing it, not only germinate, but flower and bear fruit. To prepare the future by substituting for the individual conscience structures which ignore this conscience constitutes a makeshift doomed to failure and a pathetic waste of time.

The whole world realizes the advantage which would result from the fact that the great majority of men could be trusted. There is a unanimity of thought in this which is to be found nowhere else except on the subject of the ten commandments, but the effort made to impress this idea indelibly on the minds of children in the shape of automatic conditioned reflexes is so slight that one is aghast. The equilibrium of the whole world, not only peace, but justice, commerce, industry, science, rests on the confidence in the integrity and in the word of men, and all the moral teaching given to youth in the course of ten or fifteen years of education and instruction certainly does not represent more than a few hours, in certain cases a few days. The young are stuffed with many useless details and the essential is passed over in silence. Farmers might as well be taught to grow flowers in borders without learning how to cultivate a field; or young girls be taught the art of make-up without learning how to wash. Examinations deal with a quantity of facts destined to be forgotten in three months, or which are purely technical; children are trained to behave decently in public, but nobody dreams of making them repeat daily, as a prayer: "Every promise is sacred. No one is obliged to give a pledge, but he who breaks his given word is dishonored. He commits an unpardonable crime against his dignity, he betrays; he covers himself with shame; he excludes himself from human society."

If this is not in reality a prayer it is a creed; a creed which, by expressing faith in the dignity of Man addresses itself, beyond him, to God from Whom we have received it.

In the near future the world will suffer above all from distrust. We all realize this, but what is done to dissipate or to prevent this state of things from being perpetuated? Few people worry about it. Governments think only of maintaining armies, alas necessary, and all kinds of barriers which merely intensify suspicion. Can we not find, amongst those whose voice is heard, a few men capable of looking beyond the term of their activity, beyond the miserable duration of a human life, and anxious to shape the future by preparing clear-sighted coming generations, imbued with self-respect and free from the superstitions which impede the flight of integral progress? Can we not find leaders of sufficient vision to conceive an international plan of moral development spreading over several generations, instead of economic plans of five years? It would be a magnificent task, too magnificent perhaps for our poor ambitions. The immediate problems demand temporary solutions and bring results which, though more modest, are less doubtful and less distant. God keep us from judging. Humanity has not reached the age of reason and its efforts are still on the scale of the tribe.

The reader should not let the bitterness of the foregoing lines shake his faith in the glowing destiny of Man. He should, on the contrary, find an incentive in the sadness of certain hours and be more determined to fulfill the task expected of him.

The evolved man has reached a state of development of his conscience which enables him to broaden his outlook and to become fully aware of the magnificent role he can play as a responsible actor in Evolution. Unlike the polyp who blindly fights for his life at the bottom of the sea and will never know that he is laying the foundations of a coral atoll which, in the course of centuries, will become a fertile island swarming with higher forms of life, man knows that he is the forerunner of a finer and more perfect race which will be partly his doing. He should be proud of the tremendous responsibility bestowed upon him, and his pride should be great enough to overshadow the inevitable but momentary disappointments and hardships. If only more people could grasp this, if they gloried in their work, if they rejoiced in it, the world would soon become a better world, long before the spiritual goal is reached.

Let every man remember that the destiny of mankind is incomparable and that it depends greatly on his will to collaborate in the transcendent task. Let him remember that the Law is, and always has been, to struggle and that the fight has lost nothing of its violence by being transposed from the material onto the spiritual plane; let him remember that his own dignity, his nobility as a human being, must emerge from his efforts to liberate himself from his bondage and to obey his deepest aspirations. And let him above all never forget that the divine spark is in him, in him alone, and that he is free to disregard it, to kill it, or to come closer to God by showing his eagerness to work with Him, and for Him.

PIERRE LECOMTE du NOÜY: A Biographical Sketch

DR. DU NOÜY, an internationally known French scientist, was the first of an artistic family to be attracted to science. His mother, Hermine Lecomte du Noüy, was the author of numerous novels, of which *Amitié Amoureuse* was translated into sixteen languages and ran into six hundred editions in French! His father was an architect who designed the principal cathedrals of Rumania, and his grandfather, Eugène Oudinot, was the last of the great stained-glass painters and restored the windows of Chartres and other cathedrals. Corneille was one of his ancestors.

Dr. du Noüy himself was born in Paris in 1883. He was educated at the Sorbonne and the Faculty of Law. He now holds the degrees of LL.B., Ph.B., Sc.B., Ph.D., and Sc.D. It was in 1915 that Dr. du Noüy, then an officer in the French Army, met Dr. Alexis Carrel, and through him became deeply interested in certain profound problems that appeared to have no solution. Dr. du Noüy's original work while head of the laboratory staff of a war hospital brought him to the attention of the Rockefeller Institute in New York. Indeed, he had succeeded in solving a problem which had baffled physiologists for a long time—namely, the mathematical expression of the process of healing of wounds. In other words, he had worked out an equation which made it possible to follow the process of cicatrization and to calculate in advance how long a surface wound would require to heal completely. It was the first time that mathematics had been successfully applied to a biological problem (1917). His formula took into account the age of the patient and made it possible to derive the real *physiological* age of the patient from the rate at which his wound was healing. This led him, later, to a radically new concept of "Biological Time," different from the physical time of inert things, flowing at a different rate, and according to a different law (a logarithmic instead of an arithmetic law). The main philosophical consequence was that time does not have the same value for a child and for a grownup. This revolutionary work was published in France in 1936; in London and New York in 1937. From 1920 to 1927, as an Associate Member of the Rockefeller Institute, he carried on his research mainly on the properties of the blood with special reference to the fundamental problems of immunity. He discovered a score of new phenomena, some of which are used today in clinical and industrial laboratories. As a side issue, one of the many instruments which he invented and devised for his work enabled him to measure, for the first time, the three dimensions of certain molecules and to publish a direct determination of one of the fundamental constants of physical chemistry (the Avogadro Constant). The instrument which made this possible (Surface Tension Balance) received an award from the Franklin Institute of Philadelphia in 1923 and is still being manufactured in many countries, including the U.S.A. In 1927 he returned to Paris. Until 1937 he acted as head of the important Bio-Physics division of the Pasteur Institute. In 1937 he was named a director of the "École des Hautes Études" at the Sorbonne.

He was married in 1923 to an American, Mary Bishop Harriman, who has assisted him untiringly in his researches ever since. They lived in Paris under Nazi domination in the early days of the war but escaped in August 1942, to come once again to the United States to carry on his work.

During 1944 and 1945 he made extensive tours in this country under the sponsorship of the Army and Navy department of the Y.M.C.A., speaking in scores of military camps and U.S.O. clubs on international affairs and telling of his own experiences under the Nazis. Dr. du Noüy is at present living in California.

In the course of his full life, Dr. du Noüy has studied, as a young man, with Sir William Ramsay, and with Pierre and Mme. Curie. He has published some two hundred papers, most of them of a highly technical nature, and seven books on his own researches and on the philosophy of science. One of them,

L'Avenir de L'Esprit, ran to twenty-two editions in eight months in the occupied France of 1942 and was awarded a prize by the French Academy.

Today Dr. du Noüy is widely known and respected by scientists of every land. In 1944 this respect was signalized by the University of Lausanne, Switzerland, when he was awarded the Arnold Reymond Prize for his three books, *Le Temps et la Vie, L'Homme devant la Science,* and *L'Avenir de L'Esprit,* as the most important contribution to scientific philosophy in the past ten years.

INDEX